FIND THE BUG

FIND THE BUG
A BOOK OF INCORRECT PROGRAMS

Adam Barr

✦ Addison-Wesley

Boston • San Francisco • New York • Toronto • Montreal
London • Munich • Paris • Madrid
Capetown • Sydney • Tokyo • Singapore • Mexico City

Library of Congress Cataloging-in-Publication Data

A CIP catalog record for this book can be obtained from the Library of Congress
LOC Number: 2004107316

Publisher: *John Wait*
Acquisitions Editor: *Peter Gordon*
Marketing Manager: *Chris Guzikowski*
Managing Editor: *Gina Kanouse*
Senior Project Editor: *Sarah Kearns*
Copy Editor: *Sheri Cain*
Indexer: *Christine Karpeles*
Proofreader: *Jessica McCarty*
Composition: *Interactive Composition Corporation*
Cover Design: *Chuti Prasertsith*
Manufacturing Buyer: *Dan Uhrig*

The publisher offers discounts on this book when ordered in quantity for bulk purchases and special sales. For more information, please contact:

U.S. Corporate and Government Sales
(800) 382-3419
corpsales@pearsontechgroup.com

For sales outside the U.S., please contact:

International Sales
international@pearsoned.com

Visit Addison-Wesley on the Web: www.informit.com/aw

Pearson Education, Inc.
Rights and Contracts Department
501 Boylston Street, Suite 900
Boston, MA 02116
Fax: (617) 671-3447

ISBN: 0-321-22391-8
Text printed on recycled paper
1 2 3 4 5 6 7 8 9 10—MA—0605040302
This product is printed digitally on demand.

To my wife, Maura

Acknowledgments

I'd like to thank Sheri Cain, John Fuller, Bernie Gaffney, Peter Gordon, Chris Guzikowski, Sarah Kearns, and everyone else at Addison-Wesley for helping shepherd this book to publication. Also, thanks to Mike Hendrickson for his early belief in this book.

Russ Rufer reviewed an early draft of some of the chapters and offered extremely helpful comments that dramatically improved this book's quality. Joseph White offered a good newcomer perspective on the Perl chapter. My sister Rebecca did her usual excellent job proofreading the first few chapters. My parents, Michael and Marcia, provided technical, philosophical, and grammatical assistance.

Avi Belinsky, Edward Etherington, Matt Holle, Ken Moss, and Eric Nace provided advice and support when the book was still in its formative stages.

I posted the language summaries to different Usenet groups and received helpful feedback from Greg Barron, John Bode, Josiah Carlson, Dave Cross, Malcolm Dew-Jones, Michele Dondi, Charles Falconer, Jim Gibson, Peter Hansen, Paul Hill, John Krahn, Cameron Laird, Paddy McCarthy, Tad McClellan, Mark McIntyre, Stuart Moore, Tony Morris, Ben Morrow, Tony Muler, Joona Palaste, Tassilo Parseval, Brian Quinlan, Randal Schwartz, Anno Siegel, Eric Sosman, Dave Thompson, Nils Peter Vaskinn, Mike Wahler, Jeremy Yallop, and Leor Zolman, not to mention gnari, j, John L, Moosebumps, and pete. A sincere thanks to all of you.

My children—Zachary, Madeline, Keenan, and Noah—should be mentioned here, or in some cases, have specifically asked to be mentioned here. Finally, I want to thank my wife, Maura, as always, for her support, encouragement, and love.

About the Author

Adam Barr has been programming ever since he was in high school, when his father brought home a line terminal and a 300-baud modem. This was followed by an original IBM PC with a floppy drive and copy of DOS 1.0. After college, he worked for a year and a half at Dendrite Americas, a small software company in New Jersey, and then spent ten years as a software developer at Microsoft, working primarily on the Windows NT kernel. He took some time off to work on his first book, *Proudly Serving My Corporate Masters: What I Learned in Ten Years as a Microsoft Programmer,* and to be a full-time parent. In the fall of 2003, he returned to Microsoft as a Program Manager working on Windows Server. Adam received a Bachelor of Science in Engineering degree in Electrical Engineering and Computer Science from Princeton University in 1988. He lives in Redmond, Washington with his wife and four children.

CONTENTS AT A GLANCE

TABLE OF CONTENTS

PREFACE

If you're a programmer, you've probably spent a fair bit of time looking through source code trying to find a bug. You know the routine: You've narrowed the bug down to a small code section, you know it's lurking there somewhere, but you can't see where it is. You are confident that, eventually, you will have the satisfaction of finding and fixing the bug, but for the moment all you feel is frustration.

So why, you might ask, would you voluntarily read a book that requires you to do exactly that . . . repeatedly?

The answer is that finding bugs by looking through source code is really, in the end, the only way to fix bugs. You can run your tests, gather your data, wade through a debugger session, print all the verbose text you want, but it eventually comes down to seeing where the code has to be changed. Sometimes, the bug can be glaringly obvious, but oftentimes, it is not. Given the theory that practicing something makes you better at it, it seems logical to practice a skill that makes finding bugs easier, faster, and less frustrating.

Furthermore, the more time you spend reading source code looking for bugs, the better you become at finding bugs when you first review your code, when fixing them is still cheap, as opposed to later, when the program has already been through a series of tests that need to be re-run if any code is changed—or even later, when the software has shipped and the bug is found by a disgruntled end user who wants a fix *right now*.

This book lists the source code to 50 programs. Each program has exactly one bug in it (unless I missed one).

The 50 programs consist of five chapters of ten programs each, with each chapter's programs written in one of five different languages. Don't be concerned if you are unfamiliar with some of the languages; each chapter includes a description of the relevant syntactic features of each language. The goal of these descriptions is not to present a complete tutorial, but to provide enough information to allow you to extract the logic from the code, and from there, find the flaw in the logic. If you're a programmer familiar with any language, you will be able to follow along. The specific language really doesn't matter here—the required skills are relevant to all programming languages.

For each program, I explain what it is trying to do and point out any unusual features of the language, after which comes the source code. Ideally, you will be able to find the bug by looking at the source. If you have trouble, I offer suggestions on how to approach analyzing the program, followed by hints on specific inputs to use when walking through the code. Finally, I give an explanation of the bug, and discuss how it would manifest itself (something I encourage you to come up with on your own, because it improves your understanding of the code).

The kinds of bugs vary: improperly calculated arithmetic expressions, bad algorithms, incorrect assignments, returning the wrong variable, and so on. There are no subtle tricks that are apparent only to those who are experts in a language. All the code goes through a compiler or interpreter without errors.

The inspiration for this book came from years working as a Microsoft programmer. One of the duties programmers had was interviewing candidates for programming jobs. During those interviews, employees almost always asked the candidates to write some code on the office whiteboard. The problems were not especially complicated, just simple algorithms such as sorts, linked list operations, and so on—the kind you could write, debug, and discuss in half an hour.

The code could be written in any language that the candidate felt comfortable with (as long as he or she could explain it to the interviewer). The goal was not to see if the candidate knew the precise syntax of a language, but to see if he or she could come up with something that was logically correct, and then offer a reasonable proof of it.

These coding questions were designed as a challenge for the candidates, but they also wound up being a challenge for the interviewer. Evaluating a candidate meant evaluating the code, which meant quickly understanding and analyzing whether the logic was correct so you could discuss what the candidate had written, ask about optimizations, and project an air of benevolent omnipotence. Because candidates often came up with somewhat "unique" logic, you had to do a quick job of emulating a computer and "executing" their code to see if it worked. You weren't interested in what the candidate *thought* the code was going to do, or what he or she was busy *telling* you it was going to do, or what the code *looked like* it was going to do (and I never saw a single candidate include comments in the whiteboard source code). You cared about what it *actually* did.

Emulating the computer and seeing past the surface of the code to its internal logic can be tricky. Just because someone states, "This code sorts an array," does not mean it necessarily sorts an array. Just because a variable is named `distance_from_center` does not mean it necessarily has the properly calculated distance from the center. Just because a `for` loop appears in the code does not mean that it actually loops the correct number of times.

In fact, knowing what a program is supposed to do can blind you to what the code actually does. It's hard to focus on every line of code, every assignment, every loop, every comparison, and really think about what the code actually does. Yet you have to be able to do this because that's what the computer does.

Beyond helping you debug your own programs, this practice can also help you review other people's code. Increasingly, code reviews are becoming a part of a programmer's job description, and not just informal ones to cover formatting and variable-naming conventions. Code reviewers are now asked to vouch for code quality—almost to the same extent as its original author.

Reviewing code that someone else has written (or code that you wrote long enough ago to forget the details) is an acquired skill. It has been compared to proofreading, but there is a key difference. The goal of writing is to pass information to someone who does not have it. Problems with writing, in general, often involve an imperfect simulation of the intended audience: Because the author knows the material so well, it is difficult to imagine how the writing comes across to someone lacking that knowledge. Thus, putting your writing away for a couple of weeks and then coming back to proofread it later (or reviewing someone else's writing) makes you more like the intended audience. Therefore, you can do a better job of seeing how they react than you could immediately after you wrote it.

With code, your "audience" is an infallible computer that interprets the code exactly as it is written, and in doing so, unfailingly extracts the logic contained in the code. For a person to do the same requires some careful study of the code. If code is unfamiliar, you probably don't understand the details, and thus are *less* like your intended audience. This is why code reviews are so difficult—it is hard for people to simulate the dispassionate, perfect way in which computers execute software, and easy for them to unintentionally skip mistakes.

Back when I was a candidate for a Microsoft programmer myself, I got into an argument with one of the employees who interviewed me. He asked me a typical question: Write a program to recursively reverse a sentence. I produced some code and declared it correct. He disputed my assertion and pointed out what he claimed was a bug. I responded by showing how it would work successfully on some particular sample input. He continued to insist that there was a bug. Eventually, we decided to type the program into a computer to see who was right. Unfortunately, we couldn't get it to compile for some reason, so we wound up debating the issue with only the source code as evidence, each of us simulating the computer in our minds. In the end, I convinced him I was right (I think). Well, I did get hired.

In this book, I present to you 50 programs, each of the type that was asked in Microsoft interviews (including recursive sentence reversal), although some of them are slightly longer than what would fit on a whiteboard. In the tradition of the rule that interview code could be written in any language, each chapter's 10 programs are written in a different language:

- **C.** A general-purpose language that, for years, was the language of choice for complicated systems and application development, and the language in which I wrote almost all my code for Microsoft. C was originally designed by Dennis Ritchie at Bell Laboratories.
- **Python.** An object-oriented scripting language. It's powerful, but also useful for quickly writing small pieces of code. Python was developed by Guido van Rossum.
- **Java.** An object-oriented programming language designed to allow programs to be downloaded from a network and executed on any platform. Java was invented by a team at Sun Microsystems.
- **Perl.** A scripting language that's especially optimized for processing text, and often used to write Common Gateway Interface (CGI) programs to run on web servers. Perl is the brainchild of Larry Wall.
- **x86 Assembly Language.** The native language used by the x86 family of microprocessors. It's difficult to understand and rarely written directly in nowadays, but it often needs to be read and understood by programmers analyzing code in a debugger. Intel Corporation designed this language.

If you know one of these languages well, you might be tempted to start with that chapter. This is fine, but I encourage you to also try unfamiliar languages. As previously mentioned, the summary of the language at the beginning of each chapter is enough to get you going.

The bugs in each program, I should mention, were not found "in the wild" (in code that someone else wrote). The programs were written by me. A few programs are written in a non-intuitive way (non-intuitive to some people, anyway) to showcase a feature of a particular computer language or allow a certain type of bug to be hidden. In many cases, the bugs were artificially injected; for the rest, I simply left in one of the bugs that I found when debugging the code. I usually had plenty from which to choose.

Before you get to the bugs, Chapter 2 gives you some tips on how to walk through code. If you are confident of your skills, you can skip this chapter.

In each chapter, the programs are arranged in roughly increasing order of difficulty (emphasis on "roughly" because different bugs baffle different people). The programs are mostly unrelated; you can tackle them at your leisure in any order. In a few places, programs build on previous ones to solve a larger problem.

The bugs are arranged according to a classification scheme, which is shown briefly in Chapter 1, and explained in its entirety in Appendix A. Appendix B, "Index of Bugs by Type," is an index of bugs by classification type, perfect if you want to focus only on a certain type of bug.

What is the goal of this book? First and foremost, it's a chance to improve your code reviewing and debugging skills. It's also a way to challenge yourself to solve the logic puzzle that each program represents, both in figuring out how it works and finding the bug. You might be able to gain some understanding of a programming language with which you are unfamiliar. If you're curious, it presents somewhat of a glimpse into what a programming job interview at Microsoft is like. And if you want to use the programs (after you fix the bug) for your own purposes, feel free to do so.

Please check the web site, www.findthebug.com, for updates or, if necessary, corrections to the programs. Have at them, and good luck.

Adam Barr
June 2004

Chapter 1

BUG CLASSIFICATION

This chapter covers the classification of bugs used in this book. It is based on a classification done by the computer scientist Donald Knuth. Each bug type is identified with the notation C.subcategory, where C is the initial of one of the main categories (A, D, F, or B) and *subcategory* is a descriptive name.

More details and explanations of these classifications can be found in Appendix A, "Classification of Bugs." Types of bugs marked with an [*] do not appear in any of the examples.

A–Algorithm. The algorithm that the programmer designed is incorrect.

A.off-by-one. The program makes a calculation that is off by one.

A.logic. The algorithm has a logical flaw.

A.validation. Variables are not properly checked to ensure they are valid. [*]

A.performance. The algorithm has severe performance problems. [*]

D–Data. Data is not properly processed.

D.index. An array is indexed into incorrectly.

D.limit. Processing is done incorrectly at the beginning or end of the data.

D.number. A bug related to how numbers are stored in memory.
D.memory[*]. The program mismanages memory.

F–Forgotten. Statements are not executed in the intended order.
    F.init. A variable is not properly initialized.
    F.missing. A necessary statement is missing.
    F.location. A statement is in the wrong place.

B–Blunder. A simple mistake exists in the code.
    B.variable. The wrong variable name is used.
    B.expression. The calculation of an expression has a mistake.
    B.language. A bug specific to the syntax of the language. [*]

Chapter 2

TIPS ON WALKING THROUGH CODE

This book's goal is to improve your ability to find bugs in code. Before you get to the actual code samples, this chapter offers advice on how to read code. The intent is not to provide a complete primer on debugging software, but to give you background information that will be useful when you look at the problems in the rest of this book.

In his paper, "Tales of Debugging from the Front Lines," Marc Eisenstadt discusses different ways in which bugs can be found. One of them is what he calls "gather data," which is to walk through the code in the debugger, add wrapper code, insert print statement, and so on. This can be a useful way to debug code, and in many cases, it is appropriate.

However, the problems in this book do not lend themselves to being solved by gathering data, because there is no data to gather. The programs are printed on a page and are meant to be debugged that way. You could type them into a computer and execute them if you wanted to, but that would defeat the purpose of this book.

The goal of the book is to have you debug programs by what Eisenstadt calls *inspeculation*, which he describes as "a hybrid of 'inspection' (code inspection), 'simulation' (hand-simulation), and 'speculation'. . . . In other words, [programmers] either go away and think about something else for a while, or else spend a lot of time reading through the code and thinking about it, possibly hand-simulating an execution run. The point is that this family of techniques does not involve any experimentation or data gathering, but rather involves 'thinking about' the code."

Archimedes, a mathematician who lived in the third-century B.C., was said to have reacted to his realization that the buoyancy of an object was related to the weight of fluid it displaced by running through the streets shouting, "Eureka!," which means "I have found it" in Greek. Archimedes was getting into his bath, watching water spill over the edge as his body displaced it, when he had his flash of insight. Finding bugs in code can be like that; all of a sudden, something clicks in your brain and you have your own "Eureka!" moment (running through the streets is optional).

This chapter presents a series of steps that can be followed when you walk through code. It is often not necessary to follow all the steps; at any point, the reason for the bug may suddenly pop into your mind, even if you are not directly considering the code that contains the bug. But, if that doesn't happen along the way, hopefully by the time you finish the final step, the bug will have revealed itself.

The steps are as follows:

1. Split the code into sections with goals.
2. Identify the meaning of each variable.
3. Look for known "gotchas."
4. Choose inputs for walkthroughs.
5. Walk through each section.

These steps are discussed in more detail in the following sections.

Split the Code into Sections with Goals

The first step to understanding the code is to split it into sections and identify the goals of each section.

A *section* is a snippet of code that accomplishes a specific task. No specific number of lines constitute a section; it depends entirely on the code. A section can be one statement or function call, or it can be a loop with 30 lines of code in it. We can loosely define a section to be any sequence of program statements that accomplishes enough that you should take the time to define goals for it.

The "goal" of a section of code is the set of changes that the code is intended to make to the data structures used by the program. If a section is an entire function, the name of the function usually provides a general indication of what the section is trying to accomplish, but not in a detailed-enough way to help debug it. It's more of a starting point to help you think about the goals of the entire function.

Identify the Sections in the Code

If you are familiar with the code that you are looking at, it might be easy for you to divide the code into sections because you know which parts of the code correspond to different parts of the algorithm it's implementing. If you aren't familiar with the code—either because someone else wrote it or because you wrote it so long ago that you forgot what you were thinking when you wrote it—you need to spend some time thinking about how to split up the code.

The most basic step is to locate the main part of the algorithm. Most functions begin with introductory code to handle special cases, deal with errors, and so on, and end with code that cleans up and possibly returns values to the calling function. In between these is the code that implements the main algorithm.

The main algorithm is the part that you would talk about if you were telling someone what the code did. You might say, "The function looks up a key in a dictionary," without mentioning that it first checks whether the dictionary is valid, and later frees a temporary buffer that it allocated.

Of course, the introductory and cleanup code can still harbor bugs and need to be checked as carefully as any other piece of code. However, it is true that the introductory and cleanup code usually execute on any input, so they're tested all the time. Tricky input-specific bugs might hide in the main algorithm; this is the part that actually corresponds to the mathematical algorithm that the code implements.

Therefore, it is useful to note where the introductory code ends and where the cleanup code begins. Mark the area between those as the location of the main algorithm. Consider the following code:

```
int find_largest_hash(String s[]) {
    if (s.length == 0) {
        throw new InvalidParameterException();
    }

    HashCalculator hb = new HashCalculator();
    int largesthash = hb.hash(s[0]);
    int newhash;
```

```
for (int j = 1; j < s.length; j++) {
    newhash = hb.hash(s[j]);
    if (newhash > largesthash) {
        largesthash = newhash;
    }
}

hb.flush();

return largesthash;

}
```

In this example, the code to check `s.length == 0`, plus the next three lines to define `hb`, `largesthash`, and `newhash`, are the introductory code. The call to `hb.flush()` and the `return` statement are the cleanup code. The rest, in between those, is the main algorithm.

This example also shows that you don't necessarily need to know everything about the code to figure out where the sections are. Although no information was provided for the `HashCalculator` class, it is still readily apparent where it is initialized, used in the main algorithm, and cleaned up.

If the main algorithm consists of more than just a few lines of code, it needs to be split into smaller sections. Again, consider how you would describe the algorithm to someone else: Each part of that description is probably one section. If you would describe an algorithm as "first read in the data, then organize it by key, then output it," you would try to separate the code into those three sections.

Identify Goals for Each Section

After you split the code into sections, identify the goals of each section. At the end of the section, what variables should be modified and how? What invariant conditions should be true? How should the data structures be set up?

When you have finished mentally dividing the code into sections with goals, check that each goal is well contained: Code that starts working on the next goal before it logically finishes a previous one can be prone to bugs. Some languages allow *assert* statements, which are logical expressions (usually only tested in debug versions of the code) that cause the program to halt if they are false. The gaps between sections are often a good place to put assert statements that verify if the goal of a section was properly achieved, as shown in the following code:

```
public class MyArray {
    public boolean isSorted() {
        for (j = 0; j < data.length-1; j++) {
            if (data[j] > data[j+1]) {
                return false;
            }
        }
        return true;
    }
}

MyArray ma;

// Now sort the array
ma.sort();
assert (ma.isSorted());
```

If a section of code is a loop, you need to determine the overall goal of the loop. However, you should also try to determine the goal of the loop after one iteration. For example, for a loop that sorts an array, the goal after the first iteration of the loop might be "the first element in the array holds the smallest value."

For if statements, try to state the goal of the if condition itself, as in "The if() block will execute if the user has not been validated yet."

Comments

Comments are an important part of determining the goal of a piece of code. They represent the only chance a programmer has to communicate his or her ideas in plain language.

Many programmers write comments as hints for when they come back to look at the code. In many cases, comments—particularly long comments—indicate areas that the original programmer felt were tricky, unclear, or in some other way unlikely to be obvious upon later viewing. The presence of such comments usually indicates the location of the key parts of the algorithm.

Often, comments can also help identify useful sections within the code, because many times, a multiline explanatory comment precedes a block of code worth grouping into one section, and the comment tries to explain the goal of the code.

However, it is important not to let comments mislead you. The compiler and/or interpreter ignore comments, and at times, so should you. Comments can be out of sync with more recent changes to the code, or they might have been wrong to begin with. Although they represent a starting point to understanding code, they need to be verified against the actual code to ensure their accuracy.

Some comments are done by rote, in the apparent belief that mundane operations need a comment, such as the following:

```
// add this price to the total
total += this_price;
```

These types of comments are unlikely to highlight buggy areas. On the other hand, a simple comment like the following, which is obviously wrong, is a sign that significant changes might have been made to the code since it was originally written:

```
// update the x coordinate
y_coord += delta;
```

Someone likely changed this code in a hurry, perhaps pasting it in from elsewhere and then renaming variables with the automated search-and-replace functions in an editor. The semantics and goals might have been broken in the process.

Identify the Meaning of Each Variable

After you identify the goal of each section, look at the variables used in the code and identify the "meaning" of each one.

The meaning of a variable refers to what value, conceptually, it is supposed to contain.

Variable Names

Variable names, like comments, can be both useful and misleading.

Unlike sections of code, all variables have names, which can usually be counted on to provide some hint of the variable's meaning. A variable's name is like a miniature comment from the programmer that appears every place the variable is used. As with comments, however, you have to make sure that the variable really is used the way the name indicates. Furthermore, some variables, even important ones, have single-letter or other uninformative names:

```
float average_balance;   // good
string name;             // OK, but name of what?
int k;                   // unclear; could be anything
```

Unlike comments, a compiler or interpreter does not *completely* ignore variable names, because a variable name refers to a specific piece of storage. But the compiler or interpreter doesn't care about the actual name. Naming a variable a, total, or wxyz won't affect how the compiler treats it. What matters is that a variable is properly declared, defined, and used throughout the program.

If a variable has an unclear name or a name that does not match its real meaning, you should try to come up with a new name, or at least a verbal definition of the meaning. For example, for a variable named i, you might make a note that it is only used as a loop counter, or that it stores the current user ID, or that it holds a pointer to the next line of input.

Look at the Usage of Each Variable

For each variable used in the function or block of code, see where it is used. The first step is to distinguish where the variable is used in an expression—and therefore does not change—from where it is modified to hold a new value. This is not always obvious; some variables, especially data structures, can be modified inside of the functions they are passed to as arguments. Some languages have ways to indicate that a variable will not be changed inside a function (such as the const qualifier in C and C++), but these are not always used:

```
tot += data[j];      // tot is modified, data and j are used
print(counter);      // counter is used
update(mystruct);    // mystruct may be modified
```

After you determine *where* a variable is modified, you can start to understand *how* the variable is used. Is it constant for the entire length of the function? Is it constant in one section of code? Is it used only in one part of the code, or everywhere? If it is used in more than one part, is it merely being reused to save declaring an extra variable (loop counters are often used this way), or does its value at the end of one section remain important at the start of the next section?

When looking at loops, think about the state of each variable at the end of the loop. Separate the variables into those that were invariant during the loop, those that were used only during the loop (such as variables used to hold temporary values), and those that will be used after the loop code with an expectation about their value (based on what happened during the loop). A loop counter can fall into either of those last two categories: Often, it is only used to control the loop, but sometimes, it is used after the loop is done to help determine what happened in the loop (in particular, if it terminated early):

```
for (j = 0; j < total_records; j++) {
    if (end_of_file) {
        break;
    }
}
if (j == total_records) {
    // loop did not terminate due to end_of_file
}
```

Because the return value of a function is important, note whether a variable is used temporarily inside a function, or if it is actually going to be part of the data returned to the caller of the function:

```
def sum_array( arr ):
    tot = 0
    for j in arr:
        tot = tot + j
    return tot
```

`arr` is used inside the function, but it is not modified; `j` is modified, but it is discarded at the end of the function; and `tot` is modified and then returned to the caller.

Make sure that all variables are initialized before they are used (some compilers and interpreters warn you if this is not the case). Many variables are not given an initial value when they are defined, so it is important that those variables are assigned a value, in all possible code paths, before they are used in an expression.

Restricted Variables

Restricted variables can only hold a particular subset of the values that they would normally be allowed to hold based on their type. For example, when writing a simulation of a racetrack with eight lanes, you might define an integer variable named lane. Normally, an integer could hold a large range of values, but in this case, you are restricting lane to holding values between 1 and 8, or perhaps between 0 and 7. Consider this part of the variable's meaning.

Some languages allow such variables to have their restrictions explicitly stated, but often, programmers don't take advantage of this even where it is available. For example, a programmer could define a set of enumerated constants, ONE, TWO, THREE, FOUR, FIVE, SIX, SEVEN, and EIGHT, and then state that lane can only hold one of those specific values. However, there is often a tradeoff between strict type-checking (the compiler or interpreter ensuring that lane is only ever assigned one of those eight enumerated values) and ease of programming (allowing the code to do arithmetic operations on lane, such as adding one).

Ideally, any restricted variable would be identified as such—at least in a comment when it is defined, possibly in the name of the variable itself. Restricted variables are often used in ways that cause errors if the variable ever contains a value outside of its intended set. So, it is important to determine if and how a variable is restricted:

```
char * get_lane_name(lane) {
    static char * lane_names = { "one", "two", "three",
                                 "four", "five", "six",
                                 "seven", "eight" };

    return lane_names[lane];
}
```

The preceding code will crash if the lane parameter to get_lane_name() is not between 0 and 7.

An *array index* is a form of restricted variable because the proper values are defined by the size of the array. Some languages check array access at runtime and generate an error; other languages silently access whatever memory the index winds up indicating. The runtime error is preferable because it makes it apparent that something is wrong, but both errors can occur for the same reasons.

Unfortunately, the size of an array can itself be dynamic and difficult to determine at a given point in the code. Furthermore, an array can be indexed using a complicated expression. Take the example shown here:

```
int array[100];
y = array[x];
```

It is readily apparent that at this point x is restricted to values between 0 and 99, inclusive (assuming a language with zero-based indexing). Instead, if the array access appears as

```
y = array[x-2];
```

then x is restricted to values between 2 and 101. In a statement such as this

```
y = array[somefunction(x) / 3];
```

it can be difficult to determine what the proper values for x are, especially if the number of elements in `array[]` was determined at runtime.

Invariant Conditions

Invariant conditions are a more general form of a restricted variable. An invariant condition is an expression, involving one or more variables, that is supposed to be true at any point during the execution of the program, except for brief moments when related variables are being updated. An invariant condition is usually a convention established by the programmer based on how he or she wants to manage the data structures used by the program.

When considering a variable that is a nontrivial data structure, try to think of any invariant conditions that will be true if the data structure is in a consistent state. (For example, a data structure that holds a string and a length might require that the length always contain the string's length.) Make sure that all the relevant parts of the data structure are initialized if needed. When the data structure is changed, ensure that the invariant conditions are still satisfied.

In the previous example using `lane`, the invariant condition might be stated as follows:

```
(lane >= 1) && (lane <= 8)
```

Another example, with a linked list, might be

```
if ((list_head != NULL) && (list_head->next != NULL))
    (list_head->next->previous == list_head)
```

You need to note invariant conditions where they exist because they constitute an implicit goal before and after every block of code in the program. Because goals are a theoretical idea that the compiler or interpreter is not actively concerned about, invariant conditions are also good candidates for including in `assert` statements for languages that support them.

The previous statement about invariant conditions being true "except for brief moments when related variables are being updated" is important. For multithreaded programs, take care that those "brief moments" are synchronized, so that another thread won't find the variables in a state where the invariant condition is false.

Track Changes to Restricted Variables

As previously mentioned, some variables are restricted in that they should only contain a subset of the possible values they could contain. For example, an integer being used as a Boolean value might be restricted to the values 0 or 1. Because these restrictions are usually logical rather than enforced by the compiler or interpreter, it is important to check modifications to the variable to make sure that the value remains properly restricted.

Modification of restricted variables can be checked with an inductive process. That is, before a variable is modified, if you assume that the current value is properly restricted, it is possible to prove that the value after modification is properly restricted. If you can show that the variable is initialized with a proper value, and that every modification keeps the variable properly restricted as long as it is properly restricted beforehand, you prove that the variable is always properly restricted.

For example, if a variable `grade` is supposed to contain a value between 1 and 4, the following statement

```
grade = 3;
```

always keeps `grade` within the restricted range. However, with a statement such as this

```
grade = 5 - grade;
```

it is unclear if `grade` will still be properly restricted. But, if you assume that `grade` is properly restricted to 1 through 4 beforehand, at that point, you know that the expression 5 - grade keeps `grade` in the proper range.

Look for Known Gotchas

If you have split the code into sections with goals and identified the real meaning of each variable, and nothing has jumped out as being incorrect, you can proceed to choosing inputs and walking through the code. First, however, you can quickly scan the code for a few "gotchas" without getting into the nitty-gritty details.

Loop Counters

Loop counters are often used to index into arrays. In languages that have zero-based arrays, notice if the check to exit a loop uses <= in the comparison, as opposed to <. Code such as the following

```
for (index = 0; index <= MAX_COUNT; index++) {
    j = array[index];
}
```

might be correct, but the comparison index <= MAX_COUNT is suspicious. Normally, with a zero-based array, it should be index < MAX_COUNT, so the loop would not iterate when index was equal to MAX_COUNT.

As previously mentioned, some loops logically have multiple loop counters, which can be specified in an obvious way:

```
for (j = 0, k = 0; j < MAX_SIZE; j++, k+= 2) {
    // loop body
}
```

or partly by hand:

```
k = 0;
for (j = 0; j < MAX_SIZE; j++) {
    // loop body
    k += 2;
}
```

or entirely by hand:

```
j = 0;
k = 0;
while (true) {
```

```
if (j >= MAX_SIZE)
    break;
// loop body
j++;
k+= 2;
}
```

These three code examples look the same, but the difference is that in the second and third examples, if a continue were added somewhere within the section marked "loop body", it would skip the code that modifies the loop counters. In the second example, j would be updated, but k would not be updated. In the third example, neither j nor k would be updated.

In the third example, k increments by 2 each time through the loop. Normally, this will not in itself be a bug; the normal case is to increment by 1, so if someone has gone to the trouble to increment by 2, he or she probably has a good reason. However, make a mental note that k is incremented in an unusual way.

Be aware of code that modifies the loop counter within the loop. This is usually done for a reason and (hopefully) is accompanied by a comment, but it makes it more difficult for you to think through what really happens during execution of the loop—especially if the modification is only done in certain cases (depending on the contents of the data being looped through):

```
for (p = 0; p < buffer_size; p++) {
    if (buffer[p] == '\') {
        // it's an escape character, skip to next one
        p++;
    }
    // loop body
}
```

In this example, no continue statement exists after p++; the main loop body is still executed.

Same Expression on Left- and Right-Hand Side of Assignment

The same variable or expression sometimes appears on the left- and right-hand side of assignment statements that are near each other. This can happen when the variable's value is used to calculate the value of another variable, and then the first variable is marked as empty, deleted, invalid, and so on. Typically, there is a step where the variable is used, and a step where the variable is modified (in the following example, it's cleared):

```
total += array[m];
array[m] = 0;
```

In this situation, passing a variable to a function can be the logical equivalent of having it appear on the right-hand side of an assignment statement—it's the step where the variable is used:

```
dump_contents(current_record);    // use
current_record.valid = -1;        // clear
```

The bug occurs if the two statements are swapped; the variable is cleared *before* it is used:

```
array[m] = 0;
total += array[m];    // already 0!!
```

Another case where this happens is in code that's used to swap two variables, that has a standard form:

```
temp = var1;
var1 = var2;
var2 = temp;
```

It is easy to make a mistake with those lines—either in the ordering or in what variable appears where.

Check Paired Operations

Many operations that do something in a program have a corresponding "undo" operation, which must be properly paired.

One common example is memory allocation, especially temporary memory allocated by a function. All the temporary memory that a function allocates needs to be freed before the function exits, no matter under what condition it exits.

Some languages do not have explicit memory allocation and deallocation, but certain other operations still must be paired up: acquiring and releasing locks, adding to and subtracting from reference counts, and so on. Code such as the following

```
process_record(record * rec) {
    acquire_lock(rec);
    if (somethingabout(rec)) {
        return 1;
    // rest of code
    release_lock(rec);
    return ret_val;
}
```

does not always properly pair up a call to `acquire_lock(rec)` with a call to `release_lock(rec)`. In general, in each place that the first part of a paired operation is done, you must look to ensure that the second part is always done no matter what code path is followed.

Function Calls

Function calls can be difficult to walk through because the code inside the function is not right in front of you. In the best case, you have the code for the function available, but usually, you have to trust the documentation.

A properly written function modifies only the variables that it is supposed to modify. A call to the function can be treated like a single assignment statement, although it's one that can modify multiple variables and do more complicated modifications of arrays and structures.

When you look at code that calls a function, the main thing to check is that the parameters are passed correctly. Most compilers and interpreters catch an argument of the wrong type being passed, but not the wrong argument of the correct type.

One way to pass the wrong argument is when it is an index into an array. Because every element of the array has the same type, you can pass the right type, wrong argument just by botching the index. Because the index is likely to be of a common type (typically, something that can hold an integer value), this is not difficult to do. For example, in code such as the following

```
call_func (struct_a, pointer_b, array[q]);
```

it is likely that if `struct_a` or `pointer_b` are of the wrong type to pass as parameters to the function, the compiler will complain. But if `q` is an integer and `array[q]` was really supposed to be `array[r]` or `array[s]`, the compiler won't know the difference.

17

Return Values

Although many functions manipulate structures that are passed in to them, for many others, the *return value* is what it's all about—the only permanent result of the function's execution. Therefore, all the careful code that has been written and walked through will be for nothing if the function returns an incorrect value.

The most basic mistake is simply returning the wrong variable. For example, returning a temporary pointer instead of the one you want, as shown in the following code:

```
record * find_largest(record list[]) {
    record * current_record;
    record * largest_record;
    // code to find largest_record
    return current_record;
}
```

This code probably meant to return `largest_record`. Because both variables are of the same type, the compiler has no way of knowing that the code is semantically incorrect.

Some functions have multiple `return` statements. Returning from a function at the point where the result has been found is often easier than having to check if there is still more work to do, as shown in the following:

```
def is_word(s):
    done = 0
    return_value = 0
    if len(s) == 0:
        return_value = 0;
        done = 1
    if done == 0:
        # some code that might set return_value to 0 or 1
    if done == 0:
        # some more code that might set return_value
    return return_value
```

It might be cleaner to have the `return` statement at each point where the `return_value` was set, instead of using the variable `done` to avoid the remaining code. So, the first part of the function would look like this:

```
def is_word(s):
    if len(s) == 0:
```

```
        return 0
  # function continues...
```

If you have multiple return statements, make sure that every path through the code hits one. You don't want code that looks like the following:

```
def calculate_average(l):
    if len(l) == 0:
        return 0
    # more code
    if count > 0:
        return total/count
```

The problem with this code is that it might exit the function without hitting a return statement at all. Many languages won't allow this for functions defined as returning a certain type, but in the previous example, written in Python, the function returns the built-in value None, which is presumably *not* what you want.

Finally, make sure the data being returned is still valid. Do not return a pointer to storage that has already been freed!

Code That Is Similar to an Existing Error

If you find a particular error that looks like it could be repeated somewhere else in the code, search for other locations where the error might have been made. Bugs do repeat themselves; this can be because code is duplicated, or because the original programmer tended to make the same mistake, or because of a misunderstanding about how the code worked (where the programmer was trying to consistently do the right thing, but wound up consistently doing the wrong thing).

For example, if you see the likely error

```
for (j = 0; k < MAX; k++)
```

you should probably search for other for loops that fit the same pattern to ensure that the same mistake was not made elsewhere (especially if it looks like sections of code were cut and pasted within the program).

Similarly, if you discover that the code calls a function with the arguments in the incorrect order, you must check other places where the function is called. If a boundary error is discovered in the access to an array, check other places where the array is accessed.

Choose Inputs for Walkthroughs

If you tried the preceding steps and still don't know what the bug is, you probably need to walk through the code by hand. In a sense, walking through the code is less than ideal. In a perfect world, you would prove to yourself that every section accomplishes its goal, that every variable sticks to its meaning, and that the proper value is returned or displayed, leaving no doubt that the function is correct for all inputs. Walking through the code introduces an element of uncertainty because no matter how many inputs you try, the bug might not be exposed by any of them.

Still, in many cases, the only way to unearth a bug is to walk through the code. To do this, you need to select inputs to the code. Except for short standalone programs that are hard-coded to calculate a given value (or set of values), all sections of code—be they a program, a function, or just a piece within a larger section of code—behave differently based on what input they receive.

In cases where you try to track down a bug that has been reported by someone else, that person might have provided specific inputs that cause the problem to occur. This is then your first candidate for a walkthrough. But, you need to choose your own series of inputs to figure out a hard-to-reproduce or insufficiently documented bug, to check new code before releasing it, or in cases where the reported inputs are too complicated to use. Walking through code is time consuming; you cannot walk through code with all possible inputs. Hopefully, you can walk through with a small sample that is nonetheless representative enough of all possible inputs to expose all possible bugs.

When you design inputs for code, remember that you are not limited to choosing only inputs to the outer function or the entire standalone program. In fact, it is often easier to break the code into smaller groups and walk through them first. After you are confident that these smaller groups handle various inputs correctly, you can move back and walk through larger sections of code without having to revisit the details of the sections you already checked.

The easiest way to break up code is when your functions are layered, one on top of another. Start with the lowest-level function, the one that does not make any calls to code that you are checking. Then, move up the chain, checking each outer function in turn.

You can do the same within a single function that you have split into logical sections. Pick a section that you want to check and then figure out the inputs for it. In this case, the "inputs" consist of values for all variables that are used within the section of code you are walking through. You should know which variables are relevant if you have determined the meaning of each variable.

If the program has any state data that it keeps from one execution of the code to the next, think of possible values for that as well. For example, in object-oriented languages, the function that you look at might be a method on a class; in this case, the current state of the class member variables (the ones that are used in the function) is logically part of the inputs to that function.

Finally, it should go without saying that when you select a test input, you need to know what your test output is supposed to be. Otherwise, it makes it difficult to decipher whether the program works correctly.

Code Coverage

When designing inputs with the code in front of you, you have an advantage over others who are doing "black box" testing on the code—who can execute only the code and cannot see the source. The advantage is that you can tailor your inputs to ensure that they exercise all the code. For example, if at some point in the code you have an `if()` condition that can be either true or false, you can make sure you provide at least one input that makes the condition true and one that makes it false.

It might be tempting to think that any reasonably large or diverse group of inputs will naturally cover all the code—in particular, that everyday usage for some period of time will do so. This is unlikely to be true. In fact, code that is executed on every input is more likely to be correct than code that runs rarely. This is because errors in the common code are more likely to have been found during initial development and debugging.

Consider Donald Knuth's cautionary tale about assuming code coverage, taken from his essay "The Errors of T$_e$X" (for more about this essay, see Appendix A, "Classification of Bugs"):

> *In one of my early experiments, I wrote a small compiler for Burroughs Corporation, using an interpretive language specially devised for the occasion. I rigged the interpreter so that it would count how often each instruction was interpreted; then I tested the new system by compiling a large user application. To my surprise, this big test case didn't really test much; it left more than half of the frequency counts sitting at zero! Most of my code could have been completely messed up, yet this application would have*

worked fine. So I wrote a nasty, artificially contrived program. . . and of course I detected numerous new bugs while doing so. Still, I discovered that 10% of the code had not been exercised by the new test. I looked at the remaining zeros and said, Shucks, my source code [of his test input, not the compiler itself] wasn't nasty enough, it overlooked some special cases I had forgotten about. It was easy to add a few more statements, until eventually I had constructed a test routine that invoked all but one of the instructions in the compiler. (And I proved that the remaining instruction would never be executed in any circumstances, so I took it out.)

You cannot assume that all the code has been covered by your tests; instead, choose inputs that ensure it will be.

One aspect of code that you must keep in mind is the "implied else," that is, everything that is done if an `if()` is true, is *not* done if the `if()` is false. The most obvious case of an "implied else" is where no `else` body exists at all, such as in the following:

```
if (x = 5) {
    y = 7;
}
```

In this case, the "implied else" is that if x is not equal to 5, y retains its current value. However, even if there is an explicit `else` clause, something is often implied:

```
if (total > 20) {
    total = 0;
    carry = 1;
} else {
    total = total + 1;
}
```

The implied else here is that `carry` remains unchanged.

Of course, loops can be reversed (the logical meaning of the `if()` inverted and the `if` and `else` bodies swapped), as in the following rewrite of the previous fragment:

```
if (total <= 20) {
    total = total + 1;
} else {
    total = 0;
    carry = 1;
}
```

This means that `else` clauses also have an "implied if".

In terms of choosing inputs, you have to cover the "implied else" also. If you have code such as the following

```
if (tax > 0) {
    price += price * tax;
}
```

you might think that having just one input where `tax` is greater than `0` covers all the code because each line will be executed. But, you also need to think about covering the "implied else" by having an input where `tax` is equal to `0` and the `if()` is therefore false.

Empty Input

Empty input is a situation where there is no data to work on. For example, a program to sort an array is passed an array with zero elements; or a program to operate on strings is given an empty string. Typically, a program will handle this in one of two ways: either by explicitly checking for it at the beginning

```
void sort_array(int arr[], int count) {
    if (count == 0) {
        return;
    }
    // code to sort the array
}
```

or by handling the empty case as part of the main algorithm:

```
void sort_array(int arr[], int count) {
    for (int i = 0; i < count; i++) {
        // code to sort the array
    }
}
```

If `count` is `0`, the test `i < count` fails immediately, so the main loop never iterates and the code correctly does nothing.

Whichever way the code handles the empty case, you need to determine what an appropriate empty input would be, and walk through the code with that input.

Trivial Input

Trivial input is the next step up from empty input: A possible list of items turns out to have only one item, so the work to be done is trivial or nonexistent. Examples of trivial inputs are a program that prints the first n prime numbers being asked to print the first one, or a program that removes duplicates from an array being given an array with only one element.

As with empty input, trivial input might be handled by performing a special check at the beginning, often combined with a check for the empty case

```
void remove_dups(int arr[], int count) {
    if (count < 2) {
        return;
    }
    // rest of remove_dups
}
```

or else trivial input can be taken care of as part of the main algorithm.

Again, neither way is "right" or "wrong." The goal is just to make sure the code works correctly when you walk through it with a trivial input. Especially in cases where the trivial case is handled by the main algorithm, walking through the code—even if it manages to handle the trivial case correctly—can make you aware of a situation in which it would handle a nontrivial case incorrectly.

Already Solved Input

Already solved input is for functions that are supposed to modify data in place. It refers to a situation in which nothing needs to be modified. An example of already solved input is when a function that uppercases a string discovers that the string is already uppercase.

The already solved input exercises the code that determines if something needs to be done, without (hopefully) executing the code that actually does something:

```
void upper_case(char * s, int len) {
    for (int j = 0; j < len; j++) {
        if ((s[j] >= 'a') && (s[j] <= 'z')) {
```

```
                    // code to upper-case s[j] goes here
        }
      }
    }
```

Unlike the empty and trivial inputs, it is usually impossible (or not worth the trouble) for the code to determine with an initial check whether the input is already solved. In the previous code, an input string s that was all uppercase would still cause the iteration of the entire for() loop. However, the if() on the next line would always be false, so any bugs in the code marked with the comment code to upper-case s[j] goes here would not be found.

When designing input for the already solved case, one question is how long the input needs to be. For example, with the previous code, how many characters would the string need to be to give the code an adequate workout? The answer to this question is highly relative. In general, using an input of between three and five "items" (where an item is one element in an array, one character in a string, and so on) is a good tradeoff between being short enough to feasibly walk through the code as it processes the entire input, and long enough to encounter any bugs that are dependent on the fact that a certain number of items are present in the input.

Pay attention to cases where the code seems to be doing too much in processing the already solved case. Moving data items around unnecessarily, even if they all wind up back in their original places, is certainly a performance issue, and might indicate a bug that will appear in some not already solved cases.

Error Input

Error input is input that is just plain wrong. Examples of this are a function that expects a numeric string is given a character string, or a function that expects a pointer is passed a NULL pointer.

With error input, in addition to making sure that the function handles it without crashing, a walkthrough should verify that it behaves in the correct way. In many cases, an actual error input should be handled differently from, say, an empty input, by returning a specific error value or throwing an exception.

In other situations, where a function is nested within other code that is part of the same module, an error input might be considered an error on the part of the calling function, and by design should not be handled.

Of course, some functions do not have any input that could be considered a real error. But in most cases, it should be possible to come up with an error input and walk through it.

Loops

Just as you can't walk through your code with all possible inputs, you usually can't walk through every iteration of a loop. In some cases, you can control the number of iterations of the loop by limiting the input size. With code such as the following

```
int sum_array(int arr[], int count) {
    int j;
    for (j = 0; j < count; j++) {
        // code to sum the array
    }
    // return the sum
}
```

the input to the function directly controls how many times the loop iterates. The guidelines given earlier for the number of items in the input also apply here. First, try the code with `count` equal to `0` (the empty case), then with `count` equal to `1` (the trivial case), and then with `count` somewhere between `3` and `5`.

Random Numbers

Some functions use a randomly generated number in their computations. These functions typically use a random-number package written by someone else, either part of the language, the operating system, or a separate library.

The main thing to worry about with random numbers is to check the exact range that the random number returns. Some numbers return a value that is between 0 and a specified number; others, between 0 and 1. In some cases, the top range of the random number is just less than the specified number, so they will never be equal. For example, Python has a standard import called random:

```
import random
index = int (len(my_array) * random.random())
```

The `random.random()` call returns a number between 0 and 1, but not equal to 1, so this call is a proper way to randomly pick an element out of an array. Because `random.random()` will never return exactly 1, the `index` calculated will never equal `len(my_array)` (which would be too high an index).

The value returned by the random-number generator is another input to the code, even if it appears suddenly in the middle. As such, you have to pick values for the random-number generator to return during your walkthrough.

It's best to first pick those that are at the lower and upper limits; in the case just shown, those would be 0 and a number just below 1. Picking other inputs usually depends on what is done next with the random number. If, as an example, the code does one of three things based on the result of the random number, pick three values to correspond to the three choices (it's likely that the values 0 and "just below 1" already covered two of the choices):

```
// Determine if the pitch was a ball, strike, or foul
rnd = random.random()
if rnd < 0.3:
    ball()
elif rnd < 0.75:
    strike()
else:
    foul()
```

In this case, you would want to pick one value that was less than 0.3, one that was between 0.3 and 0.75, and one that was above 0.75.

For random numbers that are used in a calculation as opposed to an explicit choice, picking a third choice that is halfway between the lower and upper limits is usually adequate.

Walk Through Each Section

To walk through code, you have to learn how to "think like a computer"—that is, how to walk through source code while tracking the exact state that the computer is in and thus, hopefully, trigger the "Eureka" moment when you realize where the actual state diverges from the intended state. In other words, you find the bug.

Emulating a computer might seem obvious, but in practice, it can be quite hard.

It can be difficult, especially after reading through lots of code, to avoid simply sliding over statements that look reasonable. Remember that the computer devotes its full attention to each statement as it is being executed, and you need to do the same. No matter if a statement seems obvious, if a constant definition looks trivial, if an expression seems correct at first glance, you have to force yourself to focus on what is actually in the code, not what is supposed to be there or what you think is there. This involves walking through the code for a specific input. You are not walking through trying to keep track of a range of possibilities based on different inputs, such as "this variable will be 0 unless the height was greater than 100, in which case, it will be 1." Every input will have an exact value, and this will determine the exact values of other variables.

Track Variables

When walking through code, you need to keep track of what value is in every variable, unless you have determined that a variable is no longer important to the function (and even then, you might discover that such a determination was false).

There are really two ways to keep track of variables:

- Say to yourself, as you begin to look at each statement, "OK, so x is 12 and `subtotal` will be 32 right here . . . ." This can work well for simple cases.
- Write down all the variables on a piece of paper. This way is better if there are many variables, or the statements contain complicated expressions where parsing would require too much brainpower for you to simultaneously remember what values were stored in every variable.

Take this example:

```
userid = get_userid();
access = (privilege > 3) ?
          max_access(userid) : (privilege << 2) + 1;
```

Hmmm, now what was the value of `userid` again?

Keep in mind that for every variable, every statement in the program either modifies the variable or does not modify the variable. The computer never loses track and forgets to modify a variable if instructed to

28

do so; writing it all down on paper helps prevent *you* from losing track. It also helps you realize which variables change during the section and which ones remain constant.

If you discover that the inputs you have selected make it too difficult to keep track of all the variables—for example, the array you have chosen is too large—you can go back and change your inputs. Keep in mind, however, that certain bugs might appear only with large enough inputs.

Code Layout

The layout of the code in most languages is intended as a hint to a person who is reading the code, but it usually is not used by the compiler or interpreter when determining how to execute a program. Unless a language specifically requires it, indentation and the placement of curly braces should not be used to infer the semantics of code; you have to check that the actual semantics are correct. Code such as the following

```
if (a == b)
    function_A();
    function_B();
```

likely has a different meaning from

```
if (a == b) {
    function_A();
    function_B();
}
```

You might need to read the code very carefully to notice it.

On the other hand, in some languages, layout issues, such as indentation or which column a character appears in, *are* significant, and can cause the opposite sort of confusion, where you miss the significance of indentation. In Python, the code

```
if a == b:
    function_A()
    function_B()
```

is different from

```
if a == b:
    function_A()
function_B()
```

29

Improperly terminated comments can also obscure the true nature of code. In the following C code fragment

```
/*
 * Add x
 *

tot += x;

/*
 * now add y;
 */

tot += y;
```

the statement

```
tot += x;
```

is not executed because it is part of a comment. If you are debugging code and you have narrowed the problem down to a small section of code, but you simply cannot determine where the bug is, some languages allow you to remove the comments (for example, running the code through the C preprocessor) to check whether the bug is related to a statement unexpectedly being commented out.

Also, be careful when reading complicated arithmetic expressions, especially those that do not use parentheses to make the order of evaluation explicit. If you are not sure how an expression will be parsed, you can add parentheses yourself in a way that you feel is correct, and then see if this changes the program's behavior.

Loops

Loops can be especially tricky to walk through because you cannot usually simulate every iteration of a loop.

With code that proceeds linearly without loops, it is often easy to spot bugs by examining each line in turn. With loops, however, it is usually impossible to walk through the entire set of instructions that will be executed when the loop is completely iterated.

With any loop, pay attention to where the loop exits and where it exits to. Normally, a loop exits at the end when the termination condition becomes false, but loops can also exit because of break statements in the middle, or return statements from inside a function. Note if a loop has a `break` statement and where it will jump to. Some languages have a way to specify code that is always executed when the loop ends, such as the `else` clause you can add to a loop in Python (it is executed if the loop ends naturally—when a `for` loop list is finished, or a `while` condition becomes false—but not if the loop is exited because of a `break` statement).

Of course, remember that the exit condition of a loop is only implicitly tested at the end of a loop. With code such as the following

```
while x > 0:
    # code block A
    if (some_condition):
        x = 0
    # code block B
```

`code block B` will still execute after `x` is set to `0`, unless an explicit `break` is added after the `x = 0` statement. You might be constantly evaluating loop exit conditions in your head, but the computer isn't. This means that, if somewhere in `code block B`, there is an assumption that `x` is always greater than `0`, then the code may break.

When the loop is done, it is important in those cases to be aware of what state a particular language will leave a loop counter in. In particular, will it be set to the value it had during the last iteration, or one more than that? The following Python loop statement

```
for i in range(3, 10):
```

and the C loop

```
for (i = 3; i < 10; i++)
```

appear to do the same thing: loop `i` through the values 3, 4, 5, 6, 7, 8, and 9. However, after the Python loop, `i` will have the value 9, whereas after the C loop, `i` will have the value 10.

When you have a loop that needs to iterate many times, you have to choose certain iterations of the loop to walk through. A good choice to begin with is to walk through the first iteration, the second iteration, the second-to-last iteration, and the last iteration. For example, in code such as the following

```
for (k = 0; k < MAX_COUNT; k++) {
    // loop body
}
```

31

walk through with k equal to 0, 1, MAX_COUNT-2, and MAX_COUNT-1. Of course, this won't catch every bug, but in general, if the loop does the right thing for those values, it probably does the right thing for the intermediate values that you don't walk through.

In cases where the result of an iteration depends on what happened in the previous iteration, you can often use an inductive process to prove to yourself that the loop is correct: Assume the loop worked correctly on the previous iteration, and then see if this implies that it will work correctly on this one.

Summary

These are the steps to take when looking at code. Keep in mind that, hopefully, you won't need to go through all the steps:

1. **Split the code into sections with goals.** Separate the code into smaller sections and determine what changes each section is supposed to make to the program's variables.
2. **Identify the meaning of each variable.** Figure out the logical meaning of each variable and note where it is used and modified.
3. **Look for known gotchas.** Do some quick checks of the code to look for some basic errors that can be found quickly.
4. **Choose inputs for walkthroughs.** Pick a good set of inputs to use when walking through the code.
5. **Walk through each section.** Carefully walk through the code, emulating each instruction in your mind and tracking what changes it makes to the variables in the program.

Chapter 3

C

Brief Summary of C

Statements in C end with a semicolon (;). C treats all whitespace as equivalent, so line breaks and indents are for readability only (with a couple of exceptions that won't matter here). Blocks of code are surrounded with braces, { and }.

Comment lines begin with the characters // and everything after that marker on a line is ignored. (This is one of the rare cases in C where a line break has a different meaning from other whitespace, because only a line break will end a // comment.) Comments can also be delimited by a starting /* and an ending */. Within those comments, a line break is like any other whitespace, and has no effect on the comment.

C code is run through a pre-processor before it is compiled. The main way in which programmers are aware of the pre-processor is that it can substitute constant definitions throughout the code; so for example, the following pre-processor statement

```
#define  ARRAY_SIZE  20
```

causes the pre-processor to substitute 20 every place it sees
ARRAY_SIZE. #define can be used to define macros with arguments
that are replaced, such as the following

```
#define   NEGATIVE(x)   (-(x))
```

but that won't be used in the examples in this chapter.

Data Types and Variables

The basic data types in C are int and char. An int holds an integer
value, whose length can vary depending on the platform; 4 bytes is typical. (None of the code here depends on the exact length of an int.) A char
is an integer that can hold a single byte. Single characters are surrounded
by single quotes, such as 'a' and 'x'; the value of a character constant
is the numeric value of the character in the machine's character set (for
example, 'A' is 65 in ASCII). There are other data types for floating-point
numbers and integers of different sizes, which are not used in this book.

Variable and function names are case-sensitive. Variables are declared
with the type followed by the name, for example:

```
int counter;
```

Multiple variables can be declared together, separated by a comma:

```
char letter, lastbyte, direction;
```

Arrays in C are denoted with square brackets and indexed from 0, so

```
int scores[20];
```

allocates room for 20 ints, of which scores[0] would be the first and
scores[19] the last.

Assignment is done with the = sign:

```
counter = 0;
```

Variables can be declared and initialized in one step:

```
int bytecount = 0;
```

Arithmetic is as expected, with expressions grouped using parentheses:

```
counter = counter + 1;
lastbyte = ((direction - 5) * 6) / 2;
```

The statement

```
++counter;
```

is shorthand for

```
counter = counter + 1;
```

Bitwise and, or, and xor can be done with the &, |, and ^ operators:

```
mask = mask & 0x07;
finished = finished | 1;
checksum = checksum ^ array[i];
```

Casting between types is done by preceding the expression with the type name in parentheses:

```
int k;
char y;
k = (int)y;
```

Strings

Strings are simply arrays of type char, with the last element containing a 0 value, written as a single character '\0'. Thus, the length of a string can be less than the size of the char array where it is stored. Declaring

```
char name[10];
```

allocates room for a string that can be up to 9 bytes long, because one byte must be left for the terminating '\0'. (You could put a different character in the tenth byte, but it would not be a properly terminated string, according to C conventions.) The code

```
name[0] = 't';
name[1] = 'e';
name[2] = 'd';
name[3] = '\0';
```

sets the name to be "ted", with the 6 extra bytes unused at that point. A string in double quotes, such as "hello", is converted by the compiler into a char array including the final '\0', so "hello" occupies 6 bytes.

Pointers

Pointers are declared with *. For example:

```
char * city;
```

This only allocates storage for the pointer itself. Pointers can be declared together with variables of the type, so

```
char * city, name;
```

declares a pointer to a char called city, and a char (*not* a pointer) called name. char pointers are often assigned from string literals. For example

```
city = "Boston";
```

automatically allocates the 7 bytes needed to store the string "Boston" and sets city to point to it.

The value NULL can be assigned to pointers to indicate that they point to nothing.

Pointers are also dereferenced with *, so *city is the first byte pointed to by city. In fact, pointers and arrays are often used interchangeably, and the first char in the city array could be referenced as city[0] or *city. Note that C does not check the validity of pointers, so *city likely causes a crash if city is uninitialized, and name[20] gives an undefined result if name is allocated as previously mentioned, with room for only 10 chars.

Pointer arithmetic is allowed and automatically compensates for the size of the element pointed to. Thus, city+2 points to 2 bytes after city because a char occupies 1 byte. But for an int array declared as the following

```
int distances[5];
```

and assuming an int occupies 4 bytes, distances+2 will be 8 bytes after distances. Thus, array[n] is equivalent to *(array + n) and is defined as such.

Structures are defined as in the following example:

```
typedef struct _record {
    int element1;
    char element2;
    struct _record * next;
} record, * record_ptr;
```

36

This code combines two things (which could be separated if desired, but won't be in this book): the definition of the structure _record, and the creation of a new type record, which is equivalent to the more cumbersome struct _record. (It also defines a new type, record_ptr, which is a pointer to a record.) Within the structure definition itself, struct _record is used because the typedef is not finished, but from then on, record can be used instead.

Variables can then be declared such as the following:

```
record current_record;
record_ptr first_record;
```

The & operator returns the address of a variable, so with the previous declarations, you could write the following:

```
first_record = &current_record;
```

or

```
int j = 7;
int * jp = &j;
```

For clarity, in this book, programs use record   * as opposed to record_ptr to indicate a pointer to a record structure. record_ptr * means a pointer to a pointer to a record.

Structures

Elements in a struct are referenced with . as

```
current_record.element1
```

For pointers, -> combines dereferencing a pointer to a structure and accessing an entry in the structure, as in the following:

```
first_record->element2;
```

This is equivalent to

```
(*first_record).element2;
```

or even

```
first_record[0].element2;
```

37

Conditionals

Conditional statements are defined as follows:

```
if (test-expression)
    true-code-block
else
    false-code-block
```

`else` and `false-code-block` are optional. The code blocks can be either a single statement, or multiple statements surrounded by braces. The `if()` is true if `test-expression` evaluates to a non-zero value (`if()` is false if it is zero). Comparisons are done with ==, !=, <, >, <=, and >=.

In C, an assignment is also an expression having the value of the left hand of the assignment. Therefore, the following assignment expression

```
c = 5
```

evaluates to 5, and you could write

```
d = (c = 5);
```

The ++ operator, which was previously shown, can be written before or after the variable. When it's written before the variable, it returns the new value, but when written after, the old value is returned. In the following example, both `k` and `m` will be set to 6:

```
j = 5;
k = ++j;
m = k++;
```

There is also a -- operator that works the same way for subtracting 1. In C, it is a common mistake to write

```
if (c = 5)
```

because the assignment always evaluates to 5; it's therefore always non-zero and always true, instead of the following:

```
if (c == 5)
```

This evaluates as expected—true if `c` is equal to 5, false otherwise.

There is no specific boolean type. Any non-zero value is considered true and zero is considered false. Therefore

```
if (c)
```

is the same as

```
if (c != 0)
```

Conditionals can be grouped together with `&&` (logical and) and `||` (logical or):

```
if ((j > 5) && (j < 10))
if ((*byte == 0) || (endoffile))
```

These are different from the `&` and `|` bitwise operators: An `&&` expression is true if the expression on both sides is non-zero; `||` is true if the expression on either side is non-zero. Furthermore, the expression on the right of `&&` is evaluated only if the expression on the left is true (otherwise there is no point in doing so, since the overall result will be false no matter what), and the expression on the right of `||` is evaluated only if the expression on the left is false (for similar reasons). So, you can write code like this:

```
if ( (openfile(a) != INVALID) && (readfile(a)) )
```

Loops

Loops can be done with a `for` statement:

```
for (init-statement ;
    test-expression ;
    iteration-statement )
    for-code-block
```

Typically, `init-statement` initializes a loop counter, `test-expression` involves the loop counter, and `iteration-statement` modifies the loop counter (but that is not always true):

```
int array[20];
for (i = 0; i < 20; i++) {
    { /* code involving array[i]; */ }
}
```

This walks through the elements of array. Note that `test-expression` is `i < 20`, not `i <= 20`, because entries in an array of size 20 are accessed as `i[0]` through `i[19]`.

`test-expression` is evaluated at the beginning of each iteration through the loop, and if it is true (non-zero), `for-code-block` is executed. At the end of the loop, `iteration-statement` is executed. From anywhere within a loop, the statement `continue` jumps to the end of the loop (causing `iteration-statement` to execute and then beginning another check of `test-expression` and possible iteration of the loop); the statement `break` immediately leaves the loop without executing `iteration-statement`.

There is also a `while` loop:

```
while (test-expression)
    while-code-block
```

This loop evaluates `text-expression` each time, and executes `while-code-block` if it is true. `continue` and `break` can also be used within `while` loops.

Functions

Functions are defined as follows:

```
return-type
function-name(type1 argument1, type2 argument2)
{
    local-variable-declarations;
    function-code;
}
```

If `argument1` is followed with `[]`, it is an array, as shown in the following example:

```
int find_largest ( int array[], int array_length )
```

`local-variable-declarations` consists of variables declarations that are local to the function.

The `return` statement exits a function. `return` should be followed by a variable of the proper `return-type` for the function. A special `return-type` of `void` in the function declaration means the function does not return a value and the `return` statement needs no arguments. Functions that return type `void` can end without a `return` statement.

❶ Selection Sort

This function sorts an array using the algorithm known as selection sort. The array is composed of elements of type int, holding a single integer. Because C has no way to determine the number of elements in an array, this is passed as a second argument to the function.

Selection sort uses two nested loops. The first time through the outer loop, the inner loop finds the element in the array that has the lowest number. It then swaps that element with the element in the first position in the array, so that the first element now has the lowest number in it. The outer loop then iterates again, finding the next lowest number in the array and swapping that into the second position, and so on.

Source Code

```
1.      void sort (
2.          int a[],
3.          int n) {
4.
5.          int current, j, lowestindex, temp;
6.
7.          for (current = 0; current < n-1; current++) {
8.
9.              //
10.             // each time through this loop, scan the array
11.             // from current+1 to the end. If we find
12.             // something lower than what is at current, then
13.             // swap it with current index. So each time
14.             // through this loop, a[current] will be
15.             // properly sorted.
16.             //
17.             // 1) first find the index of the lowest value
18.             //
19.             // If lowestindex remains unchanged, a[current]
20.             // is already sorted.
21.             //
22.
23.             lowestindex = current;
24.
25.             for (j = current+1; j < n; j++) {
26.                 if (a[j] < a[current]) {
27.                     lowestindex = j;
28.                 }
```

```
29.              }
30.
31.              //
32.              // 2) now swap a[current] and a[lowestindex],
33.              // as long as a difference was found.
34.              //
35.
36.              if (lowestindex != current) {
37.                  temp = a[current];
38.                  a[current] = a[lowestindex];
39.                  a[lowestindex] = temp;
40.              }
41.          }
42.      }
```

Suggestions

1. The code has six variables (the locals `current`, `j`, `lowestindex`, and `temp`, plus the two parameters `a` and `n`). Classify the variables according to how they change. Are they invariant throughout the entire function? Are they invariant through one instantiation of the outer loop? Are they invariant through one instantiation of the inner loop? Is their use localized to one (or more) subsections of the code?

2. This code has three main comments (two of which are next to each other). Verify that the comments match what the code attempts to do.

3. The code on lines 36–40 has several variables that appear in quick succession on the left and right sides of assignments. This is a good place to check to ensure that the logic is correct.

4. What are the empty, trivial, and already solved inputs to this function?

Hints

Walk through the code with the following parameters to the function:

1. The elements are already sorted:
```
a[0]  == 2
a[1]  == 5
a[2]  == 8
a[3]  == 20
```
`n` is equal to `4`.

2. Two values are equal:
```
a[0]  == 4
a[1]  == 2
```

```
a[2] == 3
a[3] == 4
```
n is equal to 4.

3. An array of numbers are all different and partly out of order:
```
a[0] == 3
a[1] == 1
a[2] == 2
a[3] == 4
```
n is equal to 4.

Explanation of the Bug

In the inner loop, the comparison on line 26

```
if (a[j] < a[current])
```

is incorrect. The algorithm is designed so that at the end of each iteration of the outer loop, starting at line 36, it will swap a[current] with the lowest-valued array element that appears after current in the array. But as it is written now, it will swap it with the *last* element in the array that is less than a[current].

For example, look at hint #3, where the array is equal to:

```
[3, 1, 2, 4 ]
```

During the first iteration of the outer loop, when current is 0, the end result should be to swap the 3 in the first position with the 1 in the second position, because 1 is the smallest element in the array. Consider what actually happens in the inner loop (lines 25–29), the way the code is now written. current is 0 and j loops from 1 to 3. When j is 1, the code on line 26 compares a[0] to a[1], and correctly determines that lowestindex should be set to 1 at line 27. However, when j is 2 and the code on line 26 compares a[0] to a[2], line 27 then (incorrectly) updates lowestindex to 2. When j is 3, lowestindex remains unchanged, so lowestindex is still 2 when the code reaches the swap routine at line 36. The swap code exchanges the 3 and the 2 in the array, which is incorrect.

To fix this, change the test on line 26 to the following:

```
if (a[j] < a[lowestindex])
```

This ensures that lowestindex is updated only if a new value is found that is lower than the current lowest value. This bug could either be **B.variable** or **A.logic**; it depends whether the programmer used the wrong variable by accident or on purpose.

❷ Linked List Insertion

This function inserts an entry into an ordered, singly linked list. Each entry in the list is a structure that contains an integer `key` value, a `next` pointer, and some other data. The structure is defined as follows:

```
typedef struct _entry {
    int key;
    int data;
    char name[20];
    struct _entry * next;
} entry, * entry_ptr;
```

The head of the linked list is saved in a pointer that is stored outside the list itself. Within the list, the `next` pointer in each entry points to the next element in the list. The end of the linked list is denoted by the `next` pointer of the last entry being set to `NULL`.

The order of the list is determined by the `key` value. Entries with a lower `key` value appear earlier in the list.

The function is passed a pointer to the structure that will be inserted as the new entry. The code reads the `key` value to determine the proper order in the list, sets the `next` pointer as needed, and does not change any other elements in the structure.

The function is also passed a pointer to the current head of the list, and it returns the new head of the list, because this changes if the new entry needs to be inserted at the head of the list.

Source Code

```
1.    entry *
2.    insert_linked_list(
3.        entry * current_head,
4.        entry * new_element) {
5.
6.        entry * current_element;
7.
8.        // If the list is empty, then just return
```

```
9.          // new_element;
10.
11.      if (current_head == NULL) {
12.          new_element->next = NULL;
13.          return new_element;
14.      }
15.
16.      // If new_element should be the first on the list,
17.      // attach the current list to new_element and return
18.      // new_element as the new head of the list.
19.
20.      if (new_element->key < current_head->key) {
21.          new_element->next = current_head;
22.          return new_element;
23.      }
24.
25.      // Now walk the list, comparing key values. Exit the
26.      // while loop when current_element points to the
27.      // value after which we should insert new_element.
28.
29.      current_element = current_head;
30.      while (current_element->next != NULL) {
31.          if (new_element->key <
32.                  current_element->next->key) {
33.              break;
34.          }
35.          current_element = current_element->next;
36.      }
37.
38.      // Insert new_element after current_element
39.      // and return.
40.
41.      new_element->next = current_element->next;
42.      current_element->next = new_element;
43.      return new_element;
44.  }
```

Suggestions

1. Because the function has only one local variable, `current_element`, mark the section of the function in which `current_element` is used.
2. The function has several `return` statements. Verify that they all leave the list in a consistent and correct state.

3. Identify where the main part of the algorithm is. What is the "goal" of this part of the code?
4. Where in the code is the actual modification to the list done? Is this code correct?

Hints

Walk through the code with the following parameters to the function (assume in all cases that `head` properly points to the first element, the list is ordered correctly, and the `next` pointers are correct, so the last element's `next` pointer is NULL):

1. Because the code special-cases inserting at the head of the list, try the case where the list exists with one element whose `key` value is 7, and a new entry is inserted whose `key` is 4.
2. Then test inserting in the middle of the list: A list exists with two elements, `key` values 5 and 9, and a new entry is inserted whose `key` value is 6.

Explanation of the Bug

The code is fine until the `return` statement at line 43:

```
return new_element;
```

The two special cases at the top catch both situations in which the head of the list changes to `new_element`: Lines 11–14 handle the list being empty, and lines 20–23 handle the new element becoming the head of the list. In both cases, the code immediately returns `new_element` as the new head of the list.

For example, in the first hint, the existing list is non-empty, but the new entry becomes the new head of the list, so the list is modified on line 21 and the new head is returned on line 22.

On the other hand, with the second hint, the new entry has to go between the two existing entries. The `while` loop on lines 30–36 exits with `current_element` pointing to the first entry in the list, the one with a `key` value of 5 (in fact, the `while` loop exits during the first iteration). The code on lines 41 and 42 properly inserts the new entry after the first entry and adjusts the `next` pointers.

So, if you reach the `return` statement at line 43, it will be in a situation where the head of the list has not changed. Therefore, the code has a **B.variable** error; it should return the old head of the list, not the new element. So, line 43 should be as follows:

```
return current_head;
```

❸ Linked List Removal

This code removes an entry from an ordered, singly linked list. It follows up on the previous example of a linked list of structures ordered by a key value. The structure is defined the same way:

```
typedef struct _entry {
    int key;
    int data;
    char name[20];
    struct _entry * next;
} entry, * entry_ptr;
```

The head of the linked list is saved in a pointer that is stored outside the list itself. Within the list, the next pointer in each entry points to the next element in the list; the end of the linked list is denoted by a NULL next pointer. Entries with a lower key value appear earlier in the list.

When passed a key value to look up, the function needs to remove the entry with a key equal to that value. (If multiple entries with that key value exist, it removes only the first one it finds.)

The function does not change any of the fields in the entry it removes. In the remaining list, it adjusts only next pointers as necessary.

The function is passed the current head of the list, and returns the new head of the list because the head changes if the removed entry is the current head.

The function also returns the deleted entry. It can't do this using the function return value, because that is used to return the new head of the list. Therefore, one of the function arguments is a pointer to a pointer to an entry. This is defined as a * entry_ptr, which is a good way to think of it: a location at which the function can store a pointer to the deleted entry.

Source Code

```
1.    entry *
2.    delete_linked_list(
3.        entry * current_head,
4.        int key_to_delete,
```

```
5.          entry_ptr * deleted_entry) {
6.
7.          entry * current_element, * previous_element;
8.
9.          // If the list is empty, then do nothing.
10.
11.         if (current_head == NULL) {
12.             *deleted_entry = NULL;
13.             return NULL;
14.         }
15.
16.         // Does the head of the list have key_to_delete?
17.
18.         if (current_head->key == key_to_delete) {
19.             *deleted_entry = current_head;
20.             return current_head->next;
21.         }
22.
23.         // Now find the entry that has the value
24.         // in question.
25.
26.         previous_element = current_head;
27.         current_element = current_head->next;
28.         while (current_element != NULL) {
29.             if (current_element->key == key_to_delete) {
30.                 // Delete current_element.
31.                 previous_element->next =
32.                     current_element->next;
33.                 *deleted_entry = current_element;
34.                 return current_head;  // unchanged
35.             }
36.
37.             // Advance our pointer in the linked list.
38.             current_element = current_element->next;
39.         }
40.
41.         // If we get here, we did not find the entry.
42.
43.         *deleted_entry = NULL;
44.         return current_head;
45.     }
```

Suggestions

1. The code begins with a couple of special cases. Are these the proper special cases?

2. The code from lines 26–39 is a loop. How many loop variables does it have? Are they initialized and modified correctly?
3. At line 30, what would be good inputs to the code at that point? Which variables should you consider when thinking of inputs? Which ones can be ignored?
4. The code has multiple `return` statements. Do they all "clean up" the same variables?

Hints

Walk through the code with the following parameters to the function (assume in all cases that `head` properly points to the first element, the list is ordered correctly, and the `next` pointers are correct, so the last element's `next` pointer is `NULL`):

1. The code should handle no entry being found. Try a list with three elements whose key values are 2, 4, and 9, and the function is called with `key_to_delete` equal to 5.
2. Deleting an element in the middle of the list is the most common case. Assume a list exists with three elements whose `key` values are 2, 4, and 9, and the function is called with `key_to_delete` equal to 4.
3. Try it with a longer list. The list exists with four elements whose `key` values are 2, 3, 4, and 8, and the function is called with `key_to_delete` equal to 4.

Explanation of the Bug

The `while` loop on lines 28–39 is walking through the list. Because it must keep track of the entry before the one it wants to delete (so it can fix up the `next` pointer), it keeps track of both `previous_element` and `current_element`. The initialization code just before the `while` loop, on lines 26 and 27, makes this apparent.

Therefore, both these pointers need to be advanced for each iteration of the loop. The statement on line 38

```
current_element = current_element->next;
```

is correct, but the code also needs to advance `previous_element`, so line 38 should be preceded by a new line of code:

```
previous_element = current_element;
```

49

This is an **F.missing** error. It is important that this new line precede the existing one, so the two lines appear in this order:

```
previous_element = current_element;
current_element = current_element->next;
```

Under what conditions does the code work? There are special cases handled earlier: the list being empty on lines 11–14, and the entry to delete being at the head on lines 18–21. In addition, if the entry is not found, as discussed in the first hint, the code works because the `if()` statement on line 29 is never true, so the code that follows (which uses `previous_element`) never executes. (Because the list is ordered, the code could also be optimized by inserting some code around line 36 to break out of the `while` loop if `current_element->key` is greater than `key_to_delete`.)

The code does work for the second hint, which hits none of the above exceptions. Some analysis reveals that the code works if the element to be deleted is precisely the second one on the list; the `if()` on line 29 is true on the first iteration, so the code breaks out of the `while` and `previous_element` retains its correctly initialized value from line 26.

❹ Memory Copy

This function copies an area of memory. This function is passed two blocks of memory, a target and a source, defined as type `char *` in C. It is also passed the length of the block to copy.

The copying operation is simple if the source and target do not overlap. However, if they do overlap, the copy has to be done in the correct direction—either starting at the beginning and working forward, or starting at the end and working backward—depending on how they overlap. Otherwise, bytes of data will be copied into some memory locations before the bytes that are currently at those memory locations have been moved where they belong; when the algorithm reaches that point, it will copy the new data, not the old data.

Source Code

```
1.    void
2.    copy_memory(
```

```
3.          char * target,
4.          char * source,
5.          int length) {
6.
7.          char * source_ptr, * source_end, * target_ptr;
8.          int step;
9.          int done = 0;
10.
11.         if (length < 1)
12.             return;          // nothing to copy, so exit
13.
14.         //
15.         // Normally copy forward, unless they overlap with
16.         // the source being later, in which case we want to
17.         // go backwards to avoid the copied bytes
18.         // overwriting the source bytes before they are
19.         // copied.
20.         //
21.         if ((target < source) &&
22.             ((target + length) > source)) {
23.             source_ptr = source + (length-1);
24.             source_end = source;
25.             target_ptr = target + (length-1);
26.             step = -1;
27.         } else {
28.             source_ptr = source;
29.             source_end = source + (length-1);
30.             target_ptr = target;
31.             step = 1;
32.         }
33.
34.         //
35.         // Now do the copy.
36.         //
37.         while (1) {
38.             if (source_ptr == source_end)
39.                 done = 1;
40.             *target_ptr = *source_ptr;
41.             if (done)
42.                 break;
43.             source_ptr += step;
44.             target_ptr += step;
45.         }
46.     }
```

Suggestions

1. Consider the local variable done. Where is it used? Is it used correctly?
2. The if on lines 21 and 22 is the heart of the algorithm. Is it correctly calculating whether the buffers overlap?
3. What are the empty, trivial, and already solved inputs to this program?
4. Does the comment on lines 15–19 match the code that follows?

Hints

Walk through the code with the following parameters to the function:

1. The most basic test is a non-overlapping copy. An array
   test_buffer[] contains 6 bytes:
   ```
   test_buffer[0] == 0x01
   test_buffer[1] == 0x02
   test_buffer[2] == 0x03
   test_buffer[0] == 0x04
   test_buffer[1] == 0x05
   test_buffer[2] == 0x06
   ```
   The function is called as follows:
   ```
   copy_memory(test_buffer, test_buffer+3, 3)
   ```
2. Try an overlapping copy. An array test_buffer[] contains 6 bytes:
   ```
   test_buffer[0] == 0x01
   test_buffer[1] == 0x02
   test_buffer[2] == 0x03
   test_buffer[0] == 0x04
   test_buffer[1] == 0x05
   test_buffer[2] == 0x06
   ```
   The function is called as follows:
   ```
   copy_memory(test_buffer, test_buffer+2, 4)
   ```

Explanation of the Bug

The logic about when to copy going backward is wrong. The comment on lines 15–19 and the if on lines 21 and 22 are consistent with each other

```
//
// Normally copy forward, unless they overlap with
// the source being later, in which case we want to
// go backwards to avoid the copied bytes
// overwriting the source bytes before they are
```

```
// copied.
//
if ((target < source) &&
    ((target + length) > source)) {
```

but they are both incorrect; there is an **A.logic** error that causes overlapping moves to be incorrect. In fact, the situation in which the copy should be done backward is when the *target* is later, not the source; so, the code should be changed to swap `target` and `source` wherever they appear (and the comment should also be changed):

```
if ((source < target) &&
    ((source + length) > target)) {
```

With the first hint, `source` and `target` don't overlap, so the `if` on line 21 is false and falls through to the `else` with `step` set to `1` and the copy proceeding in the forward direction (although it would work fine in the reverse direction because there is no overlap).

With the second, however, `source` and `target` do overlap. `target` is passed as `test_buffer`, `source` is `test_buffer+2`, and `length` is 4, so the `if` on lines 21 and 22 is true, resulting in `step` being set to `-1`. However, if you unwind the loop on lines 37 to 45, you can see the copy is done wrong:

Iteration 1: `target` is `test_buffer+3`, `source` is `test_buffer+5`.
Iteration 2: `target` is `test_buffer+2`, `source` is `test_buffer+4`.
Iteration 3: `target` is `test_buffer+1`, `source` is `test_buffer+3`.

This is where the bug happens: `test_buffer+3` was overwritten in iteration 1, so it does not have its original value. This copy should be done in the forward direction; `target` later than `source` is the situation that should be copied in reverse.

❺ Parse a String into Substrings

This function parses a string into substrings delimited by a specified character. The function takes as input a string, a delimiter, and an index. It splits the string into substrings that are separated by the delimiter, and returns the appropriate substring based on the index, where the first substring would be indexed as 1, the second as 2, and so on.

For example, with an input string `"This#is#a#test"` and a delimiter of `'#'`, index 2 would point to the substring `"is"`. (C strings are just arrays of type `char`; normally, the end of a string is marked by having a character with value 0, also written as `'\0'`, but in this case, to avoid having to copy the data or modify the input string, the substring is returned by indicating its starting point and length.)

Source Code

```
1.    char *
2.    parse_string(
3.        char * input_string,
4.        char delimiter,
5.        int index,
6.        int * return_length) {
7.
8.        char * curr_substring = input_string;
9.        char * curr_character = input_string;
10.       int found_so_far = 0;
11.
12.       while (1) {
13.
14.           ++found_so_far;
15.
16.           // At end of input string, exit the loop.
17.
18.           if (*curr_substring == '\0')
19.               break;
20.
21.           // If at delimiter, no need to loop through.
22.
23.           if (*curr_substring != delimiter) {
24.               curr_character = curr_substring;
25.
26.               // Not at delimeter, so loop to find it.
27.
28.               while ((*curr_character != '\0') &&
29.                      (*curr_character != delimiter)) {
30.                   ++curr_character;
31.               }
32.           }
33.
34.           if ((found_so_far == index) ||
35.               (*curr_character == '\0'))
36.               break;
37.
38.           // skip over the delimiter character
39.
40.           curr_substring = curr_character+1;
41.       }
```

```
42.
43.          if (found_so_far == index) {
44.              *return_length =
45.                  (curr_character - curr_substring);
46.              return curr_substring;
47.          } else {
48.              return NULL;
49.          }
50.      }
```

Suggestions

1. At line 33, what are the possible values for `*curr_character` (the character pointed to by `curr_character`)?
2. Because the `while (1)` loop starting on line 12 has a condition that is always true, it depends on other variables changing for it to exit. What comparisons cause the loop to exit? Are the variables being tested guaranteed to change each time through the loop?
3. What is the "implied else" of the `if` statement on line 23?
4. `found_so_far` is incremented on line 14 but is not tested until line 34. Is this correct?

Hints

Walk through the code with the following parameters to the function:

1. Normal operation that finds a substring: s is `"ab/cd/ef"`, delimeter is `'/'`, and index is 2.
2. The index is well past the last substring: s is `"t-u-v"`, delimeter is `'-'`, index is 5.
3. The index is just after the last substring: s is `"hello$"`, delimeter is `'$'`, index is 2.

Explanation of the Bug

The code on line 24 to initialize `curr_character`

```
curr_character = curr_substring;
```

has an **F.init** error; it will not execute if the `if` statements on line 18 or line 23 are false, yet `curr_character` can still be used in those situations.

The solution is to move line 24 up to around line 15, so it is always set correctly if the `while` loop exits.

The mistake can cause two different errors:

- If the `if` on line 18 is true and the `while` loop exits because of the `break` statement on line 19, `curr_character` remains set from the assignment on line 35 from the previous iteration of the `while` loop; thus, the calculation of `return_length` on line 44 evaluates to `-1`. This happens when the input string ends in a delimiter character and the index asks for the substring that goes just after that final delimiter (which is the case in the third hint).

- If the `if` on line 23 is false, `curr_character` remains unchanged for that iteration of the `while` loop. This means that the assignment of `curr_substring` on line 40 keeps its current value, so the `while` loop keeps looping until the `if` on line 34 is true because `found_so_far == index` (the other part of that if expression, `*curr_character == '\0'`, won't ever be true because `curr_character` continues to point 1 byte before `curr_substring`; thus not to a `'\0'` character). After the `while` loop exits, the calculation of `return_length` on line 44 again equals `-1`. This happens if the input string has two delimiter characters in a row.

⑥ Memory Allocator

This function is a memory allocator. Allocations are made from a chunk of memory, which in C is simply an array of `chars`. Memory is always allocated in multiples of a constant block size, so allocations are internally rounded up in size.

A consecutive group of blocks of memory, whether free or allocated, will be called a *span*. A second "in use" array tracks whether each block is allocated or freed; the "in use" array has one element per block. If a span is free, all the entries in the "in use" array that correspond to the blocks in the span contain the same positive value, which is the number of blocks in the span. If a span is allocated, all the corresponding entries in the "in use" array contain the same negative value, which is the negative of the number of blocks in the span.

The code uses some definitions interpreted by the C pre-processor:

```
#define MEMORY_SIZE 8000
#define BLOCK_SIZE 16
#define BLOCK_COUNT (MEMORY_SIZE / BLOCK_SIZE )
```

The following code allocates the main memory array and the "in use" array:

```
char array[MEMORY_SIZE];
int array_in_use[BLOCK_COUNT];
```

In addition, it assumes the following initialization function has been called, which initializes the "in use" array to show that every block is free and is part of a span that covers the entire chunk of allocatable memory:

```
void mem_init()
{
    int i;
    for (i = 0; i < BLOCK_COUNT; i++) {
        array_in_use[i] = BLOCK_COUNT;
    }
}
```

Source Code

```
1.    void *
2.    mem_alloc(int length)
3.    {
4.        int i;
5.        int blocks_needed, old_span_size;
6.        int block_index, best_fit;
7.
8.        blocks_needed =
9.            (length + (BLOCK_SIZE-1)) / BLOCK_SIZE;
10.
11.       // Now try to find the smallest free span that has
12.       // blocks_needed blocks available. best_fit stores
13.       // the index of the start of the best span found
14.       // so far.
15.
16.       block_index = 0;
17.       best_fit = -1;      // indicate nothing found so far
18.
19.       while (block_index < BLOCK_COUNT) {
20.
21.           if (array_in_use[block_index] >=
22.                   blocks_needed) {
23.
24.               if (best_fit == -1) {
25.                   best_fit = block_index;
```

```
26.                  } else {
27.                      if (array_in_use[block_index] <
28.                              array_in_use[best_fit]) {
29.                          best_fit = block_index;
30.                      }
31.                  }
32.              }
33.              // Skip to the next span
34.              block_index += array_in_use[block_index];
35.          }
36.
37.          // if best_fit stayed at -1, then nothing was found
38.          if (best_fit == -1) {
39.              return NULL;
40.          }
41.
42.          // Found a span; split it into two spans,
43.          // the allocated part and the remaining free part.
44.
45.          old_span_size = array_in_use[best_fit];
46.          for (i = 0; i < blocks_needed; i++ ) {
47.              array_in_use[best_fit + i] = -blocks_needed;
48.          }
49.          for (i = blocks_needed; i < old_span_size; i++) {
50.              array_in_use[best_fit + i] -= blocks_needed;
51.          }
52.
53.          return (array + (best_fit * BLOCK_SIZE));
54.      }
```

Suggestions

1. What is the goal of the `while` loop on lines 19–35? What variable is being set and what should it be set to when it is done?

2. The calculation of `blocks_needed` on lines 8–9 and the `return` statement on line 53 are both complicated. Verify that they are correct.

3. What is the loop counter for the `while` loop on lines 19–35? Is it properly incremented? Are the initialization and termination clauses correct?

4. For the five local variables, note any sections of the code in which they stay invariant.

Hints

Walk through the code with the following parameters to the function:

1. The initial case: Nothing has been allocated, so the `array_in_use[]` array is still set up the way it was by the `memory_init()` function:

   ```
   array_in_use[0] == BLOCK_COUNT
   array_in_use[1] == BLOCK_COUNT
   array_in_use[2] == BLOCK_COUNT
   ...
   array_in_use[BLOCK_COUNT-1] == BLOCK_COUNT
   ```

   and the function `mem_alloc(BLOCK_SIZE)` is called.

2. One block is allocated, the second block in `array[]`. Check that the code correctly picks a block that can fit the request. Therefore

   ```
   array_in_use[0] == 1
   array_in_use[1] == -1
   array_in_use[2] == BLOCK_COUNT-2
   array_in_use[3] == BLOCK_COUNT-2
   array_in_use[4] == BLOCK_COUNT-2
   ...
   array_in_use[BLOCK_COUNT-1] == BLOCK_COUNT-2
   ```

   and the function `mem_alloc(BLOCK_SIZE+1)` is called.

Explanation of the Bug

At the end of the `while` loop starting on line 19, the index of the next span to check is calculated using the knowledge that the number of blocks in this span is stored in `array_in_use[]`, on line 34:

```
block_index += array_in_use[block_index];
```

However, this only works for free spans, where the corresponding `array_in_use[]` element has a positive value.

When crossing allocated spans, where `array_in_use[]` has a negative value, the `if` on line 21 always fails because `blocks_needed` is positive. That's how the code avoids reallocating an already allocated span. However, `array_in_use[]` is negative, so to fix this **A.logic** bug, line 34 should be replaced with code like the following:

```
if (array_in_use[block_index] < 0) {
    block_index += -array_in_use[block_index];
} else {
    block_index += array_in_use[block_index];
}
```

For the first hint, no allocated spans exist, so the `array_in_use[]` values are always positive. In fact, there is only one free span, so the `while` loop iterates once, with `block_index` equal to 0; the code on line 34 adds `BLOCK_COUNT` to `block_index` (`array_in_use[0]` is equal to `BLOCK_COUNT`), at which point, `block_index` is equal to `BLOCK_COUNT` and the `while` condition on line 19 is false.

In the case of the second hint, `blocks_needed` is 2. Thus, the first span checked by the `if` on lines 21–22, with `block_index` equal to 0, won't be big enough: `array_in_use[0]` is 1, and `blocks_needed` is 2. Line 34 changes `block_index` to 1; on the second iteration of the while loop, the check on lines 21–22 is also false because `array_in_use[1]` is -1. The code to advance `block_index` on line 34, instead of changing it to 2 as it should, instead moves it back to 0. So, the `while` winds up looping forever as `block_index` ping-pongs between 0 and 1.

❼ Memory Free

This function frees memory allocated by the previous program. To reiterate, memory is allocated out of a block of memory, in multiples of a specified block size. A consecutive group of blocks of memory, whether free or allocated, is called a *span*. An "in use" array tracks whether each block is allocated or freed. If a span is free, all the entries in the "in use" array that correspond to the blocks in the span contain the same positive value, which is the number of blocks in the span. If a span is allocated, all the corresponding entries in the "in use" array contain the same negative value, which is the negative of the number of blocks in the span.

The code uses the pre-processor definitions:

```
#define MEMORY_SIZE 8000
#define BLOCK_SIZE 16
#define BLOCK_COUNT (MEMORY_SIZE / BLOCK_SIZE)
```

The following code allocates the main memory array and the "in use" array:

```
char array[MEMORY_SIZE];
int array_in_use[BLOCK_COUNT];
```

The code assumes that the buffer passed to be freed was in fact allocated by a correctly functioning version of the memory allocator, and is in the proper range and aligned correctly. It also assumes that the array_in_use array has not been corrupted.

Source Code

```
1.      void
2.      mem_free(char * buffer)
3.      {
4.          int i, buffer_index, buffer_block_count;
5.          int adjust_start, adjust_end;
6.          int adjust_value;
7.          int prev_block_count, next_block_count;
8.
9.          // Fix up array_in_use[] if the spans before and/or
10.         // after are also free.
11.
12.         buffer_index = (buffer - array) / BLOCK_SIZE;
13.         buffer_block_count = -array_in_use[buffer_index];
14.
15.         // These start out just fixing up this span --
16.         // they may grow if the previous and/or next span
17.         // has to be merged in. The fixup will be done
18.         // starting at array_in_use[adjust_start], up to
19.         // but not including array_in_use[adjust_end].
20.
21.         adjust_start = buffer_index;
22.         adjust_end = buffer_index + buffer_block_count;
23.         adjust_value = buffer_block_count;
24.
25.         // See if there is a previous span and is it free.
26.
27.         if ((adjust_start > 0) &&
28.                 (array_in_use[adjust_start - 1] > 0)) {
29.
30.             prev_block_count = array_in_use[adjust_start-1];
31.             adjust_start -= prev_block_count;
32.             adjust_value += prev_block_count;
33.         }
34.
35.         // See if there is a next span and is it free.
36.
37.         if ((adjust_end < BLOCK_COUNT) &&
38.                 (array_in_use[adjust_end+1] > 0)) {
39.
40.             next_block_count = array_in_use[adjust_end+1];
```

```
41.          adjust_end += next_block_count;
42.          adjust_value += next_block_count;
43.       }
44.
45.       // Now mark the span as free and the proper size.
46.
47.       for (i = adjust_start; i < adjust_end; i++) {
48.          array_in_use[i] = adjust_value;
49.       }
50.    }
```

Suggestions

1. What are the empty and trivial input cases for this function?
2. The code has various comments. Do the comments correctly match the functionality of the blocks they describe?
3. The code has many local variables. Which ones are used throughout the function and which ones are used only in certain blocks?
4. What are the valid values for indexing into `array_in_use`? Are they properly enforced? In cases where expressions are used, what does that imply about restrictions on the indexing variables? Are those followed?

Hints

Walk through the code with the following parameters to the function:

1. Verify that the code correctly restores all memory to be a single free span if only one allocation exists and it is freed. So, there is one allocation, starting at the third block and continuing for two blocks. `array_in_use[]` is set up as follows:
```
array_in_use[0] == 2
array_in_use[1] == 2
array_in_use[2] == -2
array_in_use[3] == -2
array_in_use[4] == BLOCK_COUNT-4
array_in_use[5] == BLOCK_COUNT-4
array_in_use[6] == BLOCK_COUNT-4
...
array_in_use[BLOCK_COUNT-1] == BLOCK_COUNT-4
```
The single allocation is freed. In effect,
```
mem_free(array + (2*BLOCK_SIZE))
```

is called, although the caller of `mem_free()` should not actually know about internal details, such as `array[]` and `BLOCK_SIZE`.

2. Test the boundary case of a single large allocated span, with one small free span at the end: There is one allocation, starting at block 0 and continuing for `BLOCK_COUNT-1` blocks, followed by one free block. Therefore, `array_in_use[]` is set up:

```
array_in_use[0] == -(BLOCK_COUNT-1)
array_in_use[1] == -(BLOCK_COUNT-1)
. . .
array_in_use[BLOCK_COUNT-2] == -(BLOCK_COUNT-1)
array_in_use[BLOCK_COUNT-1] == 1
```

The single allocation is freed. In effect,

```
mem_free(array)
```

is called.

Explanation of the Bug

The code that checks if the next span is free, on lines 37–43

```
if ((adjust_end < BLOCK_COUNT) &&
        (array_in_use[adjust_end+1] > 0)) {

    next_block_count = array_in_use[adjust_end+1];
    adjust_end += next_block_count;
    adjust_value += next_block_count;
}
```

indexes into `array_in_use[]` incorrectly. Because `adjust_end` is defined to be one more than the block number at the end of the buffer being freed, it is incorrect to add 1 to it. This is an **A.off-by-one** error that becomes a **D.index** error. The code needs to be as follows:

```
if ((adjust_end < BLOCK_COUNT) &&
        (array_in_use[adjust_end] > 0)) {

    next_block_count = array_in_use[adjust_end];
    adjust_end += next_block_count;
    adjust_value += next_block_count;
}
```

The example in the first hint works because `adjust_end` is 4 when the code arrives at line 37. The comparison on line 38 will look at `array_in_use[5]` when it should be looking at `array_in_use[4]`, but because they are both equal to the same thing (`BLOCK_COUNT-4`), `next_block_count` is set to `BLOCK_COUNT-4` on line 40, and `adjust_end` is then properly modified from 4 to `BLOCK_COUNT` on line 41.

With the second hint, `adjust_end` is equal to `BLOCK_COUNT-1` at line 37. As a result, the comparison on line 38 indexes `array_in_use[BLOCK_COUNT]`, which is past the end of `array_in_use[]`, and results in either a crash or undefined behavior, depending on whether the integer at that memory location is positive or negative.

❽ Recursive Word Reversal

This function prints out the words in a sentence reversed. The function uses recursive calls to itself. The definition of *words* is any sequence of characters delimited by one or more spaces. The resulting printout should include only one space between words, with no spaces before the first word or after the last word. Therefore, the input string can have multiple spaces between words, or before and after the string, but the result should not preserve those.

The bug does *not* involve the stack potentially overflowing because of excessive recursion—assume that is not an issue.

For this example, the length of the string is passed as an argument; thus, the string is not assumed to be terminated with a `'\0'` character. This is primarily done to make the recursion easier because it allows the recursive function calls to also specify the length of the string explicitly. Thus, it can operate on a substring of the original string without modifying or copying the string to put a final `'\0'` in.

The function uses the C standard library function `printf()` to display the string. The relevant syntax is

```
printf ("%.*s", n, s);
```

n represents a number and s is a string. This prints out the first n characters of the string s (unless s terminates earlier with a `'\0'`). The function can also print out a `'\0'`-terminated string, with no length needed:

```
printf ("%s", s);
```

or print out a literal string:

```
printf ("Hello");
```

but this example doesn't use it that way.

Source Code

```
1.     void
2.     print_reversed_string(
3.         char * inp_str,
4.         int inp_str_length) {
5.
6.         // Go to the end of the string and walk backwards.
7.         // When we hit the start of a word, print it, then
8.         // call recursively on the preceding part.
9.
10.        char * current_character;
11.        char * end_of_word;
12.
13.        // First skip any blanks at the end.
14.
15.        current_character = inp_str + (inp_str_length-1);
16.        while (current_character >= inp_str) {
17.            if (*current_character != ' ') break;
18.            --current_character;
19.        }
20.
21.        if (current_character >= inp_str) {
22.
23.            // end_of_word points to last char in the word.
24.            end_of_word = current_character;
25.
26.            // Now go back and find the beginning of the
27.            // word. We know the current is non-blank so we
28.            // can back up one right away.
29.            --current_character;
30.            while (current_character >= inp_str) {
31.                if (*current_character == ' ') break;
32.                --current_character;
33.            }
34.
35.            // current_character now points one character
36.            // before the beginning of the word -- either
37.            // a blank, or one byte before inp_str.
38.
39.            printf ("%.*s",
40.                    end_of_word - current_character,
41.                    current_character + 1);
42.
43.            if (current_character >= inp_str) {
44.
45.                // If there is more before this, then
```

65

```
46.                    // print a separator and call recursively,
47.                    // passing the previous part of the string.
48.                    printf(" ");
49.                    print_reversed_string(
50.                        inp_str,
51.                        (current_character+1) - inp_str);
52.                }
53.            }
54.        }
```

Suggestions

1. This function calls itself recursively. Under what conditions does it exit instead of making the recursive call? What guarantees are there that it will not get into an infinite set of recursive calls (by calling itself recursively with the exact same parameters that it was passed)?
2. What different types of inputs would the function need to ensure that every line of code is executed?
3. What is the useful lifetime of current_character as compared to end_of_word?
4. The calculation on line 51 is not obvious. Understand exactly where current_character is in relation to inp_str when this call is made to verify that the calculation is correct.

Hints

Walk through the code with the following parameters to the function:

1. A good test case is to have spaces at the end of the input string with multiple spaces between words, inp_str == "Hello world ", inp_str_length == 14:

```
inp_str[0]  == 'H'
inp_str[1]  == 'e'
inp_str[2]  == 'l'
inp_str[3]  == 'l'
inp_str[4]  == 'o'
inp_str[5]  == ' '
inp_str[6]  == ' '
inp_str[7]  == 'w'
inp_str[8]  == 'o'
inp_str[9]  == 'r'
inp_str[10] == 'l'
```

```
inp_str[11] == 'd'
inp_str[12] == ' '
inp_str[13] == ' '
inp_str[14] == '\0'
```

2. Test spaces at the beginning of the input string, `inp_str ==` `" qwerty uiop"`, `inp_str_length == 12`:

```
inp_str[0]  == ' '
inp_str[1]  == 'q'
inp_str[2]  == 'w'
inp_str[3]  == 'e'
inp_str[4]  == 'r'
inp_str[5]  == 't'
inp_str[6]  == 'y'
inp_str[7]  == ' '
inp_str[8]  == 'u'
inp_str[9]  == 'i'
inp_str[10] == 'o'
inp_str[11] == 'p'
inp_str[12] == '\0'
```

Explanation of the Bug

The problem occurs when spaces exist at the beginning of the string. The function is set to print nothing if all it is passed is a string full of spaces. However, at line 48, before the recursive call, it always calls

```
printf(" ");
```

Even if the string passed to the recursive call has only spaces and does nothing, the unwanted space still has been printed by line 48. This is a **D.limit** error.

The second hint shows this behavior. The first time through the function, it will back `current_character` up to point to `inp_str[7]`; that is, the space right before the word `"uiop"`. The code prints out `"uiop"`, then prints a space and calls itself recursively as `print_reversed_string(inp_str, 8)`. Inside this recursive call, it backs up `current_character` to point to `inp_str[0]`, which is the space right before the word `"qwerty"`. It prints out `"qwerty"`, the check on line 43 succeeds (`current_character` and `inp_str` will be equal, in fact), so it will print a space—the error in question—then call itself recursively again as `print_reversed_string(inp_str, 1)`. In this last recursive call, the `while` condition on line 16 becomes false after one iteration, the `if` on line 21 is false, and the function exits. But, the extra space at the end has been printed.

With the first hint, when `current_character` moves back to before `"Hello"`, the `if` on line 43 becomes false, so the extra space won't be printed.

One solution is to strip off the spaces at the end of the string before the recursive call. Between lines 41 and 43, add a repeat of lines 16–19:

```
while (current_character >= inp_str) {
    if (*current_character != ' ') break;
    --current_character;
}
```

This means the code on lines 16–19 only ever finds any spaces to strip on the first outer call to the function; on any recursive call, `inp_str_length` will have been adjusted back by the newly added code to hide any spaces.

❾ Calculate All Possible Routes

This function is a helper function for a brute force method of finding the shortest path between a set of five points. If the five points are numbered 0 through 4, a *route* is a unique ordering of the numbers 0 through 4. There are 120 such orderings (5 * 4 * 3 * 2 * 1), including ones that are the reverse of others. Each of the five positions in a route is called a *slot*, and the number in a given slot is called a *stop*.

The routes are numbered 0 through 119 and a lower-numbered route always has lower stops in earlier slots, except that a route cannot repeat a lower-numbered route. For example, the first route will be 0 1 2 3 4, the second will be 0 1 2 4 3, the third will be 0 1 3 2 4, and the last will be 4 3 2 1 0.

With 5 entries in a route, any given choice of stop in the first slot allows 24 possible choices for the others (4 * 3 * 2 * 1). So, the first 24 routes have stop 0 in the first slot, the next 24 have stop 1 in the first slot, and so on.

Then, for the 24 routes with stop 0 in the first slot, the first 6 have stop 1 in the second slot, the next 6 have stop 2 in the second slot, and so on. For the 24 routes with stop 1 in the first slot, the first 6 have stop 0 in the second slot, the next 6 have stop 2 in the second slot, and so on.

The function is passed a route number between 0 and 119. It is also passed an array that can hold 5 integers. The function should fill in the

5 places in the array with the numbers 0 through 4, arranged according to the route number. The function always fills in the array the same way for a given route number.

Source Code

```
1.     void
2.     fill_route(
3.         int route_number,
4.         int slots[5]) {
5.
6.         int stops_available[5];
7.         int i, j, k, factor, slot, this_stop;
8.
9.         for (i = 0; i < 5; i++) {
10.            stops_available[i] = i;    // all unused at first
11.        }
12.
13.        for (slot = 0; slot < 5; slot++) {
14.
15.            // For each slot, see how many consecutive
16.            // routes have the same stop in that slot. It's
17.            // the number of slots left factorial, so this
18.            // next loop calculates (4 - slot)!.
19.            factor = 1;
20.            for (j = 4-slot; j > 0; j--) {
21.                factor *= j;
22.            }
23.            this_stop = route_number / factor;
24.
25.            // Find the (this_stop+1)'th stop still left in
26.            // stops_available. The first time through the
27.            // outer loop (slot == 0) this will just be
28.            // stops_available[this_stop], but as entries in
29.            // stops_available[] are used and marked with -1
30.            // that will change.
31.            k = this_stop;
32.            for (j = 0; j < 5; j++) {
33.                if (stops_available[j] != -1) {
34.                    if (k == 0) {
35.                        stops_available[j] = -1;
36.                        slots[slot] = stops_available[j];
37.                        break;
38.                    }
39.                    --k;
40.                }
```

```
41.                    }
42.                    route_number = route_number % factor;
43.              }
44.        }
```

Suggestions

1. Note where the local variables are used, especially i, j, and k.
2. Examine the calculation of factorial on lines 20 and 21 to ensure that the algorithm is correct.
3. Think of what else acts as a loop variable for the main if from lines 13–43. Is it initialized and updated correctly?
4. Lines 35 and 36 have the same expression appearing on the left and right side of an assignment in quick succession. Is this done correctly?

Hints

1. Because the code is dividing and taking the modulo of the route number, it might be mathematically simplest to try with a route number of 0. That is, the function is called as fill_route(0, slots) where slots[] is an array of 5 ints.
2. Because there are 24 choices for a given stop in the first slot, a number just higher than 24 is a good test. Walk through the code to calculate route 25: The function is called as fill_route(25, slots) where slots[] an array of 5 ints.

Explanation of the Bug

The code to fill in slots[slot] and "use up" a stop, on lines 36 and 37,

```
stops_available[j] = -1;
slots[slot] = stops_available[j];
```

does it in the incorrect order, which is an **F.location** bug. The effect is to set slots[slot] to -1. The two lines of code need to be swapped:

```
slots[slot] = stops_available[j];
stops_available[j] = -1;
```

This manifests itself with any route number, so the same behavior should have been observed with both hints: The resulting `slots[]` array has `-1` in all five positions. However, running through the code with different route numbers should help you understand how this (admittedly confusing) algorithm works, because everything up until the actual assignment to `slots[]` is correct.

⑩ Kanji Backspace

This function backspaces within text stored using the encoding scheme known as *double-byte character sets* (*DBCS*). Although other writing systems are encoded using DBCS, this problem has acquired the name Kanji Backspace.

A text string encoded in DBCS contains a mixture of single-byte and double-byte characters. Single-byte characters are the ASCII characters that many programmers are familiar with; a capital `'A'` is represented by the single byte 65. Double-byte characters occupy 2 bytes in the encoding.

To tell them apart, single characters in DBCS are allowed to use only 7 bits, with the high bit off. In a double-byte character, the first byte has the high bit on, and the second byte can be any value.

Note

We will refer to bytes that have the eighth bit on as **high bytes** *and ones that do not have it on as* **low bytes,** *which are abbreviated as H and L. So, a double-byte character made up of a high byte followed by a low byte is called an HL character.*

Thus, moving forward through a DBCS string, it is easy to determine character boundaries: If you encounter a low byte, it is a single-byte character; if you encounter a high-byte, it is the first byte of a double-byte character; and then repeat. However, it is tricky to backspace because a low byte could be either a single-byte character or the second byte of a double-byte character.

The Kanji Backspace algorithm is based on the observation that a low byte always precedes a character boundary. That is, the byte after a low byte is always the beginning of a new character. Using this information, the code can scan backward to find a known character boundary.

The function takes the start of the string and the current location in the string as parameters. It needs the string's start because sometimes you have to walk all the way back to the start of the string to figure out the character boundaries. The function returns a pointer to the previous character.

Source Code

```
1.    char *
2.    kanji_backspace(
3.        char * string_start,
4.        char * current) {
5.
6.        char * location, * return_value;
7.        int distance;
8.
9.        if ((*(current-1)) & 0x80) { // byte before current?
10.           // H byte, must be second byte of HH character
11.           return_value = current - 2;
12.       } else {
13.           // L byte, so find a previous reliable character
14.           // boundary. The algorithm is to scan back until
15.           // we find another L byte, or hit string_start.
16.           location = current-2;
17.           while (location >= string_start) {
18.               if (((*location) & 0x80) == 0) {
19.                   break;
20.               }
21.               --location;
22.           }
23.
24.           // The byte right after location is the start of
25.           // a character. See how far it is from current.
26.           distance = (current - (location+1));
27.           if ((distance % 2) == 0) {
28.               // series of HH chars followed by HL char
29.               return_value = current-2;
30.           } else {
31.               // series of HH chars followed by L char
32.               return_value = current-1;
33.           }
34.       }
35.
36.       // Check to make sure we have not moved back before
37.       // string_start. We compare with <= because we are
```

```
38.          // going back one character.
39.          if (return_value <= string_start) {
40.              return NULL;
41.          } else {
42.              return return_value;
43.          }
44.      }
```

Suggestions

1. What are the trivial and empty inputs for this function?
2. What inputs are required to ensure full code coverage?
3. Restate the `if` statements on lines 9 and 18 in English.
4. What is the goal of `while` on line 17? What is true at line 23?

Hints

Walk through the code with the following parameters to the function:

1. Test the case where the preceding character is a single-byte character. A buffer `test_string` is set up as follows:

```
test_string[0]  ==  0x9f
test_string[1]  ==  0x68
test_string[2]  ==  0x86
test_string[3]  ==  0xa0
test_string[4]  ==  0x34
test_string[5]  ==  0x65
```

That is, it contains an HL character, an HH character, and an L character.

The function is called as follows:
```
kanji_backspace(test_string, test_string+5)
```

2. Try the case where the preceding character is a double-byte character and the first character in the string. A buffer `test_string` is set up the same way:

```
test_string[0]  ==  0x9f
test_string[1]  ==  0x68
test_string[2]  ==  0x86
test_string[3]  ==  0xa0
test_string[4]  ==  0x34
test_string[5]  ==  0x65
```

The function is called as follows:
```
kanji_backspace(test_string, test_string+2)
```

Explanation of the Bug

The check performed at the end, on line 39, to make sure that you did not step back before the beginning of the string,

```
if (return_value <= string_start) {
```

is incorrect. It is acceptable for `return_value` to point to `string_start`, if the function was called with the parameter `current` pointing to the second character in the string. This is an **A.off-by-one** bug; the check should be as follows:

```
if (return_value < string_start) {
```

The comment preceding the test

```
// Check to make sure we have not moved back before
// string_start. We compare with <= because we are
// going back one character.
```

is a red herring; although the function is indeed going back one character, that has nothing to do with whether this check should use <= or <.

With the situation in the first hint, the byte before current is a low byte (0x34). The `if` on line 9 is false and the code runs through the `else` case starting on line 12. The `while` loop starting on line 17 never finds another L character, so at line 23, after the `while` loop, `location` winds up as `string_start-1`. Because `current` was passed in as `string_start+5`, the calculation on line 26 sets `distance` to be 5; therefore, the string is as described in the comment on line 31 and `return_value` is set properly on line 32. The incorrect test on line 39 doesn't cause an error because `return_value` is greater than `string_start`.

With the second hint, the byte before `current` is an H byte, so `if` on line 9 is true and `return_value` is set correctly on line 11. However, `return_value` happens to be equal to `string_start`, so the incorrect check on line 39 is true and the function winds up incorrectly returning NULL on line 40.

Chapter 4

PYTHON

Brief Summary of Python

Python is an interpreted language. In Python, a new line terminates a statement; a continuation character \ can be used to continue a statement on a second line.

Python is sensitive not only to new lines, but also to how many spaces a line is indented. A block of code has all the lines indented the same number of spaces, and that is the only way that a block is indicated. It is illegal to change the indentation within a block of code, unless you are beginning a new inner block, such as the body of an `if` statement. There is no defined amount of spaces that the inner block must be indented, as long as it is at least one more than the outer block. A block of code ends when the indent level reverts to the level of an outer block.

Comments are denoted with a #. Everything after that symbol on a line is ignored. Comments can also be written as strings that are not assigned to any variable (for more details, see the section, "Strings").

Data Types and Variables

Python supports integers and floating point numbers; integers in an expression are converted to floating point numbers if needed.

Variable and function names are case-sensitive. Variables do not need to be declared as an explicit type; in fact, they are not declared at all. Python assignment statements associate a variable name with an object, which can be a number, string, or something more complicated. It is a mistake to use a variable in an expression if it has not been bound to an object. When the variable is used, its type will be the type of the object to which it is bound. Thus, if you wrote the following

```
i = 5
```

i points to an integer and would be used as such in any expression. If you then write the following

```
i = "Hello"
```

i now points to a string. However, Python does not convert between strings and numbers automatically. For example, if you write

```
i = "5"
```

you cannot use i somewhere that expects an integer without converting it (in this case, using the built-in int() function).

Python takes care of issues such as garbage-collecting storage used by reassigned strings.

You won't see them here, but Python also supports complex numbers. (Using the syntax 2.0+0.5j, with the j or J being a required element 2.0 is the real part and 0.5 is the imaginary part. So, 1j * 1j equals -1+0j.)

Multiple variables can be assigned at once, as in the following:

```
two, three = 2, 3
```

All the expressions on the right-hand side are evaluated before any assignments are done, so two variables can easily be swapped:

```
x, y = y, x
```

In Python, arithmetic uses the standard symbols, with % used for modulo:

```
total = (total * 3) - 4
counter = (counter + 1) % 100
```

Strings

Strings are surrounded by single or double quotes, which must match. Multiline strings are surrounded by triple quotes (either " " " or ' ' '):

```
state = "Maryland"
longstring = """This is a
    multiline string"""
```

Multiline strings are often included in Python code without being assigned to anything (which means that they have no semantic relevance). It's a way to include comments in the code:

```
""" Reinitialize the translation dictionary
"""
translations.clear()
```

Strings can be indexed into with integers (starting at zero). Indices can be negative; the index -1 refers to the last character in the string, -2 the second-to-last character, and so on:

```
testStr = "Ostrich"
testStr[0]     # "O"
testStr[6]     # "h"
testStr[-1]    # "h"
testStr[5]     # "c"
testStr[-2]    # "c"
testStr[-7]    # "O"
testStr[-8]    # ERROR!
testStr[7]     # ERROR!
```

There is no distinction between a single character and a string. Indexing into a string as shown above produces a string of length one.

The slice character, : (colon), obtains substrings by using the syntax x:y to mean "all characters from index x up to, but not including, index y."

The default for x is 0, while the default for y is the string's length. Finally, strings are concatenated using the $+$ symbol:

```
name1 = "Tom"
name2 = "Jones"
newname = name1[0] + name2[:3] + "123"
```

This code sets `newname` to `"Tjon123"`. You cannot assign directly into a substring, so

```
newname[1] = "X"   # WRONG!!
```

is illegal. Instead, you could write the following:

```
newname = newname[:1] + "X" + newname[2:]
```

The function `len()` returns the length of a string:

```
byteCount = len(buffer)
```

Lists and Tuples

Python has two types of ordered sets of elements: *lists* and *tuples*. These types function like arrays in other languages. The main difference is that a tuple cannot be modified once declared; it is "immutable," as opposed to a list, which is mutable. The elements in a list or tuple can be of any type mixed together.

A list is declared with square brackets:

```
mylist = [ "hello", 7, "green" ]
```

A tuple is declared with parentheses:

```
mytuple = ( "hello", 7, ( "red", 31 ) )
```

`mytuple` has three elements, the third of which is another tuple, which itself has two elements, `"red"` and `31`. The middle of such a declaration list (or any place in Python that is inside an expression surrounded with parentheses, curly braces, or square brackets) is one occasion where a line can be broken without adding the line-joining character, backslash (\).

Accessing lists and tuples is done the same way as strings, with zero-based integer indexing, negative indexing going backward from the end, and the slice operator:

```
firstelement = mylist[0]
lastelement = mylist[-1]
subtuple = mytuple[1:3]
```

You can assign a value to an element in a list (but not an element in a tuple because tuples are immutable):

```
mylist[1] = "newlistvalue"
```

You can also assign a list to a slice (the list doesn't have to be the same length as the slice):

```
mylist [0:3] = [ "Just one value now" ]
```

append() adds an element to a list and extend() combines two lists, as shown here:

```
mylist.append( 9 )
mylist.extend( [ "new", "entries", 50 ] )
```

Note that append() and extend() are methods on the list object, as opposed to built-in functions; in Python all variables (and literals) are objects, but in most cases we won't care about this fact.

A new list can be created from an existing list using *list comprehensions*. An example is the easiest way to show how to use this:

```
oldlist = [ 1, 2, 3, 4 ]
newlist = [ elem* 2 for elem in oldlist if elem != 3 ]
```

This sets newlist to be [2, 4, 8]. The if part of the list comprehension is optional.

The length of a list or tuple is returned using the built-in len() function:

```
print "List has", len(mylist), "elements"
```

Entries are deleted using del, which can take a single index or a slice:

```
del mylist[2]
del mylist[0:1]
```

None of the functions that modify lists are allowed on tuples.

Dictionaries

Python has a more sophisticated storage type called a *dictionary*. A dictionary is an unordered set of keys and values, in which values can be looked up by key. The keys are usually an integer or a string. The values can be any Python value, including another dictionary. Keys do not need to be in any order or of the same type.

For example, you can write the following:

```
mydict[0] = "First"
mydict[1] = "Second"
```

From then on, indexing into `mydict` looks similar to that used to access a single entry in a list or tuple:

```
newvar = mydict[1]
```

However, you don't have to use integers as keys; a key can be any immutable object, including a tuple. You could instead write the following:

```
mydict["zero"] = "First"
mydict["one"] = "Second"
```

This indexes by using the strings `"zero"` and `"one"`. You can also write the following:

```
mydict[0] = "Zero"
mydict["Name"] = "Joe"
```

You could also combine all the previous six statements. If you do that, the second assignment to `mydict[0]` would replace the value `"First"` with the value `"Zero"`.

Dictionaries are defined with curly braces, { and }, using a `key:value` syntax and separated by commas:

```
mydict = { 0 : "Zero", "Name" : "Joe" }
```

You can check the number of entries in a dictionary, delete entries from a dictionary, and check if a value exists for a given key:

```
length = len(mydict)
del mydict["Name"]
if 1 in mydict:
```

The in syntax is new in Python 2.2. Previously, the notation mydict.has_key(1) was used (has_key() was a method on the dictionary object).

The dictionary function keys() returns a list whose elements are the keys currently in the dictionary.

Conditionals

if statements end with a semicolon (:), and the body of the if is then indented. The block ends when the indentation ends. The keywords else and elif (else-if) can also be used:

```
if c == 12:
    c = 1
    print "starting over"
elif c < 12:
    c = c + 2
    if c in mylist:
        del mylist[c]
else:
    print c
```

Note that == (two equal signs) is used for comparisons. Expressions can be grouped together with and and or:

```
if (k == 4) or ((k > 10) and (k < 20)):
```

In control flow statements, the number 0, empty strings, tuples, lists, and dictionaries, and the special value None are all interpreted as false. All other values are true. Python recently added a built-in type bool that has two possible values, True and False.

Loops

Loops are done by walking through the elements in a list or a string:

```
for element in mylist:
    print element
```

The `range()` operator can easily declare a list of increasing numbers to simulate a typical `for` loop:

```
for i in range(0, 12):
    print mystring[:i]
```

This loops 12 times, with `i` having values from `0` to `11`. The first value is optional, so `range(10)` has values from `0` to `9` inclusive. A third argument to `range()` can specify the increment to use each time:

```
for j in range (5, 105, 5):
    print j
```

This counts to 100 by fives. (The top of the range could have been 101 instead of 105; the range ends when it reaches or passes the end point.)

Remember a couple of things about for loops and `range()`:

- After the loop is done, the loop counter contains the value it had on the last iteration, so in the previous example with `range(0, 12)`, after the loop is done, `i` will be equal to `11`.
- If the range turns out to be empty (the end point is less than or equal to the beginning point), the loop counter is not modified at all, so if it was not initialized before the loop, it remains uninitialized after the loop.

    `while` loops iterate as long as the specific condition is true:

```
while len(mystring) > 0:
    print mystring[0]
    mystring = mystring[1:]
```

`break` and `continue` can be used to leave a loop and continue with the next iteration, respectively. Loops can also have an `else` clause, which executes if the loop reaches its end naturally (that is, without hitting a break statement):

```
while (k < length):
    if (something):
        break
else:
    # if we get here, did not hit the break statement
```

Functions

Functions are defined with the def keyword. Only the names of the arguments are specified; the types are whatever is passed to the function at runtime:

```
def lookup_value(dict, keyvalue, defaultvalue):
    if keyvalue in dict:
        return dict[keyvalue]
    else:
        return defaultvalue
```

Functions that do not exit via a return statement, or that execute return with no arguments, actually return a built-in value called None.

Functions can have default parameters, as in the following definition:

```
def show_text (text, intensity=100):
```

Classes

Python has *classes*, as in C++ and other languages. However, this book doesn't use classes except in their most basic form, which is a way to associate named data items, the same as a struct (structure) in C. Such Python classes are declared with an empty declaration with no member functions. The Python statement pass is defined to do nothing and exists for places where the language syntax requires a statement:

```
class Point:
    pass
```

A new instance of this class is created with the syntax:

```
p = Point()
```

As with local variables, class member variables don't need to be declared ahead of time; they can simply be assigned a value:

```
Point.x = 12
Point.y = 15
```

Methods can be written to allow the class instantiation operator to take parameters, for example, Point(12, 15), but this book won't cover that or other features of Python classes.

Exceptions

Python supports exceptions. Code can be put inside a `try` block, followed by one or more `except` clauses to handle different exceptions:

```
try:
    x = int(input_buffer)
except(ValueError):
    print "Invalid input!"
```

Exceptions propagate upward if not handled; unhandled exceptions cause a program to terminate. Exceptions can be raised with the `raise` statement:

```
if (j > 100):
    raise ValueError, j
```

The statement `raise` with no arguments can be used within an exception handler to re-raise the exception.

The `except` statement can list multiple exceptions, and the last `except` clause can list no exceptions to serve as a wildcard. (This is risky because it catches all exceptions.) Exception handlers are another area where you might see the Python statement `pass`:

```
try:
    # some code
except (TypeError, NameError):
    pass
except:
    print "Unknown exception"
    raise
```

Python also supports user-defined exceptions, which this book doesn't discuss.

Importing Other Code

Code in other modules must be imported before it is used. The statement

```
import random
```

brings in the code in the standard `random` module, which has a useful function, `random()`, that returns a floating point number between 0 and

1 (but not equal to 1). Imported functions are called with the syntax `module-name.function-name()`, so in this case, `random.random()`.

Output

Output can be displayed with the `print` statement:

```
print j
```

`print` can display more complicated types, such as lists and dictionaries, with a single command.

❶ Is a Number Prime?

This function returns `1` if a number is prime; otherwise, it returns `0`.

A prime number has only two divisors: 1 and itself. (The number 1 is not prime.)

The function is only required to work correctly on positive numbers and 0. The efficiency of the function, or lack thereof, is not the bug.

Source Code

```
1.    def isPrime( number ):
2.        """ Check if a number is prime
3.
4.            number: An integer.
5.
6.            Returns: 1 if number is prime, 0 otherwise
7.        """
8.
9.        """ Special-case 0 and 1, which are not prime.
10.       """
11.
12.       if ( number == 0 ) or ( number == 1):
13.           return 0
14.
15.       """ Make a range of all numbers up to half of the
16.           one we want to check
```

```
17.              """
18.
19.              checkList = range(2, (number/2))
20.
21.              """ If we find a factor, return 0 right away.
22.                  If the loop ends first, then it is prime.
23.              """
24.
25.              for check in checkList:
26.
27.                  if ((number / check) * check) == number:
28.                      return 0
29.
30.              else:
31.
32.                  return 1
```

Suggestion

1. On line 12, an `if` statement has a logical `or` in it. Because it can be easy to accidentally invert the meaning of these, check that this line is correct.
2. The main part of the algorithm is the loop that starts on line 25. Does the loop counter look like it is used correctly?
3. Are the return statements correct? Ensure that the function follows the behavior it is defined to use (that is, make sure that it has not swapped when it is supposed to return 0 and when it is supposed to return 1).
4. What set of inputs do you need to choose to ensure that every line of code in the function is covered?

Hints

In an algorithm such as this, it's likely that any errors appear near the limit, which in this case, is with small numbers. Walk through the code with the following values for the `number` parameter to the function:

1. Test the introductory special case: Try `number` equal to 0 and 1.
2. Test the main logic with a mix of small prime and non-prime numbers: Try `number` equal to 2, 3, 4, 5, and 6.

Explanation of the Bug

The code on line 19 that creates the range of numbers to check

```
checkList = range(2, (number/2))
```

is incorrect in the case where number is equal to 4. Recall that the list returned by range() does not include the end point; therefore, range(2, 2) is an empty range. As a result, when number is 4, the for loop on line 25 immediately falls through to the else statement on line 30 and then to the return statement on line 32, and the code incorrectly reports that 4 is a prime number. It works correctly on all other positive numbers. This is a **D.limit** error because it fails only at the edge of the range of possible values.

The fix is to extend the checkList range created on line 19 by one more element, so in the case of number equal to 4, the for loop on line 25 will iterate once with a value of 2:

```
checkList = range(2, (number/2)+1)
```

The smallest value of number that isn't special-cased by the introductory code is 2; you can quickly verify that when number is 2 or 3 the checkList range will be initialized to (2,2) on line 19, meaning the for loop on line 25 never iterates and the function properly returns 1 on line 32.

❷ Find a Substring

This function finds a substring within a string. It returns a tuple with two elements:

- The first element is the part of the outer string before the substring.
- The second element is the rest of the outer string (beginning with the substring).

If the substring is not found, the first element of the tuple is the entire original string and the second element is an empty string.

Note

The standard Python string library has a function, find(), *that does essentially the same operation. (It returns the index of the first occurrence of the substring, not a tuple.) This book doesn't use that here.*

Source Code

```
1.     def findSubstring ( outerString, subString ):
2.
3.         """Finds the first occurrence of subString within
4.             outerString.
5.
6.             Returns a tuple of the part of the string
7.             before the first occurrence of subString,
8.             and the part starting at the first occurrence
9.             of subString. If not found, the second tuple
10.            is empty.
11.
12.        """
13.
14.        outerLen = len(outerString)
15.        subLen = len(subString)
16.        flag = 1
17.
18.        for i in range(outerLen):
19.
20.            for j in range(subLen):
21.
22.                if outerString[i+j] != subString[j]:
23.                    break
24.
25.            else:
26.
27.                # wind up here if for j loop terminates
28.                # naturally.
29.
30.                flag = 0
31.                break    # out of for i loop
32.
33.        return \
34.            ( outerString[:(i+flag)], outerString[(i+flag):] )
```

Suggestions

1. Consider the variable `flag`, which has a fairly unhelpful name. Determine the goal of `flag` and a better name for it.
2. What are the various situations that the code could encounter (for example, a substring that is not found at all)?
3. Look at the places where the code indexes into `outerString` and `subString`. What are the restrictions on indexing into those strings, and what does that imply about how the variables used need to be restricted?

Hints

Walk through the code with the following inputs:

1. Part of the substring matches, but not all:
   `outerString == "Hello", subString == "Hi"`
2. The substring is found in the outer string:
   `outerString == "blue", subString == "l"`
3. The beginning of the substring matches the end of the outer string:
   `outerString = "ball", subString == "llama"`

Explanation of the Bug

The problem occurs on line 22:

```
if outerString[i+j] != subString[j]:
```

Because `i` is indexing through a range that goes up to (but not including) the length of `outerString`, adding `j` to the index might make it invalid, which is a **D.index** error. This happens in the situation in the third hint, where the first N characters of `subString` match the last N characters of `outerString`, and `subString` then has at least one more character in it. When `i` is 2, the `if` on line 22 will be false (`outerString[i+j]` is equal to `subString[j]`) when `j` is 0 and 1 (the last two l's in "ball" matching the first two l's in "llama"). Because of this the inner loop will iterate again with `j` equal to 2. At that point, `i+j` is 4 and the expression `outerString[i+j]` will result in an "index out of range" error.

This could be fixed in several ways. One way would be to fix the
`range()` used in the inner `for` loop. A more obvious fix would be to
directly guard against the subscript access by checking for it just before
line 22, adding a couple of lines:

```
if (i+j) >= outerLen:
    break
```

❸ Alphabetize Words

This function is passed a string buffer. It splits the string into words and
alphabetizes them. The return value is a list containing the words in
alphabetical order.

For the purposes of alphabetizing them, strings are compared with
the Python < operator, which compares strings using the built-in `ord()`
function that winds up comparing them based on ASCII values. Thus,
upper- and lowercase letters are unequal; the uppercase letters are considered "earlier" than the lowercase ones.

Source Code

```
1.   def alphabetize ( buffer ):
2.
3.      """Split buffer into words and return a list of them
4.         in alphabetical order.
5.
6.
7.      """
8.
9.      alphaList = [ ]
10.     wordBegin = 0
11.
12.     """ NOTE: The code does not check the indexing into
13.         buffer to prevent it from pointing past the end;
14.         instead it catches the IndexError exception
15.         that is raised when it does.
16.     """
17.
18.     while True:
19.
20.         """ Find start of next word.
```

```
21.                    " " "
22.
23.              try:
24.                  while buffer[wordBegin] == " ":
25.                      wordBegin = wordBegin + 1
26.              except IndexError:
27.                  break
28.
29.              """ Find end of the word.
30.              " " "
31.
32.              wordEnd = wordBegin+1
33.              try:
34.                  while buffer[wordEnd] != " ":
35.                      wordEnd = wordEnd + 1
36.              except IndexError:
37.                  pass
38.
39.              newWord = buffer[wordBegin:wordEnd-1]
40.
41.              alphaLen = len(alphaList)
42.              for j in range(alphaLen):
43.                  if alphaList[j] > newWord:
44.                      alphaList[j:j] = [ newWord ]
45.                      break;
46.              else:
47.                  alphaList[alphaLen:] = [ newWord ]
48.
49.              wordBegin = wordEnd + 1
50.
51.
52.          return alphaList
```

Suggestions

1. What are the empty and trivial inputs for this function? Is there the equivalent of an already solved input?

2. What is the goal of `alphaList` and `wordBegin` after one iteration through the `while` loop?

3. The blocks on lines 23–27 and lines 33–37 are similar, except for a couple of differences. Because code like this might have been pasted and modified, ensure that the differences are correct.

4. Because a `while True` loop is infinite, unless a `break` statement is executed, verify that this function terminates on all inputs.

Hints

Walk through the function with the following parameters:

1. The buffer has blanks at the beginning: `buffer == "  Help"`
2. The buffer has blanks at the end: `buffer == "one two  "`
3. The buffer has one-character words with no extra spaces:
   `buffer == "A B C D"`

Explanation of the Bug

The bug is in the calculation of `newWord` on line 39:

```
newWord = buffer[wordBegin:wordEnd-1]
```

It is true that `wordEnd` points to the space after the word. However, in the slice notation in Python, the final index is not included in the slice, so the code has an **A.off-by-one** error. The code should read as follows:

```
newWord = buffer[wordBegin:wordEnd]
```

`wordEnd` itself is calculated correctly, so `wordBegin` is assigned to point to the right place on line 49, and the search for the next word begins at the correct spot. The only problem is that every word in `alphaList` has its last character truncated. (This happens even before `alphaList` is scanned to find the proper place for the new word, so the list is alphabetized correctly, just with words that are too short.) Using the input from any of the three hints shows this effect. The third hint shows the effect most dramatically because all the words are only one character long to begin with, and thus, all get truncated to empty strings.

❹ Encode Strings Using a Character Map

This function encodes strings using a simple character map. Letters are mapped to the letter that is 13 positions away in the alphabet, so A becomes N (and N becomes A), B becomes O, and so on. In addition, numbers are mapped to the symbol that occupies the same key on a standard U.S. keyboard, so 1 becomes !, 2 becomes @ (and vice versa), and so on. Other characters are left alone.

The built-in function `index()`, when called on a string, returns the index in the string of the first occurrence of a substring: It raises a `ValueError` exception if the substring is not found:

```
location = index("hey there", "th")
```

The function `ord()` converts a one-character string to its ASCII value, and `chr()` does the reverse, converting a number to a one-character string whose ASCII value is that number:

```
numA = ord("A")      # numA will be 65
strA = chr(65)       # strA will be "A"
```

Source Code

```
1.   numbers = "1234567890"
2.   symbols = "!@#$%^&*()"
3.
4.   def encode ( string ):
5.       """ Encodes string using a simple mapping
6.           string: the input string
7.
8.           Returns the mapped string.
9.       """
10.
11.      # fill in the maps; a character at a given position
12.      # in map1 maps to the character at the same position
13.      # in map2, and vice versa.
14.
15.      map1, map2 = [ ], [ ]
16.
17.      # first do the letters, put the first half of the
18.      # alphabet in map1, then the rest in map2...
19.
20.      for k in range(ord("A"), ord("A")+13):
21.          map1.append(chr(k))
22.      for k in range(ord("a"), ord("a")+13):
23.          map1.append(chr(k))
24.      map2 = [chr(ord(x)-13) for x in map1]
25.
26.      # ...now do the numbers/symbols
27.
```

```
28.        for k in range(len(numbers)):
29.            map1.append(numbers[k])
30.            map2.append(symbols[k])
31.
32.        newstring = ""
33.
34.        # now map any character in map1 to the character at
35.        # the same position in map2, and any character in map2
36.        # to the same characters in map1.
37.
38.        for c in string:
39.            if (c in map1):
40.                newc = map2[map1.index(c)]
41.            elif (c in map2):
42.                newc = map1[map2.index(c)]
43.            else:
44.                newc = c
45.
46.            newstring = newstring + newc
47.
48.        return newstring
```

Suggestions

1. As previously mentioned, the `index()` function raises a `ValueError` exception if the substring is not found. Because the program does not catch the exception, it would be an error if it were thrown. Check that this won't happen.
2. Describe precisely the intended relationship between `map1` and `map2`. Does the initialization of the two variables maintain this relationship?
3. Think of empty, trivial, and already solved inputs for this function.
4. Track where the return value `newstring` is modified and ensure that it is done correctly.

Hints

Walk through the function with the following inputs:

1. A single lowercase letter: `string == "a"`
2. A single uppercase letter: `string == "A"`
3. A mix of letters and numbers: `string == "abc123"`
4. Letters and a symbol: `string == "bye?"`

Explanation of the Bug

The code on line 24 to initialize the letter parts of map2

```
map2 = [chr(ord(x)-13) for x in map1]
```

has a **B.expression** error. The code intends to initialize map1 with the letters in the first half of the alphabet and map2 with the letters in the second half. This means that the ASCII values in map2 should be 13 *higher* than those in map1, so the code should be as follows:

```
map2 = [chr(ord(x)+13) for x in map1]
```

As a result of this error, the program maps the letters A through M, in upper- and lowercase, to a random collection of numbers, punctuation, and even other (incorrect) letters based on the happenstance arrangement of the ASCII table. All that mapping then also happens in reverse because of the way the program is designed.

❺ Print the Month and Day

This function, when passed a day within a year (January 1 is 1, February 1 is 32, and so on) prints the month name and day within the month.

This function takes an extra parameter to specify if the year is a leap year (where February has 29 days).

The function should raise the ValueError exception if the day number is invalid.

Remember that a class with an empty definition functions like a struct in C, allowing data to be accessed by name.

This excerpt from the *Python Reference Manual* helps explain one potentially confusing expression in the code:

> The expression *x* and *y* first evaluates *x*; if *x* is false, its value is returned; otherwise, *y* is evaluated and the resulting value is returned.

> The expression *x* or *y* first evaluates *x*; if *x* is true, its value is returned; otherwise, *y* is evaluated and the resulting value is returned.

Source Code

```
1.    # Month will have two members, name and days.
2.
3.    class Month:
4.      pass
5.
6.    def showday( daynumber, isleapyear ):
7.        """ Shows the month and day for a given day number.
8.
9.            daynumber: a day number within the year.
10.           isleapyear: True if the year is a leap year
11.
12.           Prints the month and day, raises ValueError if
13.           daynumber is invalid.
14.       """
15.
16.       months = [ "January", "February", "March",
17.                   "April", "May", "June",
18.                   "July", "August", "September",
19.                   "October", "November", "December" ]
20.
21.       days = [ 31 for x in months ]
22.
23.       # Let's see, 30 days hath September...
24.
25.       thirtylist = ( "April", "June",
26.                       "September", "November" )
27.
28.       for j in [ months.index(k) for k in thirtylist ]:
29.         days[j] = 30
30.
31.       # Fix up February also
32.
33.       days[months.index("February")] = \
34.             28 + ((isleapyear and 1) or 0)
35.
36.       """ daymap consists of 12 Month objects, each of which
37.           has a name/days pair in it.
38.       """
39.
40.       daymap = [ ]
41.
42.       for i in range(len(months)):
43.         newMonth = Month()
44.         newMonth.name = months[i]
```

```
45.          newMonth.days = days[i]
46.          daymap.append(newMonth)
47.
48.      if daynumber > 0:
49.        for el in daymap:
50.          if daynumber < el.days:
51.            print el.name, daynumber
52.            return
53.          daynumber = daynumber - el.days
54.
55.      raise ValueError, "daynumber"
```

Suggestions

1. Determine the goal of the code up to line 47. How many of the variables used prior to that line remain important after line 47? What are the goals of those variables? Are they properly initialized to meet this goal?
2. Verify that the expression on lines 33 and 34 works properly. What are the inputs to this line of code? How many different values are needed to test it?
3. The months list is the kind of declaration that the eye easily skips. Is it actually correct, meaning that the months are spelled correctly and listed in the correct order?
4. One test that can be done on the function is to assume that daymap is initialized correctly and just test from line 48 on. Assuming that you decide to do this with days in January (the daynumber parameter is between 1 and 31), what is a good set of values to test with?

Hints

Walk through the code with the following inputs:

1. First day of the year: daynumber = 1, isleapyear = False
2. First day of a month other than January: daynumber = 32, isleapyear = False
3. February 29: daynumber = 60, isleapyear = True
4. Last day of a leap year: daynumber = 366, isleapyear = True

Explanation of the Bug

The code on line 50

```
if daynumber < el.days:
```

checks if `daynumber` is small enough that the day falls within the month to which `el` refers. Because `daynumber` is 1-based, not 0-based, the code uses the incorrect comparison operator. Instead, the code should read as follows:

```
if daynumber <= el.days:
```

This **A.off-by-one** error manifests itself on the last day of a month. As currently written, the code reports, for example, that day 31 is `"February 0"` instead of `"January 31"`. In that example, the very first time line 50 is executed `el` will be the element representing January, so both `daynumber` and `el.days` will be 31. The comparison on line 50 will be false, and `daynumber` will be reduced to 0 on line 53. During the next iteration of the `for` loop that starts on line 49, `el` will be the element representing February. At line 50 `daynumber` will be 0, and `el.days` will be 28 (or 29 in a leap year), so the program will print `"February 0"` on line 51 and then return. Similarly, in the case of the third hint—where day 60 (in a leap year) is February 29—the code reports it as `"March 0"`.

❻ Go Fish, Part I: Draw a Card from a Deck

This function draws a card from a deck and puts it into a hand. It is meant to be a part of the game *Go Fish*, so if the resulting hand has all four suits for a given card rank, those four cards are removed from the hand. The next two programs build on this one to produce a full version of the game.

Cards are identified by their rank and suit: the rank is one of the elements of the list `["2", "3", "4", "5", "6", "7", "8", "9", "10", "J", "Q", "K", "A"]` and the suit is one of the elements of the list `["spades", "hearts", "diamonds", "clubs"]`.

A deck is a list that initially contains 52 elements. Each element of the list is a tuple with two elements: the rank and the suit. So, a single entry in the deck might be the tuple ("K", "spades"), which is the king of spades.

A hand is a dictionary. In each element of the dictionary, the key is a rank and the value is a list that contains the names of the suits that the hand holds for that rank. For example, if a hand has the 3 of spades and the 3 of hearts, and no other 3s, the key "3" has the value ["spades", "hearts"]. A key should not have an empty list associated with it; if no cards of a given rank are held, no value exists for that key.

Source Code

```
1.   import random
2.
3.   def getCard(deck):
4.
5.       """ Randomly remove a single card from the deck and
6.           return it. Assumes the deck is not empty.
7.
8.           deck: A deck as described above.
9.
10.          Returns: a single card, which is a tuple with
11.          two elements, the rank and the suit.
12.      """
13.
14.      index = int (len(deck) * random.random())
15.      newCard = deck[index]
16.      del deck[index]
17.      return newCard
18.
19.
20.  def drawCard(name, deck, hand):
21.
22.      """ Draw a new card from the deck and add it to
23.          hand. If the hand now holds the rank in all four
24.          suits, then remove them from the hand.
25.
26.          name: A string with the name of playerHand, used
27.              only for display purposes.
28.          deck: A deck as described above.
29.          hand: A hand dictionary as described above.
30.
31.          Returns: None.
32.      """
33.
```

```
34.         if len(deck) > 0:       # guard against an empty deck
35.
36.             newCard = getCard(deck)
37.             cardRank = newCard[0]
38.             cardSuit = newCard[1]
39.
40.             if cardRank in hand:
41.                 # append this suit to the list
42.                 hand[cardRank].append(cardSuit)
43.                 if len(hand) == 4:
44.                     print name, "lay down", cardRank + "s"
45.                     del hand[cardRank]
46.
47.             else:
48.                 # first of this suit, create a list
49.                 # with one element
50.                 hand[cardRank] = [ cardSuit ]
```

Suggestions

1. The return type from the function getCard() should be a tuple. Check that the return statement on line 17 actually returns a tuple (assuming the arguments to getCard() are of the proper type).
2. What is the most complicated data structure used in the program? Probably the hand dictionary. Walk through the code and look at each location that it is used, and each location it is modified, to ensure that hand is used correctly and remains consistent.
3. A random number is generated on line 14. What constitutes a good set of values to select as results of this random number when you walk through the program?
4. What set of inputs to drawCard() ensures coverage of all the code, in particular that the if on line 40 is tested both when it is true and when it is false?

Hints

Walk through the drawCard() function with the following parameters. (In all cases, deck has only one card, the 3 of hearts, for simplicity; in this situation, the randomly selected card is always the same one.) The examples show the hand dictionary using the standard Python dictionary syntax, which is `{ key1 : value1, key2 : value2 }`. In this case, the values are themselves lists:

1. Card from `deck` doesn't match existing rank in `hand`:
   ```
   deck == [ ( "3", "hearts" ) ]
   hand == { "2" : [ "hearts", "spades" ] }
   ```
2. Card from `deck` matches existing rank in `hand`:
   ```
   deck == [ ( "3", "hearts" ) ]
   hand == { "2" : [ "hearts", "spades" ],
             "3" : [ "diamonds" ] }
   ```
3. Card from `deck` is the fourth card of a rank, so that rank should be laid down:
   ```
   deck == [ ( "3", "hearts" ) ]
   hand == { "2" : [ "hearts", "spades" ],
             "3" : [ "diamonds", "clubs", "spades" ] }
   ```

Explanation of the Bug

The code on line 43 checks if the hand now has all four ranks of a given suit:

```
if len(hand) == 4:
```

This code line checks whether the length of the `hand` dictionary itself is 4, which is true if the cards in the hand happen to represent four unique ranks (for example, some number of 5s, some number of 8s, some number of Js, and some number of As). This is a **B.expression** error: The code should be checking if the particular *rank* has all four suits represented:

```
if len(hand[cardRank]) == 4:
```

Because Python uses the same operator, `len`, to test the length of a dictionary and the length of a list, and allows a list to be an element of a dictionary, it won't report an error on a mistake such as this.

The effect is that the code incorrectly detects when a draw results in the player holding all four ranks of a given suit. It misses the case shown in the third hint, where the player now has all four 3s, and yet decides that cards should be laid when the hand happens to have four unique ranks in it (which will come across to a user as apparently random behavior).

❼ Go Fish, Part II: Ask if Another Hand Has a Card

This function constitutes another component of the Python version of *Go Fish*. This function checks if the other player has any cards of a specified rank, and if so, it transfers them to the player's hand. If this results in the player having all four cards of that rank, the cards are deleted from the player's hand.

Here's a quick recap of the relevant definitions from the previous example (this function only concerns itself with hands; it does not use the deck):

- Cards are identified by their rank and suit: The rank is one of the elements of the list `["2", "3", "4", "5", "6", "7", "8", "9", "10", "J", "Q", "K", "A"]` and the suit is one of the elements of the list `["spades", "hearts", "diamonds", "clubs"]`.
- A hand is a dictionary. In each element of the dictionary, the key is a card rank and the value is a list, containing names of the suits that the hand holds for that rank. For example, if a hand has the 3 of spades and the 3 of hearts, and no other 3s, then the key `"3"` will have the value `["spades", "hearts"]`. A key should not have an empty list associated with it; if no cards of given rank are held, no value exists for that key.

The `checkCard()` function takes four parameters: The name of the player's hand (a string with the name of the hand used only for printing if cards are laid down), the player's hand, the rank of card to check, and the opponent's hand.

Source Code

```
1.    import random
2.
3.    def checkCard ( handName, playerHand,
4.                    cardRank, opponentHand ):
5.
6.       """ Check if opponentHand contains any cards of the
7.           specified rank, if it does, transfer them to
8.           playerHand.
```

```
 9.
10.        handName: A string with the name of playerHand
11.        playerHand: A hand dictionary, as described above.
12.        cardRank: A string with the name of a
13.                  card rank ("2" through "10", "J", "Q",
14.                  "K", or "A")
15.        opponentHand: A hand dictionary, described above.
16.
17.        Returns: 1 if a card is transferred, 0 otherwise.
18.    """
19.
20.    if cardRank in opponentHand:
21.
22.        transferCards = opponentHand[cardRank]
23.        # transferCards is a list!
24.        del opponentHand[cardRank]
25.        if cardRank in playerHand:
26.            playerHand[cardRank].extend(transferCards)
27.        else:    # shouldn't happen, but handle it
28.            playerHand[cardRank] = transferCards
29.
30.        if len(playerHand[cardRank]) == 4:
31.            print handName, "lay down", cardRank + "s"
32.            del playerHand[cardRank]
33.
34.        return 1
35.
36.    else:
37.
38.        return 0
```

Suggestions

1. Does the code have any implied elses? What input would cause them to execute?
2. The comment on line 23 is one of the few in the main algorithm, suggesting a non-obvious aspect of the code. Is the comment accurate?
3. Because the statement on line 28 would not normally execute in a real game of *Go Fish* (you can't ask for a given rank unless you already have a card of that rank in your hand), it is risky code. It might never have been tested, yet someone who calls this function from somewhere else might assume it works. Thus, it is a good area to check for a bug.

Hints

Walk through the `checkCard()` function with the following parameters:

1. Opponent does have a card of that rank:
```
handName == "HAND"
playerHand == { "5" : [ "spades", "hearts" ] }
cardRank == "5"
opponentHand == { "5" : [ "diamonds" ],
                  "10" : [ "clubs" ] }
```

2. Opponent does not have a card of that rank:
```
handName == "HAND"
playerHand == { "A" : [ "clubs" ] }
cardRank == "A"
opponentHand == { "2" : [ "hearts" ] }
```

3. Opponent has two cards of that rank, and the result is that player holds all four cards of that rank:
```
handName == "HAND"
playerHand == { "6" : [ "spades", "hearts" ],
                "Q" : [ "spades", "hearts" ] }
cardRank == "6"
opponentHand == { "6" : [ "diamonds", "clubs" ] }
```

4. Opponent has cards of that rank, but player does not (which should not happen in a real game of *Go Fish*):
```
handName == "HAND"
playerHand == { "J" : [ "hearts" ] }
cardRank == "2"
opponentHand == { "2" : [ "clubs", "spades" ] }
```

Explanation of the Bug

Lines 34–38 are incorrectly indented, which in Python means they are associated with the wrong block of code. Line 34, which is

```
return 1
```

should execute in all cases where the `if` on line 20 is true (a card of the specified rank is in the opponent's hand, which results in it being transferred to the player's hand, which is the defined situation where the function should return 1). Line 36 should be an else clause of *that* `if`, not from the `if` on line 30. So lines 34–38 are indented one indentation level (four spaces, given how the code is formatted) more than they should be.

As the code stands now, if `cardRank` is found in the opponent's hand but the player does not wind up with all four cards of that rank, the function returns 0 instead of 1 (as it should). If `cardRank` is not found at all in the opponent's hand, the function exits without a `return` statement. (In Python, this results in the function returning the built-in constant `None`.) This improper indenting is an **F.location** error.

❽ Go Fish, Part III: Play a Full Game

This function plays one turn of the game *Go Fish*. It uses the `drawCard()` and `checkCard()` functions (the corrected versions) defined in the previous two parts.

One turn is completed as follows: A rank is randomly selected from the ones that are in the player's hand, and the other hand is interrogated to see if it has any cards of that rank. If it does, they are transferred over. This continues with another card until no card is transferred, at which point the player has to "go fish" and draw a new card from the deck.

Note: The code does not check if the card drawn was the same rank as the last card asked for. (In traditional *Go Fish*, this gives the player another turn.) That is not the bug to look for!

To play a complete game, the code continues until both player's hands are empty.

To recap the definitions from the previous example:

- Cards are identified by their rank and suit: The rank is one of the elements of the list `["2", "3", "4", "5", "6", "7", "8", "9", "10", "J", "Q", "K", "A"]` and the suit is one of the elements of the list `["spades", "hearts", "diamonds", "clubs"]`.

- A deck is a list that initially contains 52 elements. Each element is itself a tuple with two elements: the rank and the suit. So, a single entry in the deck might be the tuple `("K", "spades")`; that is, the king of spades.

- A hand is a dictionary. In each element of the dictionary, the key is a card rank and the value is a list that contains names of the suits that the hand holds for that rank. For example, if a hand has the 3 of spades and the 3 of hearts, and no other 3s, the key `"3"` will have the value `["spades", "hearts"]`. A key should not have an empty list associated with it; if no cards of a given rank are held, no value exists for that key.

Keep in mind the definitions of the functions from the two previous parts:

```
def drawCard(name, deck, hand):

""" Draw a new card from the deck and add it to
    hand. If the hand now holds the rank in all four
    suits, then remove them from the hand.

    name: A string with the name of playerHand, used
          only for display purposes.
    deck: A deck as described above.
    hand: A hand dictionary as described above.

    Returns: None.
"""


def checkCard ( handName, playerHand,
                cardRank, opponentHand ):

""" Check if opponentHand contains any cards of the
    specified rank, if it does, transfer them to
    playerHand.

    handName: A string with the name of playerHand
    playerHand: A hand dictionary, as described above.
    cardRank: A string with the name of a
              card rank ("2" through "10", "J", "Q",
              "K", or "A")
    opponentHand: A hand dictionary, described above.

    Returns: 1 if a card is transferred, 0 otherwise.
"""
```

Source Code

```
1.    import random
2.
3.    def doTurn ( handName, deck, playerHand, opponentHand ):
4.
5.      """ Play one turn of "Go Fish". A rank in playerHand
6.          is chosen, and if any cards of that rank exist in
7.          opponentHand, they are transferred. This continues
8.          until no cards are transferred, at which point a
```

```
9.          new card is drawn from the deck into playerHand.
10.
11.         handName: A string with the name of playerHand.
12.         deck: The current deck, a list of two-element
13.                 tuples of the form [ rank, suit ].
14.         playerHand: A hand dictionary.
15.         opponentHand: A hand dictionary.
16.
17.         Returns: None.
18.     """
19.
20.     """ Loop unless the playerHand is empty. Normally this
21.         loop exits via the break statement, when
22.         checkCard() returns false meaning a card was not
23.         transferred.
24.     """
25.
26.     while len(playerHand):
27.
28.         """ Pick a random index within the current hand...
29.         """
30.         index = int (len(playerHand) * random.random())
31.
32.         """ ...and use the rank of the card at that index
33.             as the one to ask for.
34.         """
35.         rankToCheck = playerHand.keys()[index]
36.         found = checkCard( handName, opponentHand,
37.                             rankToCheck, playerHand);
38.         if found == 0:
39.             break
40.
41.     # no transfer, so "go fish"
42.     drawCard( handName, deck, playerHand )
43.
44. ranks = [ "2", "3", "4", "5", "6", "7", "8",
45.           "9", "10", "J", "Q", "K", "A" ]
46. suits = [ "spades", "hearts", "diamonds", "clubs" ]
47.
48. def playGoFish():
49.
50.     deck = []
51.     hand1 = {}
52.     hand2 = {}
53.
54.     for i in range(52):
55.         deck.append( (ranks[i % 13], suits[i % 4]) )
```

```
56.
57.     for i in range(7):
58.         drawCard("HAND1", deck, hand1)
59.         drawCard("HAND2", deck, hand2)
60.
61.     while 1:
62.
63.         doTurn ("HAND1", deck, hand1, hand2);
64.         doTurn ("HAND2", deck, hand2, hand1);
65.
66.         if len(hand1) == 0 and len(hand2) == 0:
67.             break
```

Suggestions

1. It is a good idea to move from the bottom up: verify that the doTurn() function is correct before moving on to test the playGoFish() function. Design a good set of parameters to test doTurn() with.

2. Is the test on line 66 correct? Will the game always end? Will it end at the correct time?

3. Is the initialization of the deck on lines 54 and 55 correct?

4. Look at the four parameters to doTurn(). Which ones are modified and which ones are only used?

Hints

Walk through the doTurn() function with the following parameters: The deck has only one card, to remove any randomness in which card will be picked. (These are artificial in the fact that, in a real game, the situation would not occur, but they are reasonable to test the function.)

1. Player asks opponent for a rank that results in player getting all four cards of that rank:
```
handname == "HAND1"
deck == ( ( "3", "hearts" ) )
playerHand = { "7" : [ "clubs", "spades" ] }
opponentHand = { "7" : [ "hearts", "diamonds" ] }
```

2. Player asks opponent for a rank that the opponent does not have:
```
handname == "HAND1"
deck == { ( "5", "spades" ) }
playerHand == { "10" : [ "diamonds" ],
               "K" : [ "spades" ] }
opponentHand == { "Q" : [ "clubs" ] }
```
3. Consider the following situation near the end of the game. The variables are as follows:
```
hand1 == { }
hand2 == { "4" : [ "diamonds, clubs" ] }
deck == [ ( "4", "clubs" ) , ( "4", "spades" ) ]
```
The program is just before line 61, about to iterate the `while` loop. Will the program terminate properly?

Explanation of the Bug

The call to `checkCard()` on lines 36–37 has two parameters reversed. It currently reads as follows:

```
found = checkCard( handName, opponentHand,
                   rankToCheck, playerHand);
```

However, it should read:

```
found = checkCard( handName, playerHand,
                   rankToCheck, opponentHand);
```

Because the two hands are reversed in the function, cards get transferred in the wrong direction. Because the rank to ask for (calculated on lines 30 and 35) is chosen from the correct deck, but `checkCard()` is then called with the hands reversed, it's also possible that the card asked for won't be in the receiving player's deck. As it happens, as written (see previous program), `checkCard()` does handle this case correctly, even though it is unexpected given the rules of *Go Fish*.

Even in a language that had predeclared function prototypes and strong type checking (which Python does not), this kind of **B.variable** error could easily occur because `playerHand` and `opponentHand` are of the same type.

⑨ Parse Numbers Written in English

This function, when passed a string such as "six hundred twenty two," should return the numerical value. It should handle numbers up to 999,999,999.

This function ignores the word "and" anywhere it appears in the input string.

Source Code

```
1.    """ Define a dictionary mapping between English words
2.        and the corresponding numbers.
3.    """
4.    digitmap = {
5.        "zero" : 0,
6.        "one" : 1,
7.        "two" : 2,
8.        "three" : 3,
9.        "four" : 4,
10.       "five" : 5,
11.       "six" : 6,
12.       "seven" : 7,
13.       "eight" : 8,
14.       "nine" : 9,
15.       "ten" : 10,
16.       "eleven" : 11,
17.       "twelve" : 12,
18.       "thirteen" : 13,
19.       "fourteen" : 14,
20.       "fifteen" : 15,
21.       "sixteen" : 16,
22.       "seventeen" : 17,
23.       "eighteen" : 18,
24.       "nineteen" : 19,
25.       "twenty" : 20,
26.       "thirty" : 30,
27.       "forty" : 40,
28.       "fifty" : 50,
29.       "sixty" : 60,
30.       "seventy" : 70,
31.       "eighty" : 80,
32.       "ninety" : 90
33.    }
```

```
34.
35.
36.    """ These words act as multipliers for the numbers
37.        before them.
38.    """
39.    multipliermap = {
40.        "hundred" : 100,
41.        "thousand" : 1000,
42.        "million" : 1000000
43.    }
44.
45.    def parseNumber( numberString ):
46.        """ Convert a text string into a number, up to
47.            999,999,999.
48.
49.            numberString: The English form of a number,
50.                          with spaces between each part.
51.
52.            Returns: The integer value.
53.        """
54.
55.        retVal = 0
56.
57.        """ The function split() takes a string and parses
58.            it into substrings, using a specified delimiter
59.            character (or a space delimiter if none is
60.            specified). So this next call breaks the string
61.            into a list of individual words.
62.        """
63.
64.        numberList = numberString.split()
65.
66.        """ Walk through the list of words, but with the
67.            word "and" removed.
68.        """
69.
70.        for word in [ e for e in numberList if e != "and" ]:
71.
72.            """ If word is a number, add to running total.
73.            """
74.
75.            if word in digitmap:
76.
77.                retVal = retVal + digitmap[word]
78.
79.            """ If word is a multiplier, multiply
80.                running total by the multiplier.
```

```
81.                    " " "
82.
83.           if word in multipliermap:
84.
85.                retVal= retVal * multipliermap[word]
86.
87.        return retVal
```

Suggestions

1. The declaration of `digitmap` and `multipliermap` is the kind of repetitive code that it is easy for the eyes to gloss over. Double-check that it is correct.
2. Look at the `for` loop with the list comprehension on line 70. Make sure that you understand what the goal of `numberList` is at the beginning of the loop, what the `for` loop does, and whether it is correct.
3. What are the trivial and empty cases for this function? Are they handled correctly?
4. Pick one single parameter to the function that you feel would exercise all the code.

Hints

Walk through the function with the following values for the `numberString` parameter:

1. Three consecutive nonzero digits: `"six hundred twenty two"`
2. A gap between nonzero digits: `"four thousand and five"`
3. Zero digits at the end of the number: `"four thousand five hundred"`

Explanation of the Bug

The bug lies in the code that handles the case where `word` is in `multipliermap`; that is, where the `if` on line 83 is true. A `numberString` value, such as "four thousand five hundred" (as shown in the second hint) exposes the problem: It results in a return value of 400500.

   This is a tricky **A.logic** problem: At the point where the main loop has iterated three times (having processed the words `"four"`, `"thousand"`,

112

and "five"), the running total in retVal is correctly set to 4005. However, when the word "hundred" is seen next, retVal is multiplied by 100, which results in an incorrect value of 400500.

The code that appears on line 85

```
retVal = retVal * multipliermap[word]
```

needs to be replaced. One solution is to apply a multiplier only to the part of retVal that is less than the multiplier. So, for example, when you apply a multiplier of 100, you will save off the part of retVal that is greater than 100, multiply what is left by 100, and then add them together.

The following code does that. First, it saves the "high part" of retVal (the portion of the original number greater than 100, as an example), and then it calculates the "low part" (the portion less than 100), and then it adds them back, multiplying only the low part by the multiplier:

```
multiplier = multipliermap[word]
highPart = ((retVal / multiplier) * multiplier)
lowPart = retVal - highPart
retVal = highPart + (lowPart * multiplier)
```

It isn't perfect—it doesn't handle cases like "two thousand thousand"—and it is a bit inelegant (you should probably be accumulating the numbers between multipliers in a separate variable), but it works well enough.

⑩ Assign Gift Givers

This function is for those situations where a set of people, such as office coworkers, exchange gifts among themselves, with each person assigned to buy gifts for one other person.

This function walks the list of people and assigns a gift target to each of them. It has to ensure that no one is assigned his or her own name. In particular, with a list of N people, it needs to avoid the situation where the first N-1 people are chosen to give gifts among themselves and, when it is time to process the last person on the list, no one else is left.

The program is passed as a parameter a list of names, and returns a dictionary. In the dictionary, the keys are the same list of names, and the values are the name that each person should give a gift to.

For a Python list, the function

```
mylist.count(x)
```

returns the number of times that x appears in `mylist`.
The function

```
mylist.pop(i)
```

returns the element at index i of `mylist`, and also removes it from the list.
The function

```
mylist.index(x)
```

returns the index of the first occurrence of x in `mylist`. It's an error if x does not occur in `mylist`.

Source Code

```
 1.    import random
 2.
 3.    def secretSanta( inputList ):
 4.       """
 5.          inputList: A list of names
 6.
 7.          Returns a dictionary, the keys are givers' names,
 8.             the values are receivers' names.
 9.       """
10.
11.       if len(inputList) < 2:
12.          return {}
13.
14.       returnDict = {}
15.
16.       """ Make a copy of the input list; we remove people
17.          from this list as they are assigned givers.
18.       """
19.
20.       receiversList = inputList[:]
21.
22.       for person in inputList:
23.
24.          """ If there are only two receivers left, and one
25.             of them is the last person in inputList, then
26.             assign the last person to the second-to-last
27.             person.
28.          """
29.
```

```
30.          if len(receiversList) == 2:
31.            if receiversList.count(inputList[-1]) == 1:
32.              returnDict[person] = inputList[-1]
33.              returnDict[inputList[-1]] = person
34.              break;
35.
36.          """ The typical situation, just randomly pick
37.              someone out of receiversList and give them to
38.              person. We don't want to assign someone to
39.              themselves. If that happens, we assign them the
40.              next person in receiversList.
41.          """
42.
43.          if receiversList.count(person) == 1:
44.            receiverIndex = \
45.                int ((len(receiversList)-1) * random.random())
46.            if receiversList.index(person) <= receiverIndex:
47.              receiverIndex += 1
48.          else:
49.            receiverIndex = \
50.                int (len(receiversList) * random.random())
51.
52.          returnDict[person] = \
53.              receiversList.pop(receiverIndex);
54.
55.      return returnDict
```

Suggestions

1. Two lists (inputList and receiversList) and one dictionary (returnDict) are used. State the goal of each one, and note which ones are modified and where.

2. On line 46, the index() function is used to look up person in receiverList. This implies that person must be in receiverList. Is this guaranteed to be true?

3. An invariant condition exists between returnDict and receiversList, which is that an element in one is not in the other. Check the sections of code that relate to this to ensure that the condition is always true.

4. What is the goal of the code on lines 43–50? How many different paths to walk through exist in this code?

Hints

1. Walk through one iteration of the code when the function was passed an `inputList` equal to ["Tom", "Joe", "Donna", "Susan", "Paul"].

2. Imagine the same input list, but the next iteration of the main `for` loop on line 22, where person is "Joe", and assume the remaining `receiversList` is ["Tom", "Donna", "Susan", "Paul"].

3. Consider the fourth iteration, where person is "Susan", and assume `receiversList` is now ["Donna", "Paul"].

Explanation of the Bug

The code that appears on line 33

```
returnDict[inputList[-1]] = person
```

has a bug. Although the code looks nice and symmetric with the code on line 32, it is not correct. This is shown by walking through the third hint.

The code assumes that if the main `for` loop has two people left to iterate for, the `receiversList` has those same two people on it. So, if you have Susan and Paul left, the assumption is that `receiversList` will be ["Susan", "Paul"], and you can just assign them to each other.

In fact, this is not always true (and if it does happen to be true, the standard logic on lines 43–50 will handle it correctly anyway). The problem that lines 30–34 is trying to avoid is something shown in the third hint: person is "Susan", Paul is the next (and last) person to be processed by the main `for` loop, and Paul is on `receiversList` with someone *other* than Susan (in the example shown in the third hint, Donna and Paul are on `receiversList`). What might happen is that Susan is assigned Donna; in this case, Paul is stuck with himself.

This is an **A.logic** error. Line 32 is correct because it creates a "Susan" : "Paul" element in `returnDict`. But, line 33 should be creating "Paul" : "Donna", not "Paul" : "Susan". How can the code accomplish this? We know that Paul is the last person in `receiversList` because he was last in `inputList` and `receiversList` originated as a copy of `inputList`. Because `receiversList` has two elements, and "Paul" is the last element, "Donna" must be the first one. So, line 33 should read as follows:

```
returnDict[inputList[-1]] = receiversList[0]
```

Chapter 5

JAVA

Brief Summary of Java

Java programs are compiled into an intermediate format, known as byte-code, and then run through an interpreter that executes in a Java Virtual Machine (JVM).

The basic syntax of Java is similar to C and C++. All white space is treated equally, indent level does not matter, statements end in a semicolon, and blocks of code are enclosed between { and }.

Comments are enclosed between /* and */, or else begin with //, in which case the rest of the line is a comment.

Data Types and Variables

The integer data types are `byte`, `short`, `int`, and `long`, which correspond to numbers of 8, 16, 32, and 64 bits. The types `float` and `double` store floating-point numbers; `char` stores a 16-bit Unicode character, and `boolean` can hold one of two values, `true` or `false`.

Variables are declared with a type and name, as in the following:

```
int myint;
```

They can be initialized at the same time:

```
char delimeter = '/';
boolean finished = false;
```

Variables can be declared anywhere they are used. The scope of a variable usually extends to the end of the code block it was declared in.

Java allows variables to be converted between different numeric types by casting, as in the following:

```
int a;
double d = (double)a;
```

You can also cast between objects, but that is beyond the scope of this book.

Variables can be declared as `final`, which means that their value cannot be changed after it is initialized:

```
final int MAX_LEN = 128;
```

Arithmetic expressions in Java are straightforward, with `%` used for modulo:

```
k = a + b;
remainder = tot % users;
```

The `++` and `--` operators exist. If they are used in prefix notation, the expression is evaluated after the operation is done. In postfix notation, the expression is evaluated before the operation is complete. So, with the following code

```
d = 4;
e = ++d;
f = e--;
```

e and f are both set to 5.

Strings (and Objects)

Beyond the basic data types, everything in Java is declared as a class. A *class* is a grouping of variables and methods (functions that operate on those variables). The word *object* is often used to refer to a class, but technically, a class is a description of an object and an instance is an actual object.

You can define your own classes; Java includes many predefined ones. One such class is `String` (or more precisely, `java.lang.String`), which is used to store a constant string. Strings in Java are not just arrays of characters—they are a class that has defined methods for accessing and modifying the characters.

The `String` class can serve as an example of how Java objects are used. A `String` can be created from an array of characters, as follows:

```
char[] myArray = { 'a', 'b', 'c' };
String myString = new String(myArray);
```

The expression `new String(myArray)` invokes what is called a *constructor* for the class `String`. *Constructors* create a new instance of an object, optionally taking parameters. How many parameters a constructor takes, and the type and order of those parameters, are part of the constructor's *signature*. Multiple constructors can exist for a given class as long as they have different signatures. For example, another constructor for `String` is called as follows:

```
String myString = new String(myArray, 2, 1);
```

That is, specifying an offset and count within `myArray`. You can also call

```
String myString = new String();
```

This creates an empty string. (A `String` cannot be changed after it's initialized, so it would stay empty.) The `String` class actually has nine constructors, plus two more obsolete ones.

When Java sees a literal string in double quotes, it automatically creates a `String` object, so you can write the following:

```
String newString = "text";
```

This is actually an assignment of one `String` to another. This automatic creation of an object from a literal is unique to the `String` class (all other literals, such as numbers, become primitive types), but it sure is convenient.

No destructors exist in Java; objects are destroyed by the *garbage collector* at some point after the last reference to them is removed (often because the variables holding that reference go out of scope). A variable can be assigned a keyword `null` to force a reference it is holding to be removed:

```
anotherString = null;
```

However, the garbage collector makes no guarantees about how soon an object will be destroyed once there are no references to it.

Java does not have explicit pointers; in a sense, all variables that refer to objects are pointers. When you assign between two objects of the same type, you actually assign a reference to the object on the right-hand side. To create a new instance of an object, you need to call one of its constructors:

```
myObject a, b;
a = b;                 // reference
a = new myObject(b);   // create a new object
```

Classes define methods that can be called on an instance of that class. For example, the `String` class has a method `length()` that returns the length of the string:

```
String j = "abc123";
x = j.length();
```

As previously mentioned, a `String` cannot change after it's initialized. Java has another class, `StringBuffer`, which holds strings that can change. A `StringBuffer` can be constructed from a `String`, or from a length, which specifies how many characters of capacity it should start with:

```
StringBuffer sb1 = new StringBuffer("howdy");
StringBuffer sb2 = new StringBuffer(100);
```

`StringBuffer` has a variety of methods on it:

```
sb.append("more data");
char c = sb.charAt(12);
sb.reverse();
```

In Java, the + operator can concatenate strings together. A sequence such as the following

```
String greeting = "Hello";
greeting = greeting + " there";
```

is legal. Because the original `String` that `greeting` points to cannot be modified, the concatenation actually involves the creation of a new

String, which greeting is then set to point to. Therefore, the reference to the original "Hello" string is removed, which eventually causes it to be destroyed.

Note

The concatenation statement also involves some more behind-the-scenes magic by the compiler. It creates a temporary StringBuffer*, then calls the* StringBuffer.append() *method for each expression separated by a + sign, then calls* StringBuffer.toString() *to convert it back to the result* String*. As with the automatic creation of* String *objects from constant strings, this is a special case on the part of Java, but is there because string concatenation is so useful.*

StringBuffer.append() is overloaded, so it can be passed any primitive type. Thus, you can call the following

```
int j = 4;
String b = "Value is" + j;
```

and b will equal "Value is 4". In fact, StringBuffer.append() works for any object by appending the result of the object's toString() method, which can be overridden as needed by the author of the object's class.

Arrays

Arrays in Java are declared with square brackets:

```
int[] intArray;
```

The array then has to be created:

```
intArray = new int[10];
```

intArray would then be indexed from 0 to 9.

Arrays can also be created at declaration time, if values are specified using an array initializer:

```
int[] array2 = { 5, 4, 3, 2, 1 };
```

You can't explicitly specify the length in that case because it's determined from how many values are provided.

You can get the number of elements in an array:

```
k = array2.length;
```

Note that this is not a method, so no parentheses appear after `length`. Arrays can also hold objects, so you can declare the following:

```
MyObject[] objarray;
```

This would then be created as follows (this could be combined with the declaration):

```
objarray = new MyObject[5];
```

It is important to note that this creates only the array. You still need to create the five objects:

```
for (k = 0; k < 5; k++) {
    objarray[k] = new MyObject();
}
```

To create subarrays, create an array where each element is an array. The first array can be declared and created in one step

```
int[][] bigArray = new int[6][];
```

and then each subarray needs to be created (each one can be a different length, in fact):

```
for (m = 0; m < 6; m++) {
    bigArray[m] = new int[20];
}
```

You can initialize arrays when they are declared:

```
short[][] shortArray = { { 1, 2, 3 }, { 4 }, { 5 , 6 } };
```

After that, `shortArray[0]` would be an array of three elements, `shortArray[1]` would be an array of one element, and `shortArray[2]` would be an array of two elements.

Finally, if the entries in the arrays are objects, they also have to be constructed, as shown here:

```
final int XDIM = 6;
final int YDIM = 10;
SomeObj[][] oa;
```

```
oa = new SomeObj[XDIM][];
for (int i = 0; i < XDIM; i++) {
    oa[i] = new SomeObj[YDIM];
    for (int j = 0; j < YDIM; j++) {
        oa[i][j] = new SomeObj();
    }
}
```

Conditionals

Java *conditionals* use the same if/else syntax as C:

```
if (j == 5) {
    // do something
} else {
    // do something else
}
```

The switch statement is also the same, with explicit break statements required, and a default case:

```
switch (newChar) {
    case "@":
        process_at();
        break;
    case ".":
        process_dot();
        break;
    default:
        ignore();
}
```

Loops

Looping is done with for, while, and do/while:

```
while (k > 8) {
    do_processing();
}

do {
    eof = get_line();
} while (eof != true);
```

`break` breaks out of a loop, and `continue` jumps to the next iteration. A label can be added to `break` or `continue` to specify which loop it refers to:

```
outerloop:
for (x = 0; x < 20; x++) {
    for (y = x; y < 20; y++) {
        if (something) {
            break outerloop;
        }
    }
}
```

`outerloop:` is a label for the loop and the statement `break outer-loop;` breaks out of the labeled loop. It does *not* jump to the point where the `outerloop:` label exists in the code.

Classes

A *class* is defined as follows:

```
class MyClass {
    private int a;
    public StringBuffer b;
    public MyClass(int j) {
        a = j;
        b = new StringBuffer(j);
    }
    public MyClass(String s) {
        a = s.length();
        b = new StringBuffer(s);
    }
    public int getLength() {
        return a;
    }
}
```

`a` and `b` are member variables in the class. `a` is defined with an *access specifier* of `private`, which means that it is hidden from the view of external code. `b` is `public`, which means that anyone can access it if they have an instance of `MyClass`. For example

```
MyClass mc = new MyClass("hello");
String abc = mc.b;  // this is allowed, b is public
int def = mc.a;     // this is NOT allowed, a is private
```

We'll get back to access specifiers within the next few paragraphs. For now, note that MyClass has two constructors, one of which takes an int as a parameter, and the other takes a String (the second one is the one called in the previous code sample). Both constructors initialize a and b. Variables can also be initialized when they are declared, so b could have been declared as follows:

```
public StringBuffer b = new StringBuffer();
```

Although, for this class, that would not be necessary because every constructor initializes b.

Classes can also inherit from another class. A subclass inherits all the state and behavior of its superclass (but *not* the constructors), although it can override methods by providing new ones with the same name (unless those methods were declared with the final keyword).

Inheritance is indicated by the extends keyword:

```
abstract class Polygon {
    Point[] points;
    abstract int getcount();
}

class Triangle extends Polygon {
    public Triangle() {
        points = new Point[3];
    }
    int getcount() { return 3 };
}
```

The access specifier of a class variable can be public, private, protected, or package (the default). public means that any code can access it; private means that only methods in the class itself can access it; package means that any code in the same "package" (which is a way to group classes) can access it.

A variable marked protected can be accessed by the class, subclasses, and all classes in the same package. Actually, to be more precise, subclasses can only access a protected member inherited from a superclass when the object is an instance of the subclass (which it usually will be). They can't modify an instance of the superclass itself. (If you didn't catch all that, don't worry too much about it.)

Members of a class (variables or methods) can be declared with the keyword static, which makes them "class members," as opposed to "instance members," which is the case that's been described so far. Class variables and class methods exist just once, as opposed to once per instance. For example, a class could assign unique identifiers to each instance it creates, as shown here:

```
class ImportantObject {
    private static int nextcounter = 0;
    private int counter;
    public ImportantObject() {
        counter = nextcounter++;
    }
    // continues...
}
```

Each instance of the class has its own `counter` member, but there is only one global `nextcounter`.

A method on a class can be declared `abstract`, which means that it defines the parameters and return value, but has no actual implementation. A class can also be declared `abstract`; this is required if it defines at least one abstract method. (It is also required if a class does not provide implementation for any abstract methods declared in its superclasses.) An abstract class cannot itself be instantiated—it exists to ensure that subclasses follow the "contract" that it defines.

Closely related to classes are interfaces. The main difference between an interface and an abstract class is that *all* the methods on an interface must be abstract:

```
public interface identify {
    String getName();
}
```

Other classes can now support an interface using the `implements` keyword. Unlike inheritance, where a class can only inherit from one class, classes can implement as many interfaces as they like, as long as they provide implementations of all the interfaces' methods (or are declared `abstract`):

```
class SomeClass implements identify {
    final String name = "SomeClass";
    String getName() { return name };
    // rest of class follows...
}
```

A class with only public member variables—and no methods—can be used to group variables by name, similar to C structures:

```
class Record {
    public String name;
    public int id;
    public int privilege;
}

Record r = new Record();
r.name = "Joe";
r.id = 12;
r.privilege = 3;
```

Java likely has a class for almost any standard operation you want to do; the documentation lists constructors and methods. For example, classes exist that wrap all the primitive types, such as this one that wraps the short primitive in a class called Short (note the capital "S" on the class name), and provides various useful methods:

```
Short s = new Short(12);
String str = s.toString();
```

I won't go into more details about specific classes, except as needed in the examples.

Exceptions

Java supports exceptions, which are objects that can be caught:

```
try {
    file = new FileInputStream("data.tmp");
} catch (FileNotFoundException e) {
    System.err.println("Exception " + e.getMessage());
} finally {
    // cleanup code
}
```

A try can have multiple catch blocks, each catching a different exception. (There is a hierarchy of exception classes, leading back to a class called Throwable. A catch block that catches a particular exception also catches any exceptions that are subclasses of that exception.)

If an exception happens and is caught, the `catch` block executes. The `finally` block always executes, whether or not an exception happens, and is usually used for cleanup code.

You can create and throw exceptions:

```
if (bytesleft == 0) {
    throw new EOFException();
}
```

Java requires that methods that can throw an exception specify it in the declaration of the method, using the `throws` keyword:

```
public void read_file(File file)
            throws IOException {
    if (!check_valid(file)) {
        throw new IOException("check_valid() failed");
    }
}
```

Method declarations must also list any exceptions that can be thrown by methods they call, unless they catch the exception. Thus, a method that called `read_file()` (as defined above) would need to either put it in a `try` block with an associated `catch` block that caught `IOException`, or specify in its own declaration that it throws `IOException`. (This "catch or specify" rule does not apply to a class of exceptions known as runtime exceptions, which inherit from the class `RuntimeException`. This rule is detailed in the Java documentation.)

Importing Other Code

To use a class, you must import the package that defines it. This is specified in the documentation of the class. For example, to use the `Timer` class, include the following in the code:

```
import java.util.Timer;
```

This can include a wildcard:

```
import java.util.*;
```

Command-Line Applications and Applets

The examples used in this chapter are split between command-line applications and applets designed to run in a web browser. A command-line application has to contain a class that implements a `main()` method, which must be defined as `public static`, return type `void`, and receive the command-line parameters as an array of `String` objects called `args` (the first element in `args` is the first parameter, etc.):

```
public class MyApplication {
    public static void main(String[] args) {
        for (int j = 0; j < args.length; j++) {
            System.out.println(args[j]);
        }
    }
}
```

An applet inherits from a class called `Applet`:

```
public class MyApplet extends Applet {
    public void paint(Graphics g) {
        g.drawString("Testing 123", 10, 10);
    }
}
```

The `paint()` method is overridden from a superclass a few levels up from `Applet`, and is used to display on the screen. The `Graphics` class has many methods used to draw lines and shapes, display text, change color, and so on.

❶ Is a Year a Leap Year?

This program determines if the first argument passed to it is a leap year, and prints the result.

A year is a leap year if it is divisible by 4, unless it is divisible by 100. However, years divisible by 400 *are* leap years.

The program internally uses a method that throws one of two exceptions: one if the year is a leap year, and one if it isn't. Because these exception classes don't do anything different from the built-in `Exception` class, they don't need to override any methods; they can simply be declared and used.

129

To convert the command-line parameter from a string to a number, the program uses the `static` method `parseLong()` from the class `Long`, which is a class that wraps the primitive type `long`. Because `parseLong()` is a `static` method, it is not called on an instance of the class.

`parseLong()` is defined to throw `NumberFormatException` if the input string cannot be converted to a number. Because `checkLeapYear()` throws the two user-defined exceptions and, thus, typically is called inside a `try` block, it is not too much work to also catch `NumberFormatException`.

`NumberFormatException` is a runtime exception and, therefore, does not have to be listed in the `throws` clause of the declaration of `checkLeapYear()`, but it is included because throwing that exception is the designated way to handle an invalid input.

Source Code

```
1.    public class IsLeapYear {
2.
3.        public static class LeapYearException
4.                extends Exception {}
5.        public static class NotLeapYearException
6.                extends Exception {}
7.
8.        static void checkLeapYear(String year)
9.            throws LeapYearException, NotLeapYearException,
10.               NumberFormatException {
11.
12.           long yearAsLong = Long.parseLong(year);
13.
14.           //
15.           // A leap year is a multiple of 4, unless it is
16.           // a multiple of 100, unless it is a multiple of
17.           // 400.
18.           //
19.           // We calculate the three values, then make a
20.           // 3-bit binary value out of them and look it up
21.           // in results.
22.           //
23.
24.           final boolean results[] =
25.                   { true, false, false, true,
26.                   false, false, false, false };
```

```
27.
28.        if (results[
29.            ((((yearAsLong % 4) == 0) ? 1 : 0) << 2) +
30.            ((((yearAsLong % 100) == 0) ? 1 : 0) << 1) +
31.            ((((yearAsLong % 400) == 0) ? 1 : 0) << 0)]) {
32.            throw new LeapYearException();
33.        } else {
34.            throw new NotLeapYearException();
35.        }
36.    }
37.
38.    public static void main(String[] args) {
39.
40.        if (args.length > 0) {
41.
42.            try {
43.                checkLeapYear(args[0]);
44.            } catch ( NumberFormatException nfe ) {
45.                System.out.println(
46.                    "Invalid argument: " +
47.                    nfe.getMessage());
48.            } catch ( LeapYearException lye ) {
49.                System.out.println(
50.                    args[0] + " is a leap year");
51.            } catch ( NotLeapYearException nlye ) {
52.                System.out.println(
53.                    args[0] + " is not a leap year");
54.            }
55.        }
56.    }
57. }
```

Suggestions

1. What exactly does it mean if a bit is on in results?
2. Because the value computed on lines 29–31 is immediately used to index into results, an array of size 8, is it guaranteed that this value will be properly restricted so as to not produce an invalid array index?
3. How many possible kinds of years are there, and given that it is less than the size of results, are there certain values for the index into results that will never occur?

Hints

Walk through `main()` with the following values for `args[0]`:

1. Multiple of 100 is not a leap year: `"1900"`
2. Multiple of 4 is a leap year: `"1904"`
3. Multiple of 400 is a leap year: `"2000"`
4. Any other year is not a leap year: `"2001"`

Explanation of the Bug

Not surprisingly, the problem is in the declaration of the `results` array on lines 24–26. It is reversed; that is, it is declared as if the calculation of the index on lines 29–31 had every bit flipped, which is an **F.init** error. The proper declaration should be as follows:

```
private static final boolean results[] =
    { false, false, false, false,
      true, false, false, true };
```

Alternately, the assignment of the bits on lines 29–31 could be flipped.

With the bits assigned as-is, if a year is divisible by 400, the low bit in the index will be on, which means that the index in binary is in the form xx1. Because such years are also divisible by 4 and 100, the next two bits are also on. Thus, indices 1, 3, and 5 in `results` won't ever be used. Years divisible by 400 always wind up with an index of 7 (binary 111).

If year is not divisible by 400, but is divisible by 100, the low bit is off, but the second bit is on, so the index is in the form x10. Because such a year is also divisible by 4, the index is always 6 (binary 110), and index 2 is never used.

For the rest of the years, those not divisible by 100 (or 400), the index is in the form x00. Years divisible by 4 result in an index of 4 (binary 100), and those not divisible by 4 result in an index of 0.

Therefore, the only indices that matter are 0, 4, 6, and 7. Of those, 0 and 6 should be false (not leap years), and 4 and 7 should be true (leap years). Because of the bug, those indices had their bits flipped, so 7 and 1 were false, and 3 and 0 were true. The "unused" indices (2, 4, 5, and 6) were also set to false.

Thus, the program as written would, by chance, work if a year was divisible by 100 but not by 400 (a year such as 1900), correctly reporting, based on the value of index 6, that such a year was not a leap year. It would misrepresent the years 2000 (index 7) and 2004 (index 4) as not being leap years, and the year 2001 (index 0) as being a leap year.

❷ Convert a Number to Text

This class takes a number and converts it to the equivalent text in English.

For example, the input 1 should return the string "one" and 123,456 should return the string "one hundred twenty three thousand four hundred fifty six." (The program does not try to insert the word "and" between any of the numbers.)

The class has one constructor, which takes the integer to convert as a parameter, and has a single method—getString()—that returns the string. This is not necessarily the ideal interface for such a class, but it works for these purposes.

The constructor uses the pow() method from the Math package, which raises a number to a power. It also uses the substring() method of the String class, which when called with one parameter, creates a new String starting at the specified offset in the original string. (The offset is zero-based.)

Source Code

```
1.    class EnglishNumber {
2.
3.        private static final String[] ones = {
4.            " one", " two", " three", " four", " five",
5.            " six", " seven", " eight", " nine", " ten",
6.            " eleven", " twelve", " thirteen", " fourteen",
7.            " fifteen", " sixteen", " seventeen",
8.            " eighteen", " nineteen"
9.        };
10.       private static final String[] tens = {
11.           " twenty", " thirty", " forty", " fifty",
12.           " sixty", " seventy", " eighty", " ninety"
13.       };
14.       //
15.       // A Java long can only go up to 2^63 - 1,
16.       // so quintillions is as big as it gets. The
```

```
17.        // program would automatically handle larger
18.        // numbers if this array were extended.
19.        //
20.        private static final String[] groups = {
21.            "",
22.            " thousand",
23.            " million",
24.            " billion",
25.            " trillion",
26.            " quadrillion",
27.            " quintillion"
28.        };
29.
30.        private String string = new String();
31.
32.        public String getString() { return string; }
33.
34.        public EnglishNumber ( long n ) {
35.
36.            // Go through the number one group at a time.
37.
38.            for (int i = groups.length-1; i >= 0; i--) {
39.
40.                // Is the number as big as this group?
41.
42.                long cutoff =
43.                    (long)Math.pow((double)10,
44.                                   (double)(i*3));
45.
46.                if ( n >= cutoff ) {
47.
48.                    int thisPart = (int)(n / cutoff);
49.
50.                    // Use the ones[] array for both the
51.                    // hundreds and the ones digit. Note
52.                    // that tens[] starts at "twenty".
53.
54.                    if (thisPart >= 100) {
55.                        string +=
56.                            ones[thisPart/100] +
57.                            " hundred";
58.                        thisPart = thisPart % 100;
59.                    }
60.                    if (thisPart >= 20) {
61.                        string += tens[(thisPart/10)-1];
62.                        thisPart = thisPart % 10;
63.                    }
```

134

```
64.          if (thisPart >= 1) {
65.              string += ones[thisPart];
66.          }
67.
68.          string += groups[i];
69.
70.          n = n % cutoff;
71.
72.      }
73.  }
74.
75.  if (string.length() == 0) {
76.      string = "zero";
77.  } else {
78.      // remove initial space
79.      string = string.substring(1);
80.  }
81.  }
82.  }
```

Suggestions

1. Look at the main `for` loop, running from lines 38–73. What is the goal of one iteration of this loop?
2. What is the meaning of the variable `thisPart`?
3. The functionality is split because the return string is computed in the constructor, but not returned until `getString()` is called. What variable is returned? Where is it modified?
4. What is the trivial input for this program? How is it handled in the code?

Hints

Walk through the constructor with the following inputs to the constructor, and determine what value `getString()` would return:

1. The trivial case: n == 0.
2. Test one iteration of the loop, including one case where a digit is 0: n == 102.
3. Test several iterations of the loop: n == 1234567.

Explanation of the Bug

The code indexes into the `ones` and `tens` array incorrectly. Because arrays are zero-based, the number 1 corresponds to `ones[0]`, not `ones[1]`. Thus, the various accesses need to be adjusted for this. Lines 55–57 should change from

```
string +=
  ones[thisPart/100] +
    " hundred";
```

to

```
string +=
  ones[(thisPart/100)-1] +
    " hundred";
```

Line 61 should change from

```
string += tens[(thisPart/10)-1];
```

to

```
string += tens[(thisPart/10)-2];
```

Line 65 should change from

```
string += ones[thisPart];
```

to

```
string += ones[thisPart-1];
```

This is an **A.off-by-one** error that becomes a **D.index** error. It can actually lead to an `ArrayIndexOutOfBoundsException` being thrown in certain cases. (Can you determine which ones?)

❸ Draw a Triangle on the Screen, Part I

This function draws a triangle on the screen. It becomes the core of an applet that allows the user to pick the three endpoints by clicking three times on the screen, which will be completed in the next example.

The algorithm assumes that the three points are ordered by x coordinate. It fills the triangle by drawing a series of vertical lines, 1 pixel wide. To do this, it splits the triangle into a "left" and "right" half; that is, the part from the x coordinate of the first point to the x coordinate of the second point, and the part from the x coordinate of the second point to the x coordinate of the third point. This algorithm won't work well with triangles that are extremely tall and thin, so to cover those cases, the function also draws a line between each pair of endpoints.

Applets draw to the screen by overriding a member method called paint(). This method is passed a Graphics class, which supports two methods that are used here: fillOval() (used to draw a circle) and drawLine(). The meaning of the parameters can be inferred from their use (assume that they are passed in the correct order).

In the declaration of the Triangle class, it specifies that it implements the MouseListener interface. This is explained in the next program.

Source Code

```
1.   import java.awt.event.*;
2.   import java.awt.*;
3.
4.   public class Triangle extends java.applet.Applet
5.       implements MouseListener {
6.
7.       // The rest of the applet will be in the next
8.       // example.
9.
10.      Point[] pt = new Point[3];
11.      int ptCount = 0;
12.
13.      public void paint(Graphics g) {
14.
15.          int i;
16.
17.          // Draw the points that have been selected
18.
19.          for (i = 0; i < ptCount; i++) {
20.              g.fillOval(pt[i].x - 10, pt[i].y - 10,
21.                      20, 20);
22.          }
23.
```

```
24.        if (ptCount == 3) {
25.
26.            // Connect the endpoints to handle
27.            // tall thin triangles.
28.
29.            g.drawLine(pt[0].x, pt[0].y,
30.                       pt[1].x, pt[1].y);
31.            g.drawLine(pt[1].x, pt[1].y,
32.                       pt[2].x, pt[2].y);
33.            g.drawLine(pt[0].x, pt[0].y,
34.                       pt[2].x, pt[2].y);
35.
36.            // Calculate x and y diffs between points.
37.
38.            int x0to1 = pt[1].x - pt[0].x;
39.            int x0to2 = pt[2].x - pt[0].x;
40.            int x1to2 = pt[2].x - pt[1].x;
41.            int y0to1 = pt[1].y - pt[0].y;
42.            int y0to2 = pt[2].y - pt[0].y;
43.            int y1to2 = pt[2].y - pt[1].y;
44.
45.            // Left part of the triangle.
46.
47.            if (x0to1 > 0) {
48.                for (i = pt[0].x; i <= pt[1].x; i++) {
49.                    g.drawLine(
50.                      i,
51.                      pt[0].y +
52.                      ((y0to1 * (i - pt[0].x)) / x0to1),
53.                      i,
54.                      pt[0].y +
55.                      ((y0to2 * (i - pt[0].x)) / x0to2)
56.                    );
57.                }
58.            }
59.
60.            // Right part of the triangle.
61.
62.            for (i = pt[1].x+1; i <= pt[2].x; i++) {
63.                g.drawLine(
64.                  i,
65.                  pt[1].y +
66.                  ((y1to2 * (i - pt[1].x)) / x1to2),
67.                  i,
68.                  pt[1].y +
69.                  ((y0to2 * (i - pt[0].x)) / x0to2)
```

```
70.                        );
71.                      }
72.                  }
73.              }
74.          }
```

Suggestions

1. There are several places with repetitive statements, such as lines 29–34 and 38–43. Check these lines carefully to ensure that they are correct.

2. Although the points are ordered by x coordinate, it's possible that two or three of them will have the same x coordinate. As a result, x0to1, x0to2, or x1to2 could be 0. Examine the code to ensure that the division operations on lines 52, 55, 66, and 69 would never result in an ArithmeticException due to divide by zero.

3. Look at the loops on lines 48–57 and lines 62–71. Determine what values will be passed to g.drawLine() on the first and last iteration of each of these loops to make sure that they seem reasonable. Remember how the values are related; for example, the expression pt[0].y + y0to1 is equal to pt[1].y.

Hints

Walk through the function with ptCount == 3 and the points as follows:

1. A triangle with nothing unusual:
```
pt[0].x == 0;
pt[0].y == 20;
pt[1].x == 2;
pt[1].y == 18;
pt[2].x == 4;
pt[2].y == 28;
```

2. A triangle with points that are the same in the x or y coordinate:
```
pt[0].x == 0;
pt[0].y == 10;
pt[1].x == 4;
pt[1].y == 10;
pt[2].x == 4;
pt[2].y == 0;
```

139

Explanation of the Bug

A **B.variable** error exists in the calculation of the second y coordinate in the call to `g.drawLine()` in the second loop. Lines 68–69, which read as follows

```
pt[1].y +
    ((y0to2 * (i - pt[0].x)) / x0to2)
```

should be

```
pt[0].y +
    ((y0to2 * (i - pt[0].x)) / x0to2)
```

The problem can be spotted by considering the last iteration of the loop, when `i` is equal to `pt[2].x`. In this situation, the expression as initially written becomes

```
pt[1].y +
    ((y0to2 * (pt[2].x - pt[0].x)) / x0to2)
```

which, because `pt[2].x - pt[0].x` is equal to `x0to2`, becomes

```
pt[1].y + y0to2
```

This does not make any particular sense because `pt[1].y` and `y0to2` are not related. With the fix, the expression is instead

```
pt[0].y + y0to2
```

This equals `pt[2].y`, a reasonable y coordinate for the second endpoint of the last vertical line (in fact, the y coordinate of the first endpoint of the line also evaluates to `pt[2].y`, so the "line" is actually just a single pixel drawn at the point `pt[2]`).

❹ Draw a Triangle on the Screen, Part II

This function draws a triangle on the screen, with the points selected by the user clicking three times on the screen. It uses the `paint()` method from the previous example. Because the `paint()` routine expects the points to be sorted by x coordinate, this function takes care of that.

Calling the repaint() method of the Applet class (which is actually a method of the Component class, the great-grandparent of Applet) eventually causes the paint() method to be called.

In addition to extending the java.applet.Applet class, as all applets do, the function also implements the MouseListener interface to receive mouse clicks. The only method in this interface that matters here is mousePressed(). This calls the method getPoint() (whose functionality is obvious) on the MouseEvent passed as a parameter. If an applet consumes a MouseEvent (or any event derived from its super-class InputEvent), it notes this by calling the consume() method.

The class calls addMouseListener() during initialization of the applet, and removeMouseListener() during destruction. This is how it registers to receive mouse events. These methods take, as a parameter, an object that implements MouseListener. Because the Triangle class extends MouseListener, it can pass this, that is, a pointer to the instance of the applet class itself, as a parameter.

The class should implement several methods that are not shown to save space. Applets normally implement a method getAppletInfo(), which returns the title and author of the applet. In addition, the MouseListener interface has four other methods: mouseReleased(), mouseClicked(), mouseEntered(), and mouseExited(). All these methods take a MouseEvent as a parameter, but don't need to do anything in this example.

Source Code

```
1.    import java.awt.event.*;
2.    import java.awt.*;
3.
4.    public class Triangle extends java.applet.Applet
5.        implements MouseListener {
6.
7.        Point[] pt = new Point[3];
8.        int ptCount = 0;
9.
10.       public void init() {
11.           addMouseListener(this);
12.       }
13.
14.       public void paint(Graphics g) {
15.           // See previous example for implementation
```

```
16.        }
17.
18.        public void mousePressed(MouseEvent e) {
19.
20.            if (ptCount < 3) {
21.                pt[ptCount] = new Point(e.getPoint());
22.                if ((ptCount++) == 3) {
23.                    Point p;
24.
25.                    // Order the points by x value, so
26.                    // pt[0] has the lowest x and pt[2]
27.                    // has the highest.
28.
29.                    if ((pt[1].x < pt[2].x) &&
30.                        (pt[1].x < pt[0].x)) {
31.                        p = pt[0]; pt[0] = pt[1]; pt[1] = p;
32.                    } else if ((pt[2].x < pt[1].x) &&
33.                               (pt[2].x < pt[0].x)) {
34.                        p = pt[0]; pt[0] = pt[2]; pt[2] = p;
35.                    }
36.                    if (pt[1].x > pt[2].x) {
37.                        p = pt[1]; pt[1] = pt[2]; pt[2] = p;
38.                    }
39.                }
40.            }
41.            e.consume();
42.            repaint();
43.        }
44.
45.        public void destroy() {
46.            removeMouseListener(this);
47.        }
```

Suggestions

1. Look at the code on lines 29–38. The comment on lines 25–27 states that the goal is to order the points. Is it correct? How would you describe the goal after line 35?

2. mousePressed() calls repaint() even if this is not the third point selected. Is it correct to assume that paint() is ready to be called in this situation?

3. Examine the code to swap points on lines 31, 34, and 37. Is it done correctly? How many different inputs would be needed to ensure that all these code lines were covered?

Hints

Walk through the `mousePressed()` method, passing in the third point equal to (20, 50) and with the following values for member variables:

```
ptCount == 2
pt[0].x == 0
pt[0].y == 100
pt[1].x == 10
pt[1].y == 75
```

Explanation of the Bug

The bug is on line 22, which reads as follows:

```
if ((ptCount++) == 3) {
```

When using the postfix notation for `++`, the expression is evaluated before the addition is done. Therefore, this expression is true only when `ptCount` is already 3 before it is incremented. However, the `if()` on line 20 will prevent that entire block of code on lines 21–39 from executing if `ptCount` is 3 or greater. Therefore, the entire block of code from lines 23–38 will never execute, and the variables won't ever be sorted. This leads to `paint()` being called with unordered points (unless the user happens to click them in sorted x order) which causes the algorithm to malfunction.

The code should instead read as follows:

```
if ((++ptCount) == 3) {
```

Because the increment is done at the incorrect time, you could consider this an **F.location** error, or you could describe it as **B.expression**.

❺ Reverse a Linked List

This function reverses a singly linked list by walking the list and changing pointers.

Each element in the list is an instance of a class `ListNode`. The list itself is an instance of a class `List`. `ListNode` has a `next` member that

143

points to the next element on the list. The final element on the list has a next pointer equal to null.

List has a method called Reverse(), which is the method to reverse the linked list.

Source Code

```
1.    class ListNode {
2.
3.        private int value;
4.        protected ListNode next;
5.
6.        public ListNode(int v) {
7.            value = v;
8.            next = null;
9.        }
10.
11.       public ListNode(int v, ListNode n) {
12.           value = v;
13.           next = n;
14.       }
15.
16.       public int getValue() { return value; }
17.
18.   }
19.
20.   class List {
21.
22.       private ListNode head;
23.
24.       public List() {
25.           head = null;
26.       }
27.
28.       public List(ListNode ln) {
29.           head = ln;
30.       }
31.
32.       public void Reverse() {
33.
34.           // Walk the list, reversing the direction of
35.           // the next pointers.
36.
37.           ListNode ln1, ln2, ln3, ln4;
```

```
38.
39.          if (head == null)
40.              return;
41.
42.          ln1 = head;
43.          ln2 = head.next;
44.          ln3 = null;
45.
46.          while (ln2 != null) {
47.              ln4 = ln2.next;
48.              ln1.next = ln3;
49.              ln3 = ln1;
50.              ln1 = ln2;
51.              ln2 = ln4;
52.          }
53.
54.          //
55.          // When we get to the end of the list, the last
56.          // element we looked at is the new head.
57.          //
58.
59.          head = ln1;
60.      }
61.  }
```

Suggestions

1. What are the empty and trivial cases for the Reverse() method? How will the code handle them?
2. What is the purpose of the variable ln4?
3. Describe the meaning of ln1, ln2, and ln3 after the while loop ends. Is the comment on lines 54–57 correct?

Hints

Walk through Reverse() in the following cases:

1. The list has only one element, so head.next == null.
2. The list has three elements, so head points to Node1, Node1.next points to Node2, Node2.next points to Node3, and Node3.next is null.

Explanation of the Bug

The code on line 59 is correct. The value of ln1 after the last iteration of the while() loop is the new head of the list. However, the next pointer of that element is still null because it used to be the end of the list.

In the somewhat-confusing nomenclature of this function, ln3 is the element that used to be before ln1 in the list, so to finish off the reversal, there needs to be a line added after line 59 that reads as follows:

```
ln1.next = ln3;
```

This is a **D.limit** error because the code works correctly except when handling the last element of the old list. The effect of the bug is that the last element of the old list keeps its next pointer as null. Since this element becomes the first element of the new list, this truncates the list to a single element.

❻ Check if a List Has a Loop

This function checks if a singly linked list has a loop in it.

It uses the same ListNode and List classes from the previous examples, but implements a new member method, HasLoop(). A list has a loop if there is some ListNode node in it for which node.next is equal to head.

Source Code

```
1.   class List {
2.
3.       private ListNode head;
4.
5.       public List() {
6.           head = null;
7.       }
8.
9.       public List(ListNode ln) {
10.          head = ln;
11.      }
```

```
12.
13.     public boolean HasLoop() {
14.
15.         //
16.         // The algorithm is to start two pointers
17.         // at the head of the list; as the first pointer
18.         // advances one element in the list, the second
19.         // advances by two elements. If the second
20.         // pointer hits a null next pointer, then the
21.         // list does not have a loop; if the second
22.         // pointer hits the first pointer, then the list
23.         // has a loop.
24.         //
25.
26.         ListNode ln1, ln2;
27.
28.         if ((head == null) || (head.next == null))
29.             return false;
30.
31.         ln1 = head;
32.         ln2 = head.next;
33.
34.         while (true) {
35.
36.             if (ln1 == ln2)
37.                 return true;
38.
39.             if (ln1.next == null)
40.                 return false;
41.             else
42.                 ln1 = ln1.next;
43.
44.             if (ln1 == ln2)
45.                 return true;
46.
47.             if (ln2.next == null)
48.                 return false;
49.             else
50.                 ln2 = ln2.next;
51.
52.             if (ln1 == ln2)
53.                 return true;
54.
55.             if (ln2.next == null)
56.                 return false;
```

```
57.                    else
58.                        ln2 = ln2.next;
59.
60.                }
61.            }
```

Suggestions

1. What are the empty and trivial cases for this function?
2. Because the main loop in the code is `while(true)`, why is the function guaranteed to eventually exit?
3. How many different inputs are necessary to guarantee complete code coverage?

Hints

Walk through `HasLoop()` in the following cases:

1. The list has only one element, so `head.next == null`.
2. The list has three elements, so `head` points to `Node1`, `Node1.next` points to `Node2`, `Node2.next` points to `Node3`, and `Node3.next` is `null`.
3. The list has a loop, where `head` points to `Node1`, `Node1.next` points to `Node2`, and `Node2.next` points to `head`.

Explanation of the Bug

The code returns `true`, which indicates that it has found a loop, on any list with more than one element. The reason is that the check on lines 44–45, immediately after advancing `ln1`

```
if (ln1 == ln2)
    return true;
```

is `true` when `ln1` is advanced from the first to the second element in the list. This is because `ln2` is initialized before the loop to point to the second element, and it has not moved yet.

In fact, the check is unnecessary because the code is concerned with `ln2` looping around and catching up to `ln1`, so there is no need to check for equality after `ln1` advances. This is an **F.location** error because the two lines should not exist at all.

❼ Quicksort

This function implements the quicksort algorithm.

Quicksort works by choosing an arbitrary element in the array and then dividing the array into two parts: The first part contains all elements less than or equal to the chosen element, and the second part contains all elements greater than the chosen element. The chosen element is then swapped into the spot between the two parts (known as the pivot point), which is its proper spot in the ultimately sorted array. The function is then called recursively twice—once on each part—to complete the sort.

Assume that the stack is deep enough that recursion will not cause a stack overflow when properly processing any array that is passed to the function.

The function declares an interface `quickcompare`, which has a single method `compare()`. This method is passed two instances of the class `Object` (which, in Java, is the root of the class hierarchy, and thus a superclass of any object), and returns a negative, zero, or positive number if the first parameter is less than, equal to, or greater than the second parameter, respectively. This is how the equivalent of function pointers can be supported in Java. To use the `Quicksort` class, you first declare a class that implements the `quickcompare` interface in an appropriate way for the data you want to sort, such as this one for `String` objects

```
private static class StringComp implements quickcompare {
    public int compare(Object a, Object b) {
        return ((String)a).compareTo((String)b);
    }
}
```

and then pass an instance of that class to `quicksort()`

```
public static void main(String[] args) {
    quicksort(
        args, 0, args.length-1, new StringComp());
}
```

149

(In this example, `StringComp` is declared as `static` so it can be called from `main()`, which is also `static`.)

Note that to make recursion easier, `quicksort()` defines the `end` parameter inclusively, thus the need to pass `args.length-1` in the previous call.

Source Code

```
1.   public class QuickSort {
2.
3.       public interface quickcompare {
4.           public int compare(Object a, Object b);
5.       }
6.
7.       // Declare it static since it does not operate
8.       // on class member variables (there aren't any).
9.
10.      public static void quicksort(
11.              Object[] array,
12.              int start,
13.              int end,
14.              quickcompare qc) {
15.
16.          if (start < end) {
17.
18.              Object temp;
19.              int pivot, low, high;
20.
21.              //
22.              // Partition the array.
23.              //
24.
25.              pivot = start;
26.              low = start+1;
27.              high = end;
28.              while (true) {
29.                  while ((low < high) &&
30.                          (qc.compare(array[low],
31.                                  array[pivot]) <= 0)) {
32.                      ++low;
33.                  }
34.                  while ((high >= low) &&
35.                          (qc.compare(array[high],
36.                                  array[pivot]) > 0)) {
37.                      --high;
```

```
38.              }
39.              if (low < high) {
40.                  temp = array[low];
41.                  array[low] = array[high];
42.                  array[high] = temp;
43.              } else {
44.                  break;
45.              }
46.          }
47.          temp = array[pivot];
48.          array[pivot] = array[high];
49.          array[high] = temp;
50.
51.          // Now sort before and after the pivot.
52.
53.          quicksort(array, start, high, qc);
54.          quicksort(array, high+1, end, qc);
55.      }
56.  }
57. }
```

Suggestions

1. What can you say about the relationship between low and high during the main while() loop? Can low ever be greater than high?
2. What is the goal at line 33? What is the goal at line 38?
3. At the end of the loop, how are low and high related? What types of inputs would cause different situations at the end of the loop?
4. Think of the empty, trivial, and already solved inputs for this code.
5. Because the code is called recursively, how can you be sure that it will ever terminate?

Hints

Assume an implementation of quickcompare that compares objects of type Integer. (Recall that Integer wraps the primitive int type. The array has to be of type Integer because quickcompare needs to compare a subclass of Object.) Walk through the code with the following inputs:

1. Array is unsorted, no duplicates:
   ```
   array == [ Integer(3), Integer(1), Integer(4),
              Integer(5), Integer(2) ];
   ```

```
start == 0
end == 4
```

2. Array contains only two duplicates:
```
array == [ Integer(4), Integer(4) ]
start == 0
end == 1
```

3. Array has the largest number in the first element (important because the value of the first element is the pivot chosen on the first pass):
```
array == [ Integer(6), Integer(3), Integer(5) ]
start == 0
end == 2
```

Explanation of the Bug

The first of the two recursive calls, on line 53, is too expansive. It reads as follows:

```
quicksort(array, start, high, qc);
```

Recall that the pivot element was just swapped into position `high`. Because of the way the call is written, it includes the pivot element in the elements sorted by the recursive call. Normally, this won't cause problems—the pivot element is less than any of the elements in the second group (the one recursively sorted by the call on line 54), and can be equal to elements in the first group (the one being sorted by this call), so it is technically correct to lump it in with the first group.

The problem, however, is that for certain arrays, `high` never changes from the initial value that's assigned to it (which was `end`), and `start` never changes during the function, so the recursive call might be attempting to sort the exact same range as the outer call. This means that it continues to recurse, never shortening the array it tries to sort, and eventually overflows the stack.

For example, the second hint causes infinite recursion. In practice, this bug causes infinite recursion when two or more elements of the array are of equal value (as reported by the `quickcompare` method). That's because the bug happens when `array[high]` and `array[pivot]` have the same value on some iteration of the loop.

The fix is to not include the pivot element in the recursive sort, because the pivot element is in its proper place in the array. Line 53 should read as follows:

```
quicksort(array, start, high-1, qc);
```

This bug's type could be debated, but I classify it as **A.logic** because it involves a particular set of inputs that the algorithm does not handle correctly.

❽ Play the Game *Pong*, Part I

The `PongTimerTask` class is used as the timer class for another class that plays the simple video game known as *Pong*.

The timer class extends the built-in class `TimerTask`. The base class has an abstract method `run()` that must be implemented by the class. In turn, the implementation of this method calls the `updatePosition()` method as long as the applet has focus. The `updatePosition()` method moves the ball as appropriate after one timer tick.

In the game, a ball moves down the screen toward a paddle that the player controls ("down the screen" means from lower to higher y coordinates). If the player can move the paddle sideways so the ball hits it, the ball bounces back up, possibly with a change in the angle at which it moves. The ball bounces off the edges and top of the applet window until it moves back toward the paddle. If the ball misses the paddle, the ball goes to the bottom of the applet window and the game ends.

Note that `Random.nextInt(n)` returns a number between 0 (inclusive) and n (exclusive).

The variables' names should be self explanatory, although of course, you should check them. Assume for now that the variables are initialized with reasonable values. The `paint()` method of the applet is included to provide some clarification. The first two parameters to both `fillRect()` and `fillOval()` are the x and y coordinates of the upper-left corner. The second two parameters are the width and height.

In the next example, this function is expanded into a class that plays a complete *Pong* game.

Source Code

```
1.    import java.util.Timer;
2.    import java.util.TimerTask;
3.    import java.util.Random;
4.
5.    public class Pong extends java.applet.Applet {
6.
```

```
7.      private int paddleX, paddleY, maxX, maxY;
8.      private int paddleWidth, paddleHeight;
9.      private int ballX, ballY;
10.     private int ballWidth, ballHeight;
11.     private int ballMoveX, ballMoveY;
12.     private Dimension size;
13.     boolean focus;
14.     Random random;
15.
16.     class PongTimerTask extends TimerTask {
17.
18.         void updatePosition() {
19.
20.             int highestAllowedX = maxX - ballWidth;
21.
22.             ballX += ballMoveX;
23.             if (ballX < 0) {
24.                 ballX = -ballX;
25.                 ballMoveX = -ballMoveX;
26.             } else if (ballX > highestAllowedX) {
27.                 ballX = (highestAllowedX * 2 ) - ballX;
28.                 ballMoveX = - ballMoveX;
29.             }
30.
31.             ballY += ballMoveY;
32.             if (ballY < 0) {
33.                 ballY = -ballY;
34.                 ballMoveY = -ballMoveY;
35.             } else if ((ballY + ballHeight) >= paddleY) {
36.
37.                 if ((ballY + ballHeight - ballMoveY) <
38.                         paddleY) {
39.
40.                     // Just hit the paddle in the Y
41.                     // direction -- now check if
42.                     // the middle of the ball intersects
43.                     // the paddle in the X direction
44.                     // (this check isn't perfect since
45.                     // ballMove has already been added
46.                     // to ballX, but it is good enough).
47.
48.                     int ballMiddleX =
49.                             ballX + (ballWidth / 2);
50.
51.                     if ((ballMiddleX >= paddleX) ||
52.                         (ballMiddleX <= (paddleX +
53.                             paddleWidth))) {
```

154

```
54.                          ballY =
55.                              ((paddleY - ballHeight) * 2) -
56.                              ballY;
57.                          ballMoveY = -ballMoveY;
58.                          int newX =
59.                              random.nextInt(7) + 7;
60.                          // keep moving in same X dir
61.                          ballMoveX = (ballMoveX > 0) ?
62.                                      newX : -newX;
63.                      }
64.                  }
65.              }
66.          }
67.
68.          public void run() {
69.
70.              if (focus) {
71.                  updatePosition();
72.                  repaint();
73.              }
74.              if (ballY > maxY) {
75.                  timer.cancel();
76.              }
77.          }
78.      }
79.      public void paint(Graphics g) {
80.
81.          g.setColor(Color.BLACK);
82.          g.fillRect(paddleX, paddleY,
83.                      paddleWidth, paddleHeight);
84.          g.setColor(Color.RED);
85.          g.fillOval(ballX, ballY, ballWidth, ballHeight);
86.
87.      }
88.
89.  }
```

Suggestions

1. Which member variables in the `Pong` class are potentially updated by the `updatePosition()` method, as opposed to only being used?
2. What do the calculation on line 27 and the similar calculation on lines 54–56 accomplish? What are some "inputs" that could test these single lines of code?

155

3. How are `ballX` and `ballY` restricted? Verify any modifications to these variables to ensure that the restrictions are honored.

Hints

Walk through `updatePosition()` with the following inputs. (Before you do, imagine each scenario visually. For example, the first one represents the ball bouncing off the left wall while moving downward.)

1. ```
ballX == 4
ballY == 50
ballMoveX == -6
ballMoveY == 10
```

2. ```
ballX == 146
ballY == 2
ballMoveX == 7
ballMoveY == -6
highestAllowedX == 150
```

3. ```
ballX == 50
ballY == 176
ballMoveX == 10
ballMoveY == 8
ballWidth == 10
ballHeight == 10
paddleX == 45
paddleY == 190
paddleWidth == 30
```

# Explanation of the Bug

The check on lines 51–53

```
if ((ballMiddleX >= paddleX) ||
    (ballMiddleX <= (paddleX +
        paddleWidth))) {
```

has a **B.expression** error. The logical operator || is incorrect. As written, the paddle is "unmissable"; the ball always bounces up when it reaches the level of the paddle, even if the paddle is nowhere near it. If the ball is to the right of the paddle, the first part of the || expression will be true; if it is to the left of the paddle, the second part will be true; and if it is hitting the paddle, both parts will be true. In all cases the overall expression will be true.
```

The logical operator should be `&&` instead, so the code should read as follows:

```
if ((ballMiddleX >= paddleX) &&
    (ballMiddleX <= (paddleX +
        paddleWidth))) {
```

❾ Play the Game *Pong*, Part II

This applet plays a game of *Pong* using the `PongTimerTask` class from the previous example.

The applet class implements two interfaces:

- `KeyListener` receives keystrokes. The user presses `'Z'` to go left and `'M'` to go right. (The code uses "key typed" events rather than the lower-level "key pressed" and "key released" events.)
- `FocusListener` determines if the applet's window has the focus, so that the game can be paused when the focus is lost.

The `schedule()` method on the `Timer` class, as called here, sets up a recurring task, and takes three parameters: an implementation of the `TimerTask` interface, a delay in milliseconds until the first execution of the task, and a delay in milliseconds between subsequent executions of the task. The implementation of `PongTimerTask` is not shown. Assume that it uses the code from the previous example (with the bug fixed). Recall that the timer calls the `run()` method of `PongTimerTask`, which calls `updatePosition()` if `focus` is `true`.

By design, the applet does not deal with the size of the applet window changing in the middle. (If you want to enhance it to handle this, applets can implement the `ComponentListener` interface to receive notifications of resizing.)

Source Code

```
1.    import java.awt.event.*;
2.    import java.awt.*;
3.    import java.util.Timer;
4.    import java.util.TimerTask;
```

```
5.      import java.util.Random;
6.
7.      public class Pong extends java.applet.Applet
8.          implements KeyListener, FocusListener {
9.
10.         private int paddleX, paddleY, maxX, maxY;
11.         private int paddleWidth, paddleHeight;
12.         private int ballX, ballY;
13.         private int ballMoveX, ballMoveY;
14.         private int ballWidth, ballHeight;
15.         boolean focus;
16.         Random random;
17.
18.         class PongTimerTask extends TimerTask {
19.             // Implementation is in previous example.
20.         }
21.
22.         PongTimerTask timerTask;
23.         Timer timer;
24.
25.         public void init() {
26.
27.             random = new Random(System.currentTimeMillis());
28.
29.             Dimension size = getSize();
30.             maxX = size.width;
31.             maxY = size.height;
32.             paddleWidth = 80;
33.             paddleHeight = 20;
34.             ballX = 0;
35.             ballY = 0;
36.             ballMoveX = random.nextInt(7) + 7;
37.             ballMoveY = 10;
38.             ballWidth = 20;
39.             ballHeight = 20;
40.
41.             addKeyListener(this);
42.             addFocusListener(this);
43.
44.             focus = hasFocus();
45.
46.             timerTask = new PongTimerTask();
47.             timer = new Timer();
48.             // schedule it ten times per second
49.             timer.schedule(timerTask, 100, 100);
50.
51.         }
```

```
52.
53.        public void paint(Graphics g) {
54.
55.            g.setColor(Color.BLACK);
56.            g.fillRect(paddleX, paddleY,
57.                    paddleWidth, paddleHeight);
58.            g.setColor(Color.RED);
59.            g.fillOval(ballX, ballY, ballWidth, ballHeight);
60.
61.        }
62.
63.    public void destroy() {
64.        timer.cancel();
65.        removeKeyListener(this);
66.        removeFocusListener(this);
67.    }
68.
69.    // KeyListener methods
70.
71.    public void keyPressed(KeyEvent e) {
72.
73.    }
74.
75.    public void keyReleased(KeyEvent e) {
76.
77.    }
78.
79.    public void keyTyped(KeyEvent e) {
80.
81.        char c = e.getKeyChar();
82.
83.        if ((c == 'z') || (c == 'Z')) {
84.            paddleX =
85.                (paddleX > 10) ? (paddleX - 10) : 0;
86.        } else if ((c == 'm') || (c == 'M')) {
87.            paddleX =
88.                (paddleX < (maxX - (paddleWidth + 10))) ?
89.                    (paddleX + 10) : (maxX - paddleWidth);
90.        }
91.        repaint();
92.
93.    }
94.
95.    // FocusListener methods
96.
97.    public void focusGained(FocusEvent e) {
98.        focus = true;
```

```
99.            }
100.
101.       public void focusLost(FocusEvent e) {
102.            focus = false;
103.       }
104.    }
```

Suggestions

1. Describe the exact meaning of each variable declared on lines 10–14.
2. Look at lines 83–90. What is the goal of this section?
3. Based on your understanding of updatePosition() and how positions are stored, is 0 a valid initialization value for ballX and ballY?

Hints

With the values initialized as they are in init():

1. Walk through keyTyped() for three different values for e.keyGetChar(): 'z', 'M', and 'a'.
2. Walk through the first iteration of updatePosition() (refer to previous example), assuming that focus is true.

Explanation of the Bug

There is an **F.init** error. paddleX and paddleY are never initialized.

The paddle position can be initialized as desired. The following code, added anywhere in the init() method (although between lines 31 and 32 would be the logical place), puts the paddle in the middle of the applet (left-to-right), and the bottom of the paddle 50 pixels from the bottom:

```
paddleX = (size.width - paddleWidth) / 2;
paddleY = size.height - (paddleHeight + 50);
```

⑩ Compute Bowling Scores

This program computes the score of a bowling game.

To quickly recap the rules, bowling is played in 10 frames. At the beginning of each frame, 10 pins are set up, and the bowler is given two rolls to knock them all down. The score for a frame is the total number of pins knocked down by the two rolls. However, if all the pins are knocked down by the first roll (known as a *strike*), the score for the frame is increased by the total number of pins knocked down by the next two rolls. If all the pins are knocked down by the first and second roll combined (known as a *spare*), the score for the frame is increased by the number of pins knocked down by the next roll.

Thus, the maximum score for a frame is 30 points, which happens when the bowler records a strike in this frame and in the next two frames. If the bowler records a spare or a strike in the 10th frame, he or she gets to roll one or two more balls, respectively, to have the proper chance to get bonus points added on to the 10th frame score (the pins knocked down on those extra balls don't count by themselves, only as bonuses on the 10th frame score).

The program does not simulate rolling the ball and knocking down pins. It prompts the user with the number of pins left and asks how many were knocked down. It does know when it is time to move to the next frame, and when extra rolls are needed after the 10th frame. It also prints the total score of the game when it's over.

The program reads input using an object declared as the following:

```
BufferedReader bufrd =
    new BufferedReader(
        new InputStreamReader(System.in));
```

You can assume this works as expected, but if you want more detail: System.in is the "standard input" stream, which is an instance of the class InputStream. BufferedReader, which provides the useful readLine() method, is a subclass of Reader, which is a different class for reading character streams. InputStreamReader is another subclass of Reader, which is passed an InputStream in its constructor and thus converts between the two classes. (The constructor for BufferedReader is defined to take a Reader as a parameter. The fact that it can take an InputStreamReader, which is a subclass of Reader, demonstrates the power of class inheritance.)

161

In the case of an I/O error, `BufferedReader.readLine()` throws an `IOException` exception. Because this is not expected, rather than put the `readLine()` call inside a `try/catch` block, the declaraton of `main()` specifies that it can throw `IOException` also. On the other hand, the code does catch the `NumberFormatException` that is thrown by `Integer.parseInt()` because this occurs if the user enters a non-number, including a blank line.

If you want to delve a bit deeper into Java (and object-oriented programming in general), understand why the `Bowling` class declares a `static` member variable called `b`:

```
static final Bowling b = new Bowling();
```

The instance `b` has to exist to create `Frame` objects. Because `Frame` is a nested class within the `Bowling` class, Java needs to associate an instance of `Bowling` with each `Frame` created. This is done automatically when the `Frame` is created within a non-static `Bowling` member method, which is why `Frame` objects have their own creation method, `Bowling.newFrame()`. But, although `main()` is a member method of `Bowling`, it is declared `static`, so you cannot simply call `newFrame()` because there is no `Bowling` object to call it on. The static `b` is created for this purpose, allowing the program to call `b.newFrame()` from within `main()`.

Having gone to the trouble of creating `b`, it would be possible to change the static member variables in `Bowling`, such as `rolls`, to be non-static, and then refer to `b.rolls` instead, but either way works.

Source Code

```
1.      import java.io.*;
2.
3.      public class Bowling {
4.
5.          static final int MAXFRAMES = 10;
6.          static final int MAXROLLS = (MAXFRAMES * 2 + 1);
7.          static int[] rolls = new int[MAXROLLS];
8.          static Frame[] frames = new Frame[MAXFRAMES];
9.
10.         static final Bowling b = new Bowling();
11.
12.         class Frame {
13.             public int[] rollindex = new int[3];
```

```
14.
15.             public Frame() {
16.                 for (int i = 0; i < 3; i++) {
17.                     rollindex[i] = -1;
18.                 }
19.             }
20.
21.             public int getTotal() {
22.                 int tot = 0;
23.                 for (int i = 0; i < 3; i++) {
24.                     if (rollindex[i] != -1) {
25.                         tot += rolls[rollindex[i]];
26.                     }
27.                 }
28.                 return tot;
29.             }
30.         }
31.
32.         public Frame newFrame() {
33.             return new Frame();
34.         }
35.
36.         public static void main(String[] args)
37.                 throws IOException {
38.
39.             String inputline;
40.             int nextroll = 0;
41.             int i, pinsleft, hitpins;
42.             boolean extrarolls = false;
43.
44.             for (i = 0; i < MAXROLLS; i++) {
45.                 rolls[i] = 0;
46.             }
47.
48.             BufferedReader bufrd =
49.                 new BufferedReader(
50.                     new InputStreamReader(System.in));
51.
52.     nextframe:
53.             for (int frame = 0; frame < MAXFRAMES; frame++) {
54.
55.                 frames[frame] = b.newFrame();
56.                 pinsleft = 10;
57.                 for (int roll = 0; roll < 3; roll++ ) {
58.
59.                     // Get number of pins hit from user
60.                     while (true) {
```

163

```
61.        System.out.println(
62.            "Frame " + (frame+1) +
63.            ", roll " + (roll+1) +
64.            ", pins left " + pinsleft +
65.            ". How many hit?");
66.        inputline = bufrd.readLine();
67.        try {
68.            hitpins =
69.                Integer.parseInt(inputline);
70.        } catch (NumberFormatException e) {
71.            continue;
72.        }
73.        if ((hitpins >= 0) &&
74.            (hitpins <= pinsleft)) {
75.            break;
76.        }
77.    }
78.
79.    rolls[nextroll] = hitpins;
80.    frames[frame].rollindex[roll] =
81.        nextroll;
82.
83.    // If all pins down and this is not an
84.    // extra roll, set it to add bonus rolls
85.    int frametot = frames[frame].getTotal();
86.    if ((frametot == 10) &&
87.        (extrarolls == false)) {
88.        for (int t = roll+1; t < 3; t++) {
89.            frames[frame].rollindex[i] =
90.                nextroll + (i - roll);
91.        }
92.    }
93.    ++nextroll;
94.    pinsleft -= hitpins;
95.
96.    // two rolls, pins left, frame over
97.    if ((roll == 1) &&
98.        (frametot < 10)) {
99.        continue nextframe;
100.    }
101.
102.    // all pins knocked down...
103.    if (frametot == 10) {
104.        if (frame < (MAXFRAMES-1)) {
105.            continue nextframe;
106.        } else {
107.            // ...and last frame
```

```
108.                              extrarolls = true;
109.                          }
110.                      }
111.                      if (extrarolls && (pinsleft == 0)) {
112.                          // new pins if needed
113.                          pinsleft = 10;
114.                      }
115.                  }
116.              }
117.
118.              int total = 0;
119.              for (i = 0; i < MAXFRAMES; i++) {
120.                  total += frames[i].getTotal();
121.              }
122.              System.out.println("Game total is " + total);
123.          }
124.      }
```

Suggestions

1. Because the `Frame` class is nested within the `Bowling` class, it makes sense to understand it first. What exactly is the meaning of the `rollindex[]` array?
2. Verify that the comments on lines 59, 83–84, and 96 match the code that follows them.
3. The loop that starts on line 57 terminates when `roll` reaches 3. Under what conditions will the loop iterate with `roll` equal to 2?
4. The loop on lines 88–90 is probably the most visually confusing part in the code. How many times will the loop iterate if the bowler has just rolled a spare? What if the bowler has just rolled a strike?

Hints

1. Walk through the loop that starts on line 57, assuming `frame` is 0, `nextroll` is 0, and `extrarolls` is `false`, and that the user specifies that 10 pins are hit on the first roll. Continue until `frame` is incremented.
2. Walk through the loop that starts on line 57, assuming `frame` is `MAXFRAMES-1`, `nextroll` is `frame*2`, `extrarolls` is `false`, and the user specifies that 10, 10, and 4 pins are knocked down by successive rolls. Continue until the loop that starts on line 57 finishes iterating.

Explanation of the Bug

The code on lines 88–90, to set up the addition of the bonus rolls to a frame total, in the event that a spare or strike was rolled

```
for (int t = roll+1; t < 3; t++) {
    frames[frame].rollindex[i] =
        nextroll + (i - roll);
```

has a **B.variable** error in it. Unlike the other minor loops in the code, which use the loop variable i, this one uses t, but the code within the loop still uses i, which in this case, will have the value MAXROLLS, left over from the initialization loop that terminated at line 46. This causes an ArrayIndexOutOfBoundsException if a player rolls a spare or strike.

Chapter 6

PERL

Brief Summary of Perl

Perl acts like an interpreter. You type the source into a file and then tell the Perl program (usually called `perl` or `perl.exe`) to execute it. Actually, Perl compiles the program before it runs it, but the user doesn't really notice this. The only difference from a true interpreter is that syntax errors anywhere in the program cause an error before execution starts.

Perl generally treats all white space, including new lines, equally. Blocks of code are enclosed between { and }, and statements usually end with a semicolon (;).

Comments are marked with a # symbol—anything following that symbol on a line is ignored.

Data Types and Variables

Variables do not need to be declared; they can simply be used. Variables that have not been assigned a value evaluate to the special reserved value, `undef`.

A variable that holds one value is known as a *scalar*. The scalars used in this book are all numbers or strings. Scalar variable names start with a $. Perl distinguishes between strings and numbers in literals, so you can assign one or the other to a scalar variable:

```
$x = "Hello";
```

or

```
$y = 5;
```

Numbers can be treated as if they were all floating-point numbers; Perl automatically converts between integers and floating-point numbers as needed. In addition, Perl converts between strings and numbers, depending on which operator is being used. For example, the + operator is defined to be a numeric addition of two scalars, so the following statement

```
$x = 5 + "7";
```

sets $x to 12. The string "7" is automatically converted to the number 7. Similarly, the operator . concatenates two strings together, so the following statement

```
$x = 5 . "7";
```

sets $x to "57".

In practice, this means that you can almost always treat a number and its string representation as the same. When converting a string to a number, only the characters up to the first non-numeric one are evaluated, so the string "123ABC" evaluates as the number 123. A variable that is undef does the "right thing" when used in an expression, evaluating to the number 0 or an empty string as appropriate.

Assignment is done with the = sign, as previously shown, and the assignment returns a value, so you can use an assignment anywhere you would use a variable:

```
$x = ($y = 4);     # $x will be 4 also
```

Perl uses +, -, *, and / for the basic mathematical operations. % is modulo (numbers are truncated to integers first) and ** is the exponentiation operator, for example 2**16. ++ and -- work as they do in C/C++ and Java. Perl supports binary assignment operators such as +=, -=, %=, and even .= and **=:

```
$x += 5;
$mystring .= "(s)";
```

Strings

Strings can be quoted with either single or double quotes. Within single quotes, the only special characters in a string are the backslash and the single quote. \\ represents a single backslash, and \' represents a single quote, as shown in these examples:

```
$directory = 'windows\\system32';
$answer = 'I don\'t agree';
```

Within double quotes, you can specify backslash escapes such as \n and \t. Perl also does variable interpolation within double-quoted strings, which means that scalar variables (and some others) are replaced with their values:

```
$prompt = "Enter your name\n";
$name = "Sally";
$reply = "Hello, $name!";
```

The length() function returns the length of a string. substr() returns a part of a string, and index() finds the index of a match within a string. String positions are zero-based, so the first character is at position 0. You can use negative numbers to count backward from the end, with index -1 as the last character in a string. With these built-in functions, as with most functions in Perl, the parentheses around the arguments are optional, as long as the fact that it is a function call is unambiguous (nonetheless, I will continue to append () to indicate functions):

```
$j = length $somestring;
$secondfivechars = substr ($x, 5, 5);
$lastchar = substr $inputline, -1;
$firstspace = index($text, " ");
```

Function parameters can be optional; if the third parameter to substr() is not provided, the rest of the string is returned. index() can also take a third parameter, which is the offset within the string to start searching.

You can modify a string by assigning to a substring, even if the new string is not the same length as the substring:

```
substr($currency, index($currency, "$"), 1) = "<dollar>";
```

Lists

Perl uses the term *list* to describe an ordered collection of scalars. An *array* is a variable that contains a list, so the terms array and list are often thought of as being the same.

A list is specified using comma-separated scalars within parentheses, which can then be assigned to an array variable:

```
@mylist = (1, 2, 3);
```

An entire array is referenced by preceding the name with @. If a list is included in another list, the elements in the list are included—not the list itself—so you don't get the "list member that is itself a list":

```
@listA = ('A', 'B', 'C');
@listB = (@listA, 'D', 'E');
```

@listB is now a list with five elements: ('A', 'B', 'C', 'D', 'E').

The range operator (..) can be used as a shortcut for a list that is a sequence of numbers (or letters):

```
@numbers1to5 = (1..5);
```

Access to elements in an array uses zero-based indexing, and supports negative numbers to indicate counting back from the end. When indexing into an array, the array name is preceded with $, not @, except for certain circumstances that this book doesn't cover:

```
$firstel = $mylist[0];
$lastel = $mylist[-1];
```

The index of the last element in an array can be retrieved with $#arrayname. This is one less than the size because arrays are zero-based. You can assign to this value to chop the end off an array:

```
$array[$#array+1] = $value    # extend array by one
$#myarray = 3;    # drop all elements after the fourth one
```

Consistent with being one less than the size of the array, $#arrayname will be −1 for an empty array.

You can assign to an element of an array past the current size. The array is extended and any intervening elements return the value `undef` if accessed (as will any elements past the new end of the array):

```
$array[0] = "A";
$array[1] = "B";
$array[25] = "Z";    # array[2] through array[24] are undef
$k = $array[26];     # this is undef also
```

You can also assign to a list containing variable names, which lines up the values as you would expect. Including `undef` in the list means no assignment is done:

```
@numarray = (1..5);
($a, undef, undef, $b, undef) = @numarray;
```

This code sets `$a` to 1 and `$b` to 4.

You can "slice" a list by specifying a list of indices into a list or array to produce a smaller list or array. For example:

```
($a, $b) = @arr[2, 3];    # $a = $arr[2], $b = $arr[3]
print @arr[0..4];         # print first five elements
```

The range is evaluated before the slice. Because the range `[0..-1]` is empty, the slice `@arr[0..-1]` is also empty (despite the temptation to think that the `-1` would refer to the last element in the list and that slice would therefore contain every element in the list).

The `shift()` function takes an element off the beginning of a list (index 0) and `pop()` takes an element off the end (index -1). `unshift()` and `push()` place an element or list of elements back on the list at the beginning or end:

```
$next = shift @mylist;
push (@mylist, $newelement);
$last = pop (@biglist);
unshift @numberlist, (1, 2, 3);
```

Hashes

A Perl *hash* is similar to a list, except it is indexed using strings known as *keys*. The entries are also unordered. To access an element of a hash, the key is surrounded by curly braces:

```
$iphash{"router"} = "192.0.0.1";
```

There can be only one value for a given key. It is replaced if a new value is assigned.

The entire contents of a hash are referred to by preceding the name with %. The functions `keys()` and `values()` return lists of the keys and values of a hash:

```
@machinenames = keys %iphash;
@ipaddrs = values %iphash;
```

Although the hash is unordered, the elements in the lists returned by `keys()` and `values()` line up as long as the hash is not modified in between.

Conditionals

Conditionals can be tested with the `if` statement, which is followed by a block of code inside curly braces (which are required even if the block has only one line of code):

```
if ($i == 5) {
    $i = 0;
}
```

A scalar that is equal to `undef` evaluates to false, as will an empty string and the number 0. To preserve the rule that a number and its string representation can be treated as equivalent, the string `"0"` also evaluates to false. Everything else evaluates to true. No specific boolean type exists.

If a string has a number in it, Perl does not know whether to compare it as a number or a string. Therefore, there are two complete sets of comparison operators. Numeric comparisons are done using `==`, `!=`, `<`, `>`, `<=`, and `>=`, and string comparisons are done using `eq`, `ne`, `lt`, `gt`, `le`, and `ge`. Thus, with the following assignments

```
$a = "5";
$b = "10";
```

(`$a < $b`) is true, but (`$a lt $b`) is false.

Perl uses `||` and `&&` for logical *or* and logical *and*. It guarantees that in the following expression

```
if ((expr1) || (expr2)) {
```

expr2 is only evaluated if expr1 is false. (Similarly, in the case of ((expr1) && (expr2)), expr2 is only evaluated if expr1 is true.)

Perl also supports the words or and and. The difference is that or and and have lower precedence than || and &&. In particular, the = assignment operator has higher precedence than or and and but lower precedence than || and &&. Therefore, a test such as the following

```
($j = myfunc() || $x)
```

won't do what you probably expect, but

```
($j = myfunc() or $x)
```

will.

Perl supports else and elsif (note the spelling) blocks after if statements:

```
if ($command eq "sort") {
    do_sort();
} elsif ($command eq "print") {
    do_print();
} else {
    invalid_command();
}
```

Perl also supports unless, which is like if except that the sense is reversed—the unless block executes if the condition is false:

```
unless (defined($name)) {
    $name = "default";
}
```

(defined() is a built-in function that returns false if the argument is undef.) An unless statement can have elsif and else clauses, but the meaning is not reversed for those:

```
unless ($age < 21) {
    print ("can drive and vote\n");
} elsif ($age >= 16) {
    print ("can drive but not vote\n");
} else {
    print ("cannot drive or vote\n");
}
```

Loops

Perl has several ways to loop. The `while` loop works as it does in many other languages:

```
while ($k < 100) {
    $k = $k + 1;
}
```

There are also `until` loops, which execute as long as their test is false (`while` and `until` are related the same way as `if` and `unless`), and also `do/while` and `do/until` loops.

Perl has `for` loops that look the same as C and Java:

```
for ($j = 0; $j < 10; $j++) {
    print $j;
}
```

Perl also has `foreach` loops that loop through a list:

```
foreach $counter (0..9) {
    print $counter;
}

foreach (@mylist) {
    print $_;
}
```

The second example shows the Perl default variable $_. If a `foreach` loop does not specify the name of its loop control variable, the control variable is stored in a variable named $_. Perl uses the $_ default in other places, too. For example, by default, the `print()` function takes $_ as its parameter. Thus, the body of the second loop could simply have been `print;`.

Perl allows `if`, `unless`, `while`, `until`, and `foreach` to be written as modifiers to expressions, which can sometimes be easier to read:

```
$x += 1 unless $x > 100;
print $_ foreach (1..10);
```

This is just a reordering of the traditional way of writing the code. In particular, the conditional is still evaluated before the code is executed, even though it is to the right of it. With `foreach` written as a modifier, the control variable can't be named; it is always $_.

Inside a loop, the `last` statement exits the loop (which is similar to `break` in some other languages), the `next` statement moves to the next iteration of the loop (which is similar to `continue` in some other languages), and the `redo` statement restarts the current iteration without changing the control variable.

Subroutines

Perl user-defined functions (called *subroutines*) are declared using `sub`. The parameters to the subroutine are passed in the `@_` array:

```
sub addtwo {
    return $_[0] + $_[1];
}
```

A `return` statement at the end of a subroutine is actually optional. If it is missing, the subroutine returns the value of the last expression calculated, or `undef` if no expressions were calculated.

Variables local to a function can be declared with the `my` operator, so the previous function could be written as follows:

```
sub addtwo {
    my ($a, $b);      # declare them local
    ($a, $b) = @_;    # list assignment
    return $a + $b;
}
```

You don't have to put `my` on a separate line. Instead, it can be applied the first time the variables are used:

```
my ($a, $b) = @_;
```

There is also a `local` operator, which is an older Perl operator that works sort of like `my`, except instead of creating a truly local variable for the subroutine, it reuses a global variable (if one exists with the same name), but saves the current value of the global until the subroutine is complete. If that wasn't clear, it really matters only if the subroutine calls another subroutine that accesses the global variable by name. (For reasons that are best left to Perl wizards to explain, you can't use `my` on a file handle (see "File Handles" on the next page); you have to use `local`.)

Scalar Versus List Context

An important concept in Perl is scalar context versus list context. This refers to where an expression is used. For example, when assigning to a scalar, the right side of the assignment statement is in scalar context. When assigning to a list, the right side of the assignment statement is in list context. The conditional expression of a `while` statement is in scalar context, but the expression controlling a `foreach` loop is in list context.

This matters because certain expressions, such as the name of an array, produce different values in list context versus scalar context. In scalar context, the name of an array returns the number of values, but in list context, it returns the entire array. Thus, you can say both of the following:

```
$arraysize = @myarray;  # scalar context - length of array
```

and

```
@arraycopy = @myarray;  # list context - entire array
```

File Handles

Scalar versus list context also matters when you deal with *file handles*. The most commonly used file handle is `STDIN`, which is the standard input to the Perl program. File handles are accessed by enclosing the handle between < and > and assigning the result to a variable. In scalar context, a file handle returns the next line of a file, or `undef` when the end of a file is reached. In list context, it returns every line of the file. Thus, you can loop through standard input with either of the following code lines:

```
while (<STDIN>) {   # scalar context
    process($_);
}
```

or

```
foreach (<STDIN>) {   # list context
    process($_);
}
```

But, in the first case, only one line of the input is read into memory at a time. In the second, the entire input is read into a list, which is then stepped through.

When Perl reads a line from a file handle, it includes the newline character ('\n') at the end. Because it is common to want to remove this, Perl provides a built-in function chomp(), whose only function is to remove the last character from a string if it is '\n'. (chomp() actually can be used to remove an arbitrary string from the end of a string, but removing '\n' is the default behavior.)

Of special note is the diamond operator, which is called that because of its appearance: <>. The diamond operator is used for programs that specify a list of files as command-line parameters. It is a magic file handle that reads in turn from each file specified on the command line, or from standard input if no files were specified:

```
while (<>) {
    lookformatches($matchstring, $_);
}
```

The diamond operator follows the UNIX convention that a filename that is a single hyphen refers to the standard input stream. The diamond operator uses the @ARGV array (discussed under "Command-Line Parameters," later in this chapter) to determine which files to read, so you can tweak @ARGV as you like before invoking the diamond operator.

Regular Expressions

Perl includes built-in *regular expression* matching. The simplest form is an if that contains only the regular expression. This compares it to the value of $_:

```
while (<>) {
    if (/hello/) {
        ++$hellolinecount;
    }
}
```

In addition to matching literal strings, the regular expressions can include the following:

- . Matches any character except newline.
- \ Escapes the next character (so \. matches only a period).

177

- () Groups parts of a regular expression.
- * Match the previous item zero or more times.
- + Match the previous item one or more times.
- ? Makes an item optional. It can appear zero or one time.
- {n} Match the previous item n times.
- {n,m} Match the previous item between n and m times.
- | Between two items, it means to match either one.
- [abcd] Matches any of the characters listed.
- [a-z] Matches any character in a range.
- [^abcd] Matches any character except the ones listed.
- \d Matches any digit, same as [0-9].
- \w Matches a word character, same as [a-zA-Z0-9_].
- \s Matches white space, same as [\f\t\n\r].
- \D, \W, and \S Match any character except their lowercase equivalent.
- ^ Matches the beginning of the string.
- $ Matches the end of the string.

Thus, you can get sophisticated with your matching (the *binding operator*, =~, matches a string against a regular expression):

```
if ($phone =~ /\d{3}-\d{4}/) {
    print ("$phone contains a US phone number\n");
}
if ($number =~ /^([0-9a-fA-F]+)$/) {
    print ("$number is a valid hexadecimal number\n");
}
if ($inputline =~ /^#/) {
    print("comment line, ignored");
}
```

Beyond grouping, parentheses (()) around a part of the match string tell Perl to remember what part of the string matched that part of the regular expression. The escape \1 can be used later in the match string to refer to the first grouped match. So, the match string /(.)\1/ matches any character repeated twice in a row. Furthermore, the part of the string that matched is put in a special variable, $1. The same goes for \2 and $2, \3 and $3, and so on:

```
if ($word =~ /([aeiou])\1/) {
    print("$word has a repeated vowel: $1\n");
}
```

When a match is complete, the part of the string that matched the regular expression is stored in `$&`, the part before is stored in `$``, and the part after is stored in `$'`:

```
if ($text =~ /[\w\.]+\.(com|org|net)/) {
    print ("$`<a href=\"$&\">$&</a>$'");
}
```

Finally, the `/i` modifier after the match string makes the matching case-insensitive. Perl regular expressions allow even more escapes and modifiers, but this book doesn't use them.

Output

Printing in Perl is done with the `print()` function, which was shown in previous examples. More sophisticated printing can be done with `printf()`, which does formatting similar to the C `printf()`, and its relative `sprintf()`, which returns the formatted string rather than printing it:

```
printf  "The date is %2d/%2d/%4d\n", $day, $month, $year;
$time = sprintf "%2d:%2d:%2d", $hour, $minute, $second;
```

Command-Line Parameters

When a program is invoked, the list `@ARGV` contains the command-line parameters that were passed to it:

```
$firstarg = shift @ARGV;
```

Unlike in the `argv[]` array in C, which stores the name of the program in `argv[0]` and the first argument in `argv[1]`, the first element in `@ARGV` is the first argument to the program; the name of the program is stored in the variable `$0` (that's the number 0, not the letter O).

❶ Sort a File by Line Length

This function reads lines from standard input and outputs them sorted by length.

For each line of text, it inserts a string in a new array. This string consists of the length of the line of text, concatenated with the vertical bar (' | ') character, concatenated with the index of the line of text in the original array. The program sorts the new array, and then uses the results to display the original lines in sorted order.

This depends on the fact that when Perl converts a string to a number, it stops the conversion when it hits a non-numeric character, but still returns the number converted so far. Converting these artificially fabricated `"length|index"` array strings back to a number returns the length of the line of text because conversion stops (but does not fail) when it hits the vertical bar character.

Remember that `index()` returns the zero-based index of the first occurrence of a string in another string, and `substr()` with two parameters returns a substring from the specified index to the end.

This program uses Perl's built-in `sort()` function. By default, it sorts a list in ASCII order:

```
@sortedlist = sort @unsortedlist;
```

However, you can also specify a subroutine to use for comparisons. This can be a named subroutine, or it can be specified inline as a parameter to `sort()`. The semantics of the subroutine are that it always has two arguments—$a and $b—and it should return −1, 0, or 1, respectively, if $a should be sorted before, at the same place, or after $b. For your convenience, Perl defines two built-in operators that have these same semantics: <=> (known as the "spaceship" operator) does numeric comparisons and `cmp` does string comparisons. Thus, the following line of code

```
@sortarray = sort { $a <=> $b } @sortarray;
```

replaces the list @sortarray with its numerically sorted equivalent.

Source Code

```
1.    # read in the entire input
2.
3.    @lines = <STDIN>;
4.
5.    #construct the array with the length prepended
6.
```

```
7.      foreach (0..$#lines) {
8.          $sortarray[$_] = length($lines[$_]) . "|" . $_;
9.      }
10.
11.     # sort using numeric comparison
12.
13.     @sortarray = sort { $a <=> $b } @sortarray;
14.
15.     # display results
16.
17.     foreach (@sortarray) {
18.         print $lines[substr($_, index($_, "|"))];
19.     }
```

Suggestions

1. How will it affect @sortarray if one of the elements in lines has a | character in it?
2. What are the empty and trivial cases for this function? How are they handled?
3. Is the assignment in line 3 done in scalar context or list context?

Hints

Walk through the function with the following lines of input:

1. The trivial case:
   ```
   abc
   ```
2. Check if the program handles an empty line:
   ```
   this
   is

   test
   ```
3. See if the program handles an already sorted file:
   ```
   1
   22
   333
   ```

Explanation of the Bug

The problem is in the display of the text at the end, on line 18:

```
print $lines[substr($_, index($_, "|"))];
```

An element in @sortarray will be of the form "12|3", which means the fourth entry in @lines was 12 bytes long. The index() function returns the location of the '|' character, but the code needs to index into @lines using the "3" part of the string, so it needs to add one to the value that index() returns:

```
print $lines[substr($_, index($_, "|") + 1)];
```

This is your basic **A.off-by-one** error. As it is currently written, the function attempts to display $lines["|3"], which converts to $lines[0]. It displays the first line of the file over and over, as many times as there were lines in the file.

❷ Print the Prime Factors of a Number

This function prints out the prime factorization of a number passed as an argument.

It uses a simple algorithm that loops through all possible factors (between 2 and the number itself), from smallest to largest, and divides the number by each factor that is found until it reaches 1. The factors should be printed out on one line, with a space separating each factor. Note: The inefficiency of the algorithm is not considered a bug.

Source Code

```
1.   # number to factor is passed as an argument
2.   $number = $ARGV[0];
3.
4.   # $left is the unfactored part that remains
5.   $left = $number;
6.
7.   # loop through all possible factors
8.   foreach $test (2..$number) {
9.
```

```
10.        # exit when no factoring left to do
11.        if ($left == 1) {
12.            last;
13.        }
14.
15.        # does $test divide $left?
16.        if ($left % $test == 0) {
17.
18.            $left /= $test;
19.
20.            # print a space between factors
21.            unless ($first) {
22.                print(" ");
23.            } else {
24.                $first = 1;
25.            }
26.
27.            # now print the factor
28.            print ("$test");
29.
30.            # try this factor again
31.            redo;
32.        }
33.    }
34.
35.    print ("\n") unless $first;
```

Suggestions

1. Under what circumstances will the foreach loop on lines 8–33 exit by hitting the end of its list, as opposed to the explicit last statement on line 12?
2. Prove to yourself that the algorithm employed is correct.
3. When should the final "\n" not be printed by line 35?

Hints

Walk through the program with the following parameters:

1. A value that should print nothing: 1
2. A prime number: 7
3. A number with unique prime factors: 30
4. A number with repeated prime factors: 36

183

Explanation of the Bug

The variable $first is not used properly. The intention of this variable is to distinguish the first prime factor from the rest because, after the first factor, a space should be printed before each succeeding factor. However, because the variable is not initialized, it begins as logically false, which means that $notfirst would be a better name. Ignoring the variable name, this is an **A.logic** error. The check on line 21

```
unless ($first) {
```

is true to begin with, and because the else clause of this if is the only place that first is ever set to 1, $first remains undef (therefore, false) forever. As a result, a space is printed in front of every factor, including the first. The statement on line 35 also makes the same mistake:

```
print ("\n") unless $first;
```

This is attempting to only print out the "\n" if any factors were found, but it winds up always printing it since $first always remains undef.

One fix is to change the unless to an if on line 21

```
if ($first) {
```

and line 35

```
print ("\n") if $first;
```

This preserves the misnaming of the variable. Another approach is to add an initialization statement to set $first to 1 at the beginning of the program, and then change line 24 to set $first to 0, which matches the name of the variable to its meaning.

❸ Tab Expansion

This function expands tabs in the STDIN passed to it.

The function is passed a numeric tab stop, indicating how many spaces separate each tab. A tab character in the input is expanded out to the correct number of spaces to move the line to the next tab stop.

In Perl, the character `"\t"` denotes a tab.

Perl's `x` operator repeats a string a specified number of times:

```
" " x ($tabwidth - ($cur % $tabwidth));
```

Therefore, this code repeats the left-side string argument (a single space, in this case) as many times as what's specified by the right side's numeric argument (which is the rest of the glop on that line).

Source Code

```
1.     # tab stop is the argument to the program
2.
3.     $tabwidth = shift @ARGV;
4.
5.     while (<STDIN>) {
6.
7.         # loop through each character of the input line
8.         foreach $cur (0..(length($_)-1)) {
9.
10.            # examine current character
11.            $thischar = substr($_, $cur, 1);
12.
13.            # if a tab, replace with spaces
14.            if ($thischar eq "\t") {
15.                substr($_, $cur, 1) =
16.                    " " x ($tabwidth - ($cur % $tabwidth));
17.            }
18.        }
19.
20.        # print out the modified input line
21.        print;
22.    }
```

Suggestions

1. What is the already solved input to this program?
2. What can be said about `$_` after one iteration of the `foreach` loop on lines 8–18?
3. How does the program behave if `$tabwidth` is 8, and an input line has eight characters and then a tab? What is the value of `$cur` at line 15 when the program encounters the tab?

Hints

Walk through the program with the following input lines, assuming that $tabwidth is 8. (Note that each line of input is handled completely separately, so all the hints are only one line.) Tabs are denoted with \t:

1. One tab in the middle: ABCDEFG\tH
2. Tab at the beginning of the line: \tAB\tCD\tEF
3. Two tabs at the beginning of the line: \t\t\tABCD
4. Tab at the eighth character ($tabwidth is 8): ABCDEFGH\tABCDEFG

Explanation of the Bug

The program contains an **A.logic** error. The problem occurs in the way the foreach loop is defined on line 8:

```
foreach $cur (0..(length($_)-1)) {
```

This statement calculates a list from the specified range and then iterates through the list. The list is not changed after it is created. However, the length of $_ can change as tabs are expanded into spaces, which leaves unprocessed data at the end of the string.

For example, with an input line containing only two tab characters, length($_) will be 2 at the time the list is constructed on line 8, so the list controlling the foreach loop will be (0, 1). However, after the replacement of the first tab with the spaces is complete, the string becomes longer and the second tab is now further out in the string. (For example, assuming a tab stop of 8, the second tab would now be the ninth character.) The foreach loop exits after $_ is equal to 1, and the second tab character is never expanded.

The solution is to replace the foreach on line 8 with a for loop that recalculates length($_) each time:

```
foreach ($cur = 0; $cur < length($_); $cur++) {
```

❹ Simple Database

This function is a simple file-driven database. Entries in the database are identified by a name. The program reads a file that contains lines of the form:

```
put name value  # assign entry "name" the value "value"
get name        # prints the value of entry "name"
delete name     # removes the entry "name"
length name     # prints the length of entry "name"
dump            # displays the entire database
```

To make processing easier, the names are defined to be "Perl words" (which means that they contain letters, numbers, and/or underscores—the characters that the `\w` regular expression escape matches). The spaces in between operators and names can be any number of "Perl spaces" (spaces, return, tab, or formfeed—the characters that the `\s` regular expression escape matches, except for newline, which will delimit an entire line). For the "put" operation, "value" is whatever is left on the line after the spaces following "name" have been skipped; "value" might be empty if nothing more is specified on the line after "put name".

The program uses regular expression matches and particularly the memory variables, which are expressions grouped in parentheses that, in the event of a successful match, result in the match text being stored in variables named $1, $2, and so on.

Entries in the database are stored in a hash with the name used as the key.

Recall that an `if` test containing only a regular expression compares it to $_ and that /i following a regular expression indicates that the match should be case insensitive.

The `exists()` function checks a hash for the existence of an element with a given key:

```
if (exists $table{$1})
```

`delete()` removes an element from a hash, given its key (it does nothing, silently, if no element exists for that key):

```
delete $table{$1};
```

187

The `each()` function iterates through the key-value pairs in a hash, as in the following code:

```
while ( ($key, $value) = each %table )
```

This causes the loop to exit after every element of `%table` has been iterated through. (This code also shows how the two-element list returned by `each()` is assigned to a two-element list containing two variables.)

Source Code

```
1.    # loop through stdin processing commands
2.
3.    while (<>) {
4.        if (/get\s+(\w+)/i) {
5.            if (exists $table{$1}) {
6.                print "$1: $table{$1}\n";
7.            }
8.        }
9.        elsif (/put\s+(\w+)\s+(.+)/i) {
10.            $table{$1} = $2;
11.        }
12.        elsif (/dump/i) {
13.            while ( ($key, $value) = each %table ) {
14.                print "$key: $value\n";
15.            }
16.        }
17.        elsif (/delete\s+(\w+)/i) {
18.            delete $table{$1};
19.        }
20.        elsif (/length\s+(\w+)/i) {
21.            if (exists $table{$1}) {
22.                $len = length $table{$1};
23.                print "length($1): $len\n";
24.            }
25.        }
26.        else {
27.            print("Syntax error: $_");
28.        }
29.    }
```

Suggestions

1. Read through each regular expression carefully to be sure that you understand exactly which strings it will match.
2. What happens if a particular name is "`put`" if it already exists in `%table`?
3. Lines returned by `<>` still have the '`\n`' at the end. Does the program deal with this correctly?
4. Does the program correctly ignore extra data at the end of an input line?

Hints

Walk through the function with the following inputs:

1. Add one element, operate on it, and delete it:
   ```
   put Name Smith
   get Name
   length Name
   delete Name
   ```
2. Add one element and then add it again blank:
   ```
   put ID 1234
   length ID
   put ID
   length ID
   ```
3. Add two elements and then delete one:
   ```
   put A A
   put B B
   delete A
   dump
   ```

Explanation of the Bug

The statement on line 9 that matches the `put` operation

```
elsif (/put\s+(\w+)\s+(.+)/i) {
```

does not correctly handle the case where there is no value. The match string (.+) requires one or more characters, but there might not be more characters. As a result, a line such as the following

```
put ID
```

is reported as a syntax error on line 27.

The regular expression on line 9 needs to be changed:

```
elsif (/put\s+(\w+)\s+(.*)/i) {
```

This change allows the value to be an empty string. This bug could be classified as either **D.limit** or **B.expression**.

➎ Find Repeating Part of a Fraction

This function takes two parameters, the numerator and denominator of a fraction, and determines the repeating part of the fraction (if one exists).

The logic is simple: After removing any part of the result that is a whole number, it begins dividing the denominator into the numerator and tracking the remainder after each digit. If the remainder becomes 0, then the function is done. Otherwise, when a remainder repeats, it has found the repeating part.

Because Perl treats all numbers as floating-point numbers, the easiest way to truncate a number to its integer part is to sprintf() it into a string using the "%d" conversion.

Source Code

```
1.    # use sprintf to truncate to an integer
2.
3.    sub idiv {
4.        sprintf("%d",($_[0] / $_[1]));
5.    }
6.
7.    # usage is "repeat.pl num denom"
8.
9.    $num = shift @ARGV;
10.   $denom = shift @ARGV;
11.
```

```
12.      # first display and chop off integer part
13.
14.      $div = idiv($num,$denom);
15.      $currdecimal = "$div";
16.      $num = $num - ($div * $denom);
17.      $currdecimal .= "." unless ($num == 0);
18.      $digits = 0;
19.
20.      until ($num == 0) {
21.
22.          # store where we saw this remainder
23.          $array[$num] = $digits;
24.
25.          # calculate next digit
26.          $num *= 10;
27.          $div = idiv($num,$denom);
28.          $currdecimal .= $div;
29.          ++$digits;
30.
31.          # find new remainder
32.
33.          $num = $num - ($div * $denom);
34.
35.          # did we see this before?
36.          if ($array[$num]) {
37.              $repeatlen = $digits - $array[$num];
38.              $plural = "s" unless ($repeatlen == 1);
39.              print ("$currdecimal: last $repeatlen"
40.                     . " digit$plural repeated\n");
41.              last;
42.          }
43.      }
44.
45.      if ($num == 0) {
46.          print ("$currdecimal\n");
47.      }
```

Suggestions

1. The program displays its results in two places, lines 39–40 and line 46. How does it guarantee that one—and only one—of those will be executed?

2. What is the meaning of an entry in the @array array?

3. What can you say about the relative values of `$num` and `$denom` at the start of the `until` loop on line 20? What guarantee is there that line 28 will add only one more digit to `$currdecimal`?

4. What does it mean if the `if` on line 36 is true?

Hints

Walk through the code with the following inputs:

1. A result with no fractional part:
   ```
   $num   == 8
   $denom == 2
   ```

2. A result that has a non-repeating fractional part:
   ```
   $num   == 3
   $denom == 4
   ```

3. A result with a single repeating digit, and a few leading zeros:
   ```
   $num   == 1
   $denom == 300
   ```

4. A result with a two-digit repeating part:
   ```
   $num   == 1
   $denom == 11
   ```

Explanation of the Bug

The bug is in the `if` on line 36:

```
if ($array[$num]) {
```

The code uses the automatic support for sparse arrays in Perl. It indexes into `$array` using the current remainder, and knows it has found a repeat when the entry already exists. The problem is that what is being stored in the array for a given remainder is the digit number (with the first digit after the decimal place considered number 0) where the remainder previously occurred. Thus, for the first remainder, the value in the array will be 0 (just consider the effect of line 18 and then line 23 during the first iteration of the loop). This means the program will not notice a repeat if that remainder previously happened in the first fractional digit. Hint #4, 1 divided by 11, shows this; the program will report that the result is 0.090 with the last two digits repeating, instead of 0.09 with the last two digits repeating.

This bug would either be **A.logic** or **B.expression**, depending on whether the programmer made this mistake "intentionally" (realizing that the code was checking the value, but not realizing that it could ever be 0) or not. The fix is to change line 36 to read as follows:

```
if (defined($array[$num])) {
```

❻ Expand Indented File List to Full Paths

This function walks through a file that has paths indicated by indentation level, as shown in the following example:

```
lang
    perl
        src
            math.pl
            input.pl
            readme
        lib
            tools.pm
    c
        inc
            profile.h
            names.h
        src
            update.c
        readme
```

The program is passed a match string as an argument. It scans the result of the diamond operator (<>) input (either STDIN, or filenames passed as the arguments following the match string), and for every match, it prints out the full path of the matched line. For example, if it were asked to find "readme" with the previous example as input, it would print out the following:

```
lang/perl/src/readme
lang/c/readme
```

The program tracks the text printed at each unique indent level up to the indent of the current line; if the current line is less indented than previous lines, any previous indents of an equal or greater number of spaces are no longer tracked. It uses the Perl feature that you can truncate an array by assigning to `$#array`, which is the variable that holds the index of the last element of the array.

Source Code

```
1.      # arguments: matchstring [filename1 [filename2 ...]]
2.
3.      $match = shift @ARGV;
4.
5.      while (<>) {
6.
7.          # remove \n from input
8.          chomp;
9.
10.         # process all lines except completely blank ones
11.         unless (/^\s*$/) {
12.
13.             # how many initial spaces in the line?
14.             /( *)/;
15.             $spaces = $1;
16.
17.             # chop the array at that point
18.             $#indentlabels = $spaces;
19.
20.             # save line text after spaces
21.             $indentlabels[$spaces] = $';
22.
23.             # does the line match the match string
24.             if (/$match/) {
25.
26.                 # display path
27.                 foreach $l (@indentlabels) {
28.                     print $l if defined($l);
29.                 }
30.                 print "\n";
31.             }
32.
33.             # add the separator for future printing
34.             $indentlabels[$spaces] .= "/";
35.         }
36.     }
```

Suggestions

1. Check the regular expressions on lines 11 and 14 to ensure that they are correct.
2. What number of spaces at the beginning of a line is most likely to cause problems? Probably zero. Walk through the code with a line that has no spaces at the beginning.
3. How long will a particular entry remain in the `@indent_labels` array?

Hints

Walk through the code with the following match strings and input files:

1. Match twice at different indents:
   `match eq "abc"`, file contains:
   ```
   abc
           abc
   ```
2. Match once at indent after outdent:
   `match eq "abc"`, file contains:
   ```
   test
             directory
       xyz
           abc
   ```
3. Match is substring of actual value:
   `match eq "abc"`, file contains:
   ```
   ab
       cd
           abcd
   ```

Explanation of the Bug

Line 15 has a **B.expression** error:

```
$spaces = $1;
```

At line 15, the `$1` string contains the piece of the string that matched the part of the regular expression on line 14 that was in parentheses. In this case, the regular expression is `(  *)`, so `$1` contains a certain number of space characters. However, it is used in the program as if it contained the *number* of spaces as an integer. The actual spaces always evaluates to 0 when converted to an integer. Therefore, the program will treat every line as if it were indented 0 spaces, which means it will keep chopping @indentlabels back to one element and never display full paths as it is supposed to.

Line 15 needs to be changed to read as follows:

```
$spaces = length($1);
```

❼ Sort All the Files in a Directory Tree

This function sorts all the files in a directory tree by modification time.

To obtain the modification time, the program calls the built-in function stat(). This returns a list with 13 elements. The modification time is the 10th element of this list; the rest can be ignored.

To display the modification time, the program calls localtime(), which returns a nine-element list. The program cares only about the first six, which are seconds, minutes, hours, day, month, and year, except the month is zero-based and the year has 1900 subtracted from it. (The other three elements in the list are day of the week, day of the year, and a flag for daylight savings time.)

The program prints the name of each directory in the tree as it processes it and then prints an ordered list of all the files with their modification time.

Directories are read using the functions opendir(), readdir(), and closedir(), which are fairly self-explanatory. A handle is passed to opendir() and then used as a parameter to readdir() and closedir(). Similar to reading data from file handles such as STDIN, calling readdir() in scalar context returns the name of a single file, while calling it in list context returns the entire file list. Just the filename is returned, with no path component.

Keep in mind that when you scan a directory, two special names are returned: "." and "..", which correspond to the current and parent directory. These two names should be ignored; otherwise, the program would loop forever and never terminate.

The program assumes that the path separator is a backslash, although this is simple to change.

Recall from an earlier program that Perl's built-in sort() function takes an optional subroutine as a parameter. This subroutine is passed the two elements to compare in the variables $a and $b, and should return -1, 0, or 1, depending on the appropriate ordering of the two elements. The <=> operator returns the same three values after doing a numeric comparison, so it is often used as it is in this line of the program:

```
@filelist =
  sort { $filetimes{$a} <=> $filetimes{$b} } @filelist;
```

Also, recall from an earlier program that the x operator, as used in

```
" " x $depth
```

produces the number of spaces specified by $depth.

Perl has a series of tests that can be performed on a file, which are all specified by a hyphen and a letter followed by a filename or file handle. Among these tests are -f, which is true if the filename refers to a plain file, and -d, which returns true if the filename refers to a directory:

```
if (-f $fullname) {
    # it's a plain file
} elsif (-d $fullname) {
    # it's a directory
}
```

Some of the other tests (which aren't used here) return numeric values, such as -s, which returns the size of a file in bytes:

```
if (-f $file) {
    print ("$file is a plain file\n");
    $size = -s $file;
    print ("Size is $size bytes\n");
}
```

Source Code

```
1.    # this function processes a directory; for all
2.    # subdirectories it calls itself recursively, and
3.    # for all files it adds the filename to the
4.    # @filenames directory and the file modification
5.    # time to the %filetimes hash.
6.    sub adddir {
7.        # save these in locals since it recurses
8.        my $depth = $_[0];
9.        my $path = $_[1];
10.       my ($filename);
11.       local(*DH);      # my doesn't work for handles
```

```
12.
13.         # show the directories as we process them
14.         print (("  " x $depth) . "$path\n");
15.
16.         # open the directory and scan each file in it
17.         if (opendir DH, $path) {
18.             foreach $filename (readdir DH) {
19.
20.                 # skip . and ..
21.                 unless (($filename eq ".") ||
22.                         ($filename eq "..")) {
23.                     my $fullname = "$path\\$filename";
24.
25.                     # it it a file?...
26.                     if (-f $fullname) {
27.                         push (@filelist, $fullname);
28.                         # store modification time in hash
29.                         $filetimes{$fullname} =
30.                             (stat $fullname)[9];
31.                     # ...or a directory?
32.                     } elsif (-d $fullname) {
33.                         adddir ($fullname, $depth+1);
34.                     }
35.                 }
36.             }
37.         }
38.         closedir DH;
39.     }
40.
41.     # determine the start directory, default to current
42.
43.     $startdir = $ARGV[0];
44.     $startdir = "." unless defined($startdir);
45.
46.     # this call does all the work recursively
47.     adddir($startdir, 0);
48.
49.     @filelist =
50.       sort { $filetimes{$a} <=> $filetimes{$b} } @filelist;
51.     foreach (@filelist) {
52.         ( $sec, $min, $hour,
53.           $day, $mon, $year,
54.           undef, undef, undef ) = localtime $filetimes{$_};
55.         printf("%02d/%02d/%4d  %02d:%02d:%02d  ",
56.             $mon+1, $day, $year+1900, $hour, $min, $sec);
57.
58.         # if the program was called with . as the argument
```

198

```
59.        # (or default), then all paths will have .\ at the
60.        # beginning, so remove that when printing.
61.        if ($_ =~ /^\.\\/) {
62.            print(substr($_, 2) . "\n");
63.        }
64.        else {
65.            print("$_\n");
66.        }
67.    }
```

Suggestions

1. A hash can have only one value for a given key. Does the program ensure that it never accidentally replaces an element in %filetimes?
2. Because the adddir() function calls itself recursively, does it ensure that it never calls itself recursively with the same parameters that were passed (which would lead to an infinite loop)?
3. Does the initialization of $startdir on lines 43–44 properly handle the initialization of the variable to the default value (the current directory) if it was not provided as an argument?
4. Check the code on lines 61–62 to ensure that it runs in the proper situations and performs the correct modification of the output string.

Hints

Walk through the program with a directory named abc, which contains the following:

1. Nothing.
2. Three files named d.txt, e.txt, and f.txt.
3. Two files called jones and thompson, and a directory named smith, which contains two files named joe and john.

Explanation of the Bug

The initialization of the local variables that hold the parameters to adddir(), on lines 8–9

```
my $depth = $_[0];
my $path = $_[1];
```

has an **F.init** error. The first parameter is the path and the second is the depth, so the code should read as follows:

```
my $path = $_[0];
my $depth = $_[1];
```

The code as it reads now just won't work; since the initial depth is passed as 0, with the parameters to `adddir()` being swapped, the code tries to open a directory called `"0"`, which probably doesn't exist.

❽ Calculate Student Test Averages

This function calculates averages from a file containing student test results.

The file contains sections in the following format:

```
testname: maximumscore
studentname1 score1
studentname2 score2
```

The `"testname"` line indicates the start of a new section. (Note that those lines have a colon (`:`) in them, while score lines do not.)

In the file, `testname` and `studentname` must be a single word, and the scores must be numeric.

A student does not necessarily have a score for each test. If the line is missing, it indicates that the student did not take the test.

When the program is done processing the file, for each student, it prints his or her average for taken tests, and his or her overall average (counting missed tests as 0).

The program uses memory variables: The fact that if a regular expression is matched, parts of the pattern that were in parentheses are automatically stored in variables named `$1`, `$2`, and so on.

The Perl built-in function `split()` splits a string into arrays by using a separator defined by a regular expression (in this case, the vertical bar character):

```
@teststaken = split /\|/, $studenttesttaken{$_};
```

Because it matters in this particular program, note that `split()` does return empty fields at the beginning of the string it is splitting, so `split(/:/, ":a:b")` returns three elements (`""`, `"a"`, and `"b"`). In contrast, by default, it does *not* return empty fields at the end of the string.

Source Code

```
1.    # score file is of the form
2.    # testname: maximumscore
3.    # studentname score
4.
5.    $currenttest = -1;
6.
7.    while (<>) {
8.        $thisline = $_;
9.
10.       # does this line have a testname on it?
11.       if ($thisline =~ /\s*(\w+)\s*:\s*(\d+)/) {
12.           ++$currenttest;
13.           $testnames[$currenttest] = $1;
14.           $testmaximums[$currenttest] = $2;
15.           $thistestname = $1;
16.           $thistestmaximum = $2;
17.       }
18.
19.       # or does it have a score in it?
20.       if ($thisline =~ /\s*(\w+)\s*(\d+)/) {
21.           $studentpoints{$1} += $2;
22.           $studentmaximums{$1} += $thistestmaximum;
23.           $studenttesttaken{$1} .= "|$thistestname";
24.       }
25.   }
26.
27.   # find the total maximum score
28.
29.   foreach (@testmaximums) {
30.       $totalmaximum += $_;
31.   }
32.
33.   # now print results
34.
35.   foreach (keys %studentpoints) {
36.       @teststaken = split /\|/, $studenttesttaken{$_};
37.       $testcount = $#teststaken;
38.       print("student name: $_\n");
39.       print("total tests taken: $testcount\n");
40.
41.       $testaverage =
42.           $studentpoints{$_} / $studentmaximums{$_};
43.       $testoverall = $studentpoints{$_} / $totalmaximum;
44.       printf("average in tests taken: %d%%\n",
```

```
45.                    $testaverage * 100);
46.           printf("average in all tests: %d%%\n",
47.                    $testoverall * 100);
48.        }
```

Suggestions

1. What happens to input lines that do not match either of the regular expressions on lines 11 or 20?
2. What happens if the program receives an empty file as input? What about a file with testname lines, but no student score lines?
3. Confirm that testcount is set correctly on lines 36–37.
4. How many different meanings is $_ used for in the program?

Hints

Walk through the program with the following input files:

1. One test, two students:
   ```
   test1: 10
   joe 5
   susan 8
   ```
2. Two tests, one student per test:
   ```
   test1: 10
   joe 6
   test2: 20
   susan 15
   ```
3. Two students, different number of tests:
   ```
   test1: 10
   joe 6
   susan 10
   test2: 20
   susan 18
   ```

Explanation of the Bug

The check for a score line on line 20

```
if ($thisline =~ /\s*(\w+)\s*(\d+)/) {
```

might also match a test line, which confuses the program into thinking that a new student has taken the test.

Keep in mind that the regular expression does not have to match the entire line, just a part of it (unless it is anchored to the ends with ^ and $).

A test line of the form

```
test: 20
```

matches the regular expression on line 20. It would consider the student name to be `"2"` and the score to be `"0"`. In the specific hints given, the lines with `"test1"` or `"test2"` in them result in a student named `"test"` being credited with a score of 1 or 2.

This is an **F.location** error because the test for a score line should not be done if a line has already been determined to be a testname line. The `if` should be changed to an `elsif`, although the regular expression on line 20 could also be tweaked to require a space between the student name and the score:

```
elsif ($thisline =~ /\s*(\w+)\s+(\d+)/) {
```

❾ Merge Sort of Multiple Files

This function merges multiple sorted files into one large sorted result. It sorts in ascending order.

The program opens all the files and stores the handles in an array. It has a corresponding array that contains the current line in each file. When the end of a file is reached, it closes the file and takes its slot out of both arrays, so the sort then proceeds with one fewer file.

The handles are stored in variable names, but other than that, reading from the file is as usual in Perl. An assignment from the handle to a string reads a single line into the string, as shown in the following line:

```
$firstline = <$thishandle>;
```

The read returns `undef` when the end of file is reached.

The program assumes that the input files are already sorted in ascending order. The behavior is undefined if they are not.

This program opens files using the `open()` function, which takes a file handle and a filename. A file handle has no prefix character, and it is usually written in all uppercase for clarity. After the file is opened, the file handle is used the same as the STDIN file handle, and then closed with the close() function:

```
open FH, "logfile";
while (<FH>) {
    chomp($_);
    process($_);
}
close FH;
```

In the program here, the name of the handle is stored in a string variable and the code uses the variable in place of the handle

```
$thishandle = "FH$_";
open $thishandle, $thisfile;
```

to open the handles FH1, FH2, and so forth.

As with STDIN, when end-of-file is reached, reading from the file handle in scalar context returns undef.

Source Code

```
1.  # open a handle to each file and read the first line
2.
3.  for (0..$#ARGV) {
4.      $thisfile = $ARGV[$_];
5.      $thishandle = "FH$_";
6.      open $thishandle, $thisfile;
7.      $firstline = <$thishandle>;
8.      if (defined($firstline)) {
9.          push @handlenames, $thishandle;
10.         push @currentlines, $firstline;
11.     } else {
12.         close $thishandle;
13.     }
14.  }
15.
16.  # now keep going until no more files have data left
17.
18.  while (@handlenames > 0) {
19.
```

```
20.        # find the file whose current line is first
21.
22.        $smallest = 0;
23.        for (1..$#handlenames) {
24.            if ($currentlines[$_] lt
25.                    $currentlines[$smallest]) {
26.                $smallest = $_;
27.            }
28.        }
29.
30.        # display that line and read the next one
31.        print $currentlines[$smallest];
32.        $thishandle = $handlenames[$smallest];
33.        $currentlines[$smallest] = <$thishandle>;
34.
35.        # if no line was read, then close this file
36.        unless (defined($currentlines[$smallest])) {
37.            close $thishandle;
38.
39.            # take it out of @handlenames and @currentlines
40.            $justbefore = $smallest-1;
41.            $justafter = $smallest+1;
42.            @handlenames =
43.                ( @handlenames[0..$justbefore] ,
44.                  @handlenames[$justbefore..$#handlenames]);
45.            @currentlines =
46.                ( @currentlines[0..$justbefore] ,
47.                  @currentlines[$justbefore..$#currentlines]);
48.        }
49.    }
```

Suggestions

1. What is the trivial case for this program?
2. The `@handlenames` and `@currentlines` arrays need to be synchronized so they are always the same length and the entries at the same index correspond. To ensure that this is correct, verify every place where they are modified.
3. When will the main `while` loop, starting at line 18, terminate?
4. What is the goal of the loop on lines 22–28?

Hints

Walk through the program with the following inputs:

1. A single file containing three lines with the words apple, carrot, and eggplant.
2. Three files, each with one line, containing the words, respectively, tomato, cucumber, and parsley.
3. Two files, the first containing three lines with the words airplane, boat, and train, the second containing two lines with the words car and helicopter.

Explanation of the Bug

The code on lines 42–47, to remove a file from the @handlenames and @currentlines arrays, has a **B.variable** error (or two, actually). The code

```
@handlenames =
  ( @handlenames[0..$justbefore] ,
    @handlenames[$justbefore..$#handlenames]);
@currentlines =
  ( @currentlines[0..$justbefore] ,
    @currentlines[$justbefore..$#currentlines]);
```

is using the wrong variable for the start of the second range. The code actually duplicates an element in the array, instead of removing an entry, and since the undefined entry at $currentlines[$smallest] will keep being determined to be the "smallest" by the code on lines 22–28, the program will loop forever printing out undefined strings and then increasing the size of the arrays by one.

It should use $justafter, not $justbefore, so lines 42–47 should read:

```
@handlenames =
  ( @handlenames[0..$justbefore] ,
    @handlenames[$justafter..$#handlenames]);
@currentlines =
  ( @currentlines[0..$justbefore] ,
    @currentlines[$justafter..$#currentlines]);
```

⑩ Play the Game *Mastermind*

This function plays the game *Mastermind*.

Mastermind is played with small pegs of different colors. One player creates a secret code, which consists of a sequence of colored pegs. (The standard game has four pegs in the code and six colors to choose from, but other variations exist.) The other player attempts to decipher the secret code by making guesses at the sequence. After each guess, the first player assigns a score to the guess by using a second set of pegs that are black and white. The score is one black peg for each peg in the guess that matches up exactly with a peg in the secret (same color, same location) and one white peg for each guess that matches up improperly with a peg in the secret (same color, different location).

Each peg in the guess gets only one score peg, either black or white. If it is credited with a black peg, for example, it cannot also receive a white peg for matching the same color in a different location.

In the program, the user is the keeper of the secret, and the program is the guesser. The program creates a list of all possible guesses, and simply walks through the list, guessing each one in turn. However, after each guess, it prunes its list of possible guesses down to those that would have given the same score if they were the secret. Eventually, the list of guesses that satisfy all the previous scores is narrowed down to one, and that must be the secret.

To ensure that the user doesn't make a mistake in scoring, after the program prompts the user for the secret it checks each score given by the player to ensure that it is accurate. However, the program doesn't cheat by looking at the secret.

The program uses secrets of length 3. The colors are specified in an array that currently has six elements, but could be arbitrarily expanded. Colors are specified by a single letter, and scores are specified by a combination of the letters `"B"` (black) and `"w"` (white).

The Perl `splice()` function takes a set of elements in an array and replaces them with new elements, or removes them if new elements are not provided, as used in this function:

```
splice(@colorarray, $index, 1);
```

This removes from `@colorarray` the single element indexed by `$index`.

The `join()` function converts an array back to a string using a separator specified by a string, which in the example used in this program is an empty string:

```
$allcolors = join "", @colors;
```

This string runs all the elements in @colors together with no separator. This program uses the shortcut qw (the letter q followed by the letter w), which allows you to define a list of strings without including the quotes around each one. (The strings cannot contain white space for obvious reasons.) In this case, the list has six elements, each a string of length one:

```
@colors = qw/ R P V O Y B /;
```

Source Code

```
1.    # score a single guess
2.
3.    sub score {
4.      # $_[0] is the secret value, $_[1] is the guess
5.      my $result = "";
6.      my $secret = $_[0];
7.      my $guess = $_[1];
8.      my $index;
9.
10.     for ($index=0; $index < length($secret); $index++) {
11.         if (substr($secret, $index, 1) eq
12.                 substr($guess, $index, 1)) {
13.             $result .= "B";
14.             # remove it once it is matched
15.             substr($secret, $index, 1) = "";
16.             substr($guess, $index, 1) = "";
17.             $index--; # since iteration will add one back
18.         }
19.     }
20.     for ($index=0; $index < length($secret); $index++) {
21.         my $loc =
22.             index($secret, substr($guess, $index, 1));
23.         if ($loc != -1) {
24.             $result .= "w";
25.             # remove it once it is matched
26.             substr($secret, $loc, 1) = "";
27.             substr($guess, $index, 1) = "";
28.             $index--; # since iteration will add one back
29.         }
```

```
30.        }
31.      return $result;
32.    }
33.
34.    # colors are Red, Pink, Violet, Orange, Yellow, Blue
35.
36.    @colors = qw/ R P V O Y B /;
37.    $allcolors = join "", @colors;
38.    $numcolor = @colors;
39.    print("Possible color choices: @colors\n");
40.
41.    # fill @colorarray with all possible choices
42.
43.    for (0..((3**$numcolor)-1)) {
44.        $colorarray[$_] =
45.            @colors[$_ / ($numcolor**2)] .
46.            @colors[($_ / $numcolor) % $numcolor] .
47.            @colors[$_ % $numcolor];
48.    }
49.
50.    # ask user for secret code, until valid one entered
51.
52.    do {
53.        print("Enter your secret code:\n");
54.        chomp ($code = <STDIN>);
55.    } until ($code =~ /^[$allcolors]{3}$/);
56.
57.    # now play the game until @colorarray has only one left
58.    # or we happen to guess the secret
59.
60.    while (@colorarray >= 2) {
61.        $guess = $colorarray[0];
62.        do {
63.            print("I guess $colorarray[0]; score is?\n");
64.            chomp ($score = <STDIN>);
65.        } until ($score eq score($code, $guess));
66.
67.        if ($score eq "BBB") {
68.            print ("I guessed it!\n");
69.            last;    # got it!
70.        }
71.
72.        # guess was wrong, so take it out of @colorarray
73.        shift @colorarray;
74.
75.        # remove all guesses that would not score the same
76.        $index = 0;
```

```
77.          while ($index < @colorarray) {
78.              if (score($colorarray[$index], $guess) ne
79.                  $score) {
80.                  splice(@colorarray, $index, 1);  # remove
81.              } else {
82.                  $index++;
83.              }
84.          }
85.      }
86.
87.      if (@colorarray == 1) {
88.          print("Your code is $colorarray[0]\n");
89.      }
```

Suggestions

1. Pick values to test the score() function that will result in the following results: "", "www", "BBB", "Bww".
2. How many different variables called $index are used in the program, and what scope do they have?
3. What variables in the program hold codes or guesses? What restrictions are there on such variables? Are these restrictions enforced properly?
4. The result of the game can be printed out on either line 68 or 88. Can you be sure that only one of those two lines will be executed?
5. The program has the number of elements in the secret hardcoded at 3, but is designed to make the number and names of the colors completely dependent on the declaration of the @colors array on line 36. Does it accomplish this goal?

Hints

Walk through the code for the following secrets:

1. The trivial case where the secret is "RRR", which will be the first secret guessed because it's the first entry in @colorarray.
2. The secret is "RRP", which is the second entry in @colorarray.
3. The secret is "PPP", which is the first entry in the @colorarray that does not contain an "R".

Explanation of the Bug

The bug is in the initialization of `@colorarray`. Line 43 reads as follows:

```
for (0..((3**$numcolor)-1)) {
```

It is wrong. With three pegs, each of which can have one of `$numcolor` colors, the number of possible choices is `$numcolor * $numcolor *numcolor`. In other words, line 43 should read as follows:

```
for (0..(($numcolor**3)-1)) {
```

With three pegs and six colors, the bug causes the initialization loop on lines 43–48 to execute 729 times instead of 216. The array index on line 45 (`$_ / ($numcolor**2)`) winds up being larger than the size of `@colors`, which leads to entries in `@colorarray` that only have two characters. (The second and third characters in the `@colorarray` entries, calculated on lines 46 and 47, continue to cycle through all possible values in an orderly fashion because of their use of the modulo operator.) The program won't crash, but it winds up with many extra, malformed entries in `@colorarray`, which causes it to take longer than necessary to find the secret. (It eventually does prune out the two-character elements because they won't ever score the same as a three-character guess that scores at least `"www"`.)

This error could be classified as either **A.logic** or **B.expression**. As with many errors that are in that situation, it depends on what the programmer was thinking when he or she wrote the code.

Chapter 7

x86 Assembly Language

Brief Summary of x86 Assembly Language

Assembly language is converted into executable code by a program called an *assembler*. There is no fundamental difference between an assembler and a compiler. They both take source code as input and produce machine code that the computer can execute. However, a single line of assembly language generally produces a single line of machine code, whereas a single line of code in a higher-level language can produce multiple lines of machine code.

As a result of this, assembly language is more primitive than higher-level languages. Constructs such as loops, functions, and strings must be supported with only the barest of help from the language.

Another result of the close relationship between assembly language and machine language is that different families of microprocessors support different assembly languages. This chapter uses x86 assembly language, which originated with the Intel line of chips that includes the 80386, 486, and Pentium microprocessors.

Rules about how statements are separated and the like are up to the individual assembler. The programs in this chapter follow the common convention that each statement is on a line by itself, and a comment begins with a semicolon (after which everything else on the line is ignored).

Data Types and Variables

A microprocessor can access data either in memory or in registers. Registers are storage locations, but they are located on the microprocessor itself. It is faster to perform operations on registers than on memory. In addition, some instructions are defined to only work on registers.

The x86 microprocessors have four general-purpose registers named eax, ebx, ecx, and edx. These are 32 bits each. The low 16 bits can be addressed as ax, bx, and so on; you can't address the high 16 bits directly. Within the 16 bits of ax, the low 8 bits (1 byte) are addressed as al and the high 8 bits are addressed as ah, and similarly for the other registers. An 8-bit quantity is known as a byte, a 16-bit quantity is known as a word, and a 32-bit quantity is known as a doubleword (dword).

Memory locations can be declared as follows:

```
done    db 0    ; a byte (8 bits), initialized to 0
length  dw ?    ; a word (16 bits), uninitialized
count   dd 0    ; a dword (32 bits), initialized to 0
name    db 40 dup(?)   ; 40 bytes, uninitialized
```

x86 assembly language instructions are generally in this form (an immediate value is a constant, such as a number):

```
opcode register
opcode register, memory
opcode memory, register
opcode register, register
opcode register, immediate
```

For example, one of the most basic instructions moves a value into a register or memory location. The value can come from another register, a memory location, or an immediate value. (But you can't move directly from memory location to memory location. It is a general rule in x86 assembly language that both operands can't be memory locations.) The opcode is mov and what data is moved is specified by the operands that come after the opcode. The destination of the move comes first after the opcode, as shown in the following:

```
mov ax, bx      ; ax = bx
mov ecx, 0      ; ecx = 0
```

The number of bits moved depends on the operands. Because ax and bx are both 16 bits, the first instructions move 16 bits. ecx is a dword, so the second instruction moves 32 bits. It is illegal for mov to have operands of different sizes.

Immediate values can be decimal numbers. They can also be hexadecimal numbers if they begin with 0x, or characters in single quotes, which are converted to their ASCII equivalent. (Some assemblers require that decimal numbers be followed by a d and hexadecimal numbers be followed by an h, as in 100d or f5h.)

The x86 microprocessors support a stack, which is stored in memory. The stack grows downward (toward lower memory addresses). The two main instructions for accessing the stack are push and pop, which affect the lowest location on the stack:

```
push eax   ; put value of eax on the stack
pop ebx    ; take element off the stack and store in ebx
```

The push and pop opcodes can be used to temporarily store data on the stack if you don't have a spare register to use. Just be sure to push and pop in the proper order (which means that the last value pushed is the first one popped).

The address of the current location of the stack is stored in another register, esp, which can be directly read or written. Because esp is the current location, push first subtracts from esp, then stores the pushed value at the current location of esp. pop reads the value at the current location of esp and then adds to esp.

Square brackets around a register indicate indirect addressing: Treat the contents of the register as the memory address of a value. This is equivalent to a pointer in some other languages. Because esp is a register, you can access values on the stack without using pop:

```
mov eax, [esp]   ; like pop eax, but esp is not changed
```

The number of bits to move is usually implied by the other operand (for example, eax in the previous case implies 32 bits), but in the case of instructions that don't have another operand (or have a constant operand whose size is not known), you can use the following syntax to specify it:

```
mov byte ptr [esi], 0   ; move a single byte
mov dword ptr [eax], 1  ; move a dword
inc word ptr [ebx]      ; increment a word by one
```

When writing in x86 assembly language, it can be important to know that the x86 family is "little-endian." This means that the least significant byte of a number is stored first. Understand the following sequence:

```
mov dword ptr [eax], 0x12345678
mov bx, word ptr [eax]     ; bx is now 0x5678
mov cl, byte ptr [eax]     ; cl is now 0x78
```

Indirect addressing also allows you to specify a displacement from the register, as shown in the following:

```
mov ebx, [esp+4]   ; get the second dword on the stack
```

You can modify esp the same as any other register, so the following is equivalent to pop edx

```
mov edx, [esp]
add esp, 4
```

and push ax is the same as the following

```
sub esp, 2
mov [esp], ax
```

This also shows the add and sub opcodes, which do addition and subtraction. The destination (where the result goes) is the first operand. These are discussed more in the next section.

The lea (load effective address) instruction loads the address of a memory variable, as shown in the following:

```
buffer db 80 dup(?)
lea esi, buffer
mov byte ptr [esi], 0  ; store 0 in first byte of buffer
```

lea can also be used to assign an offset from another register in a single instruction:

```
lea esi, [edi+8]
```

This is the same as the following:

```
mov esi, edi
add esi, 8
```

Other registers on the x86 microprocessors include esi, edi, and ebp. These have rough meanings assigned to them, which can manifest themselves as implied parameters to an instruction (esi and edi are always used to specify the source and destination in certain string operations) or in more efficient execution. (ebp is often used as the stack-frame base pointer, and instructions that access offsets in the stack frame using ebp as the base can be encoded more efficiently.) However, you can use the registers for simple operations without adhering to those meanings. The examples explain situations where an instruction either requires or assumes particular operands. The esi, edi, ebp, and esp registers all have separate names for the low 16 bits (si, di, bp, and sp), but do not have the equivalent of al and ah for directly accessing the low bytes within those registers.

The x86 microprocessors have six segment registers that give programmers more flexibility in addressing memory. The examples ignore the segment registers. The final two registers to worry about are the flags register, which is discussed next, and eip, which holds the instruction pointer—the location at which the processor is executing code. There are also control, debug, and test registers, which are used for things such as setting watchpoints (which trigger when a certain address is accessed). This book doesn't get into those.

Arithmetic Operations

Previous examples used the add and sub instructions, which do addition and subtraction. The result goes in the first operand:

```
add ebp, eax          ; ebp = ebp + eax
add byte ptr [esi], 5 ; [esi] = [esi] + 5
sub cl, ch            ; cl = cl - ch
sub mybyte, al        ; mybyte = mybyte - al
```

To remember that the result goes in the first operand, it might be helpful to think of these as the equivalent of the binary assignment operators (such as +=) in some languages. In other words, add ebp, eax is the same as ebp += eax.

x86 assembly language also supports opcodes for multiplication and division, but they are not as generic as addition and subtraction. The `mul` instruction, which performs an unsigned multiply, works only on `al`, `ax`, or `eax`, and the result goes in a specific location:

```
mul al, bl      ; ax = al * bl
mul ax, cl      ; dx:ax = ax * cl
mul eax, ebx    ; edx:eax = eax * ebx
```

In the comments, the notation `dx:ax` (or `edx:eax`) indicates that the high 16 (or 32) bits of the result are stored in `dx` (or `edx`), and the low 16 (or 32) bits of the result are stored in `ax` (or `eax`).

Similarly, `div` performs an unsigned divide with the dividend specified as one of the same combinations of `eax` and `edx`, and quotient and remainder being stored in the same place. (For example, `div eax, ebx` divides `edx:eax` by `ebx`, and stores the quotient in `eax` and the remainder in `edx`. You can figure out the equivalent with 8- and 16-bit divisors by working backward from how `mul` works.) An `imul` instruction does signed multiplication and is more generic about which opcodes are allowed, but it does not offer the 32-bit ¥ 32-bit = 64-bit form that `mul` does. (`idiv`, which does signed division, takes the same operands as `div`.)

x86 assembly language allows shifting to the left and right by a specified number of bits. Shifting a number 1 bit to the left multiplies it by 2, and shifting it 1 bit to the right divides it by 2:

```
shl eax, 4           ; eax = eax * 16
shr al, 1            ; al = al/2
```

Numbers can be incremented, decremented, and negated:

```
inc eax              ; eax = eax + 1
dec word ptr [esi]   ; [esi] = [esi] - 1
neg ah               ; ah = 0 - ah
```

Bitwise logical operations can be performed:

```
and eax, ebx           ; eax = eax & ebx
or al, ah              ; al = al | ah
xor edx, dword ptr [edi]  ; edx = edx ^ [esi]
not dx                 ; dx = ~dx
```

If you `xor` a number with itself, it converts it to zero. On some microprocessors in the x86 family, a statement in the following form

```
xor eax, eax
```

is faster than

```
mov eax, 0
```

Therefore, you often see xor used to zero out a register.

Flags, Conditionals, and Jumps

There is a special register on the x86 microprocessors that contains flags. A subset of the flags are known as *status flags*, and most status flags are set after arithmetic operations, depending on whether it makes sense for a particular operation. The status flags that are important in this book are as follows:

- **Carry flag (CF)**. Set if there was a carry from (addition) or borrow into (subtraction) the high-order bit. Otherwise, it's cleared.
- **Zero flag (ZF)**. Set if the result was zero. Otherwise, it's cleared.
- **Sign flag (SF)**. Set equal to the high-order bit of the result (0 means it was positive; 1 means it was negative).
- **Overflow flag (OF)**. Set if the signed result is too large (for positive numbers) or too small (for negative numbers). Otherwise, it's cleared.

The flags will not be set after an instruction such as mov. Because it is often desirable to set the flags without actually performing an operation, the cmp instruction does this. (It sets the flags the same as if a sub had been performed, without actually doing the subtraction operation.) There is also the test instruction, which performs a logical and, then sets the flags (again, without actually modifying the operands).

The flags are paired with conditional jump instructions that transfer control to any point in the program. For example

```
sub ecx, 1
jz mylabel
```

jumps to the instruction labeled with mylabel if the result of sub ecx, 1 is zero. As another example

```
test eax, 0x02
jz mylabel
```

jumps to mylabel if the second bit of eax is off.

Labels have a colon after their names, as shown in the following:

```
mylabel:     ; ecx is now zero
      mov ecx, 0xff
```

The `jz` instruction is one of the conditional jumps supported. It performs the jump if the zero flag (ZF) was set. This matches the likely thought process used in the previous code, where you subtract one from `ecx` and then test if it is zero. However, if you instead do a `cmp` instruction,

```
cmp eax, ebx
```

the zero flag is set if the result of a `sub` would have been zero. This does not mean that `eax` or `ebx` are necessarily zero—just that they are equal. For this situation, x86 assembly language also has the `je` conditional jump, which matches up more logically with the intent of the programmer, but turns out to be the same as `jz`; it jumps if the zero flag is set.

This is a partial list of the conditional jump instructions:

equal/unequal:
```
je/jz     equal/zero (ZF = 1)
jne/jnz   not equal/not zero (ZF = 0)
```

unsigned comparison:
```
ja/jnbe   above/not below or equal (CF = 0 and ZF = 0)
jae/jnb   above or equal/not below (CF = 0)
jb/jnae   below/not above or equal (CF = 1)
jbe/jna   below or equal/not above (CF = 1 or ZF = 1)
```

signed comparison:
```
jg/jnle   greater/not less or equal (ZF = 0 and SF = OF)
jge/jnl   greater or equal/not less (SF = OF)
jl/jnge   less/not greater or equal (SF != OF)
jle/jng   less or equal/not greater (ZF = 1 or SF != OF)
```

For the comparisons, the two forms simply mean the same thing: "greater" is the same as not less or equal.

The x86 stores numbers in two's complement format, which is covered in more detail in Appendix A, "Classification of Bugs." The key takeaway about two's complement numbers is that negative numbers have the high bit turned on. It can be amusing, or occasionally challenging, to sit down and work out why exactly "signed less" corresponds to the sign flag being different from the overflow flag after a subtraction (one example of non-obvious status flag values), but it isn't really necessary.

It is enough to know that in a comparison/jump sequence such as the following

```
cmp ecx, edx
jng somewhere
```

you can read the meaning of the code by placing the jump condition between the first and second operand, as in "jump if ecx is not greater than edx."

Other conditional jump instructions are explained as needed.

Finally, an unconditional jump, opcode jmp, always jumps. This often follows a conditional jump and corresponds to the else case, if you think of the conditional jump as corresponding to the if case:

```
cmp ebx, 4
jne not4   ; if (ebx != 4) jmp not4
jmp is4    ; else jmp is4
```

Loops

There is no direct support for loops as you think of them in other languages. You must construct them on your own:

```
    mov ecx, 10
topofloop:
    ; some operations
    sub ecx, 1
    jnz topofloop
```

However, a loop opcode exists that assumes ecx is being used as the loop counter. In one operation, it decrements ecx and jumps to a label if the result is nonzero. So the previous loop could be rewritten as follows:

```
    mov ecx, 10
topofloop:
    ; some operations
    loop topofloop
```

Note

Other forms of loop *check the zero flag before looping, but they aren't used in the book. (The value of the zero flag is checked before* ecx *is decremented, so the decrement of* ecx *won't affect the flag for this purpose.)*

The prefix `rep` can be used to repeat string instructions. The string instructions used in the book are `cmps` (compare), `movs` (move), `scas` (compare a string to a value), and `stos` (store a value in a string).

Those four string instructions can be used without the `rep` prefix: `cmps` compares `[esi]` to `[edi]`, `movs` moves `[esi]` to `[edi]`, `scas` compares `eax` to `[edi]`, and `stos` stores `eax` in `[edi]`. The opcodes are usually written with a `b`, `d`, or `w` tacked at the end to specify if the operation works on bytes, words, or dwords. In the case of byte or word operations, this implies that a subset of the `eax` register is used. For example

```
scasd    ; compares eax to dword ptr [edi]
scasb    ; compares al to byte ptr [edi]
movsw    ; moves word ptr [esi] to word ptr [edi]
```

The key to the string instructions is what happens at the end; they increment `edi` (and `esi` in the case of `cmps` and `movs`) at the end of the instruction. This is most useful when combined with the `rep` instruction prefix, which repeats a string operation as long as `ecx` is non-zero, decrementing it each time. For example, the following code moves 10 dwords (40 bytes) from `[esi]` to `[edi]`:

```
mov ecx, 10
rep movsd
```

This initializes 15 bytes starting at `[edi]` with 0:

```
mov ecx, 15
mov al, 0
rep stosb
```

At this point, it's worth mentioning that there is also a `lods` instruction that is the opposite of `scas` (`scas` stores at `[edi]`, while `lods` reads from `[esi]`). It can be used with a `rep` prefix, but it makes more sense to use it with `loop` because you usually want to do some processing on each value as it is loaded into `al/ax/eax`. For example, you could `xor` together 10 dwords starting at `[esi]`:

```
    mov ecx, 10
    mov ebx, 0
xorloop:
    lodsd
    xor ebx, eax
    loop xorloop
```

For the `cmps` and `scas` instructions, there are two other forms of `rep`: `repe` (repeat while equal) and `repne` (repeat while not equal). In addition to exiting the `rep` loop when `ecx` reaches zero, these also check after each `cmps` or `scas` instruction and exit the loop if the zero flag is 0 (in the case of `repe`), or if the zero flag is 1 (in the case of `repne`). If you have trouble grasping that, remember that "equality" implies the result of the comparison is zero, which means that the zero flag is 1. If that doesn't help, just know that they work "as expected" in code such as the following, which searches for the character `'A'` in a 5-byte string:

```
mov ecx, 5
mov al, 'A'
repe scasb
jz foundA       ; exited early, found an 'A'
```

Of course, when it comes to debugging the programs in this chapter, don't assume they work as expected.

The order of suboperations each time through a `rep scas` or `rep cmps` loop is

1. Check if `ecx` is 0; if it's not, move to step 2.
2. Perform the primitive instruction (meaning the `scas` or `cmps`).
3. Decrement `ecx` (but without modifying the status flags).
4. Check the zero flag to see if the loop should exit.

When applied to `scas` or `cmps`, the `rep` prefix is the same as `repe` (which means it exits if the zero flag is 1 after the primitive instruction). Also, the language provides `repz` and `repnz` as aliases for `repe` and `repne`, although these are somewhat superfluous. With `rep scas` and `rep cmps`, you usually think about equality, not "zeroness."

There is a special conditional jump instruction, `jecxz`, which jumps if `ecx` is zero. This is the "didn't match" result of a `rep/repe/repne`; it means the instruction terminated naturally. For example, the previous line that read as follows

```
jz foundA       ; exited early, found an 'A'
```

might have been replaced with the following line

```
jecxz noA       ; didn't exit early, didn't find an 'A'
```

For completeness, it's necessary to mention that the direction of the string operations is actually controlled by the direction flag, a control flag in the flags register. The direction flag can be cleared with the `cld` instruction and set with the `std` instruction. It is normally cleared, and the examples will assume it is. If it is set, the string operations go in reverse, which means that `edi` (and `esi`) are decremented—rather than incremented, as assumed in the previous examples—by 1, 2, or 4 after each string operation. This is useful for certain overlapping memory moves, to compare strings starting at the end, and so on.

Procedures

Procedures (also known as functions or subroutines) can be called using the `call` instruction, which takes the address of the procedure:

```
call myfunction
```

The only thing `call` does is push `eip` on the stack and then jump to `myfunction`. To return from a procedure, use the `ret` instruction all by itself:

```
ret
```

`ret` pops the top value off the stack and jumps to that address. Because it assumes the value on the stack is correct, this usually results in a crash if the stack is incorrect:

```
push 0
ret             ; will try to jump to 0
```

Note

More dangerously, modifying the stack so that `ret` jumps to an unexpected instruction is a key technique used by exploits, malicious code that tries to gain control of a machine by pointing `eip` to externally injected instructions.

Beyond `call` and `ret`, constructs such as parameters and return value are up to the author of the code.

Higher-level languages have standards on how they pass parameters to procedures. They are passed on the stack, in registers, or a combination of both. The key is that the caller of the procedure follows the same conventions as the procedure itself. For parameters passed on the stack, the two important questions are whether the parameters are pushed left-to-right or right-to-left, and whether the caller or the procedure cleans up the stack at the end.

For example, in the C language calling convention known as stdcall, parameters are pushed on the stack from right to left, which means that code such as the following

```
my_func (a, b, c);
```

results in assembly language instructions ordered as follows

```
push c
push b
push a
call my_func
```

stdcall also specifies that the procedure cleans up the stack, which means that the procedure must pop those three values off the stack before it returns. (The ret instruction can take an optional argument of the number of bytes to pop to make this easier.)

Meanwhile, in the cdecl calling convention, arguments are still pushed right to left, but the calling code is responsible for cleaning up the stack.

In both cases, return values are usually passed back in eax—if they are small enough to fit.

Because parameters are pushed on the stack, procedures index off of esp to obtain the parameters. Because call pushes the return value on the stack, it is at the current stack location when the procedure begins. The parameters pushed on the stack before the call are just above the return value, starting at [esp+4]. For example, if the calling code calls a procedure with

```
push param2
push param1
call proc
```

proc would access the parameters by indexing off of esp

```
mov eax, [esp+4]    ; eax = param1
mov ebx, [esp+8]    ; ebx = param2
```

If a procedure wants room for local variables, it can decrease the stack pointer and then index off of it. For example, it could begin with the following code

```
sub esp, 8
```

and then have room for two dwords, which would be addressed (assuming `esp` did not change) as `[esp]` and `[esp+4]`. Procedures must be careful to put `esp` back before they call `ret`, so that the return value is at the top of the stack. Also, such variables initially contain whatever value happened to be at that location on the stack from the execution of previous code.

It is a general rule that a procedure that uses registers will save the old values and restore them, generally by pushing them on the stack at the beginning, and popping them off at the end. As a result, procedures often start with code such as the following

```
push ebp
mov ebp, esp
push ebx
push esi
push edi
```

and then end with

```
pop edi
pop esi
pop ebx
pop ebp
```

The reason for saving `esp` in `ebp` is that parameters on the stack can then be accessed by indexing from `ebp`, which means that you don't have to worry about the offset of the parameters changing (as it would if you indexed directly off of `esp` and happened to push or pop during the procedure). In this case, `ebp` would have captured `esp` just after the old `ebp` was pushed. This means that `[ebp]` holds the old `ebp`, `[ebp+4]` has the return value, and parameters start at `[ebp+8]`. Meanwhile, local variables—if room was allocated for them by subtracting from `esp` after it was saved in `ebp`—would be accessed with negative indices from `ebp`.

But, these are all just conventions. If you are writing your own assembly-language code and do not have to interoperate with any other code in any other language, you can handle parameters, stack cleanup, register preservation, return values, and all that in whatever way you want.

Output

There is no code in the book that accepts input from the keyboard or produces output to the screen. A Perl function such as `print()` actually hides a lot of operating-system–specific code that is required underneath to produce a character on the screen. To keep our assembly language somewhat generic, the examples are restricted to procedures or blocks of code that accept parameters and return values in specified ways. It is certainly possible to call operating system input/output routines from assembler as long as the calling conventions are respected.

❶ Make Change for a Dollar

This function returns the change from a dollar for a specified number of cents.

The number of cents is the only argument and it is pushed on the stack. The valid range for this argument is between 0 and 100 (inclusive). The procedure is not responsible for checking that the argument is in the proper range.

The coin values are 25 cents, 10 cents, 5 cents, and 1 cent. The procedure returns as many of the largest coins as possible, then the next largest, and so on.

The procedure returns a dword in `eax`. The high byte is the number of quarters, then the number of dimes and nickels, and the low byte is the number of pennies. To calculate the result, it uses the magic-looking hexadecimal number `0x190a0501`, which has the face value of each coin in each corresponding byte (face value of a quarter in the high byte, and so on).

The procedure is responsible for removing the argument from the stack. It does not worry, however, about preserving the passed-in values of registers.

The program uses the `rol` instruction "rotate left". The rotate instructions, `rol` and `ror`, are like `shl` and `shr` (shift left and shift right), except that they wrap the bits that are shifted out the top or bottom around to the other end. For example, if `al` has the binary value `01001100`, after

```
rol al, 2
```

it will have the value `00110001`.

Source Code

```
1.    make_change:
2.        sub esp, 4        ; local variable
3.        mov dword ptr [esp], 0x190a0501
4.                          ; coins are 25, 10, 5, 1
5.        mov eax, 100      ; change is from 100 cents
6.        sub eax, [esp+8]  ; [esp+8] is the parameter
7.
8.        ; al holds the amount of money that we are trying
9.        ; to total the coins up to; as a new coin is added,
10.       ; we subtract its face value from al.
11.
12.       mov ebx, 0        ; ebx will hold the result
13.
14.   top:
15.       cmp dword ptr[esp], 0  ; done with all coins?
16.       je done
17.       rol ebx, 8        ; new coin, save old counts
18.
19.   testagain:
20.       cmp al, byte ptr [esp]  ; is al < current coin?
21.       jl nextcoin       ; yes, so try the next smaller coin
22.
23.       inc bl            ; count one of current coin...
24.       sub al, byte ptr [esp]
25.                         ; ...and subtract from amount left
26.       jmp testagain
27.
28.   nextcoin:
29.       shr dword ptr [esp], 8  ; done with that coin
30.       jmp top
31.
32.   done:
33.       add esp, 4        ; remove local variable
34.
35.       mov eax, ebx
36.       ret 4             ; take argument off the stack
```

Suggestions

1. What is the "loop counter" of the `top` loop, running from lines 14–30? Where is this loop counter changed? How many times will this loop iterate?

2. In the trivial case, there will be no change returned, which means that `eax` should be zero at the end (no quarters, no dimes, no nickels, and no pennies). What input causes this to happen? Does the code handle it correctly?

3. Does the use of the `al` variable match how it is described in the comment on lines 8–10?

Hints

Walk through the function with the following value pushed on the stack as the parameter:

1. The maximum amount of change: 0
2. Almost the maximum amount of change: 1
3. Skip all face values but the smallest one: 99
4. Change has at least one of every coin: 58

Explanation of the Bug

The value of all the possible coins is initialized incorrectly on line 3:

```
mov dword ptr [esp], 0x190a0501
```

It does correctly correspond to the expected result in that the high byte has the face value of a quarter and the result is supposed to have the number of quarters in the high byte. However, the program later accesses this data by using `byte ptr [esp]`, rotating it through after each coin. Because the x86 stores numbers in little-endian format, the first time through the `top` loop, `byte ptr [esp]` will be `0x01`, not `0x19`.

This is a **D.number** error because of the way numbers are stored in memory. The fix is to swap the bytes in the number. So, the initialization on line 3 becomes the following:

```
mov dword ptr [esp], 0x01050a19
```

The effect of the code as written is that it initially tries to make change with pennies, which means that it determines that the proper change for any number n is n pennies. However, it then stores this count in the high byte of the result, indicating that it feels that the proper change is n quarters.

❷ Multiply Two Numbers Using Shifts

This function multiplies two numbers using shift and add operations.

The parameters are passed on the stack. The procedure stores the two parameters in the word registers bx and dx, and accumulates the result in eax, providing 16 bit ¥ 16 bit = 32-bit multiplication. For each bit that is on in dx, it adds the value "bx shifted left the appropriate number of bits" to eax. When it has checked every bit in dx, the correct result will be in eax, which is where the procedure is defined to return it.

The procedure does preserve the passed-in value of registers, and is responsible for popping parameters off the stack. Note that the two numbers are pushed on the stack as words, not dwords.

The test instruction sets the flags as if it were a logical and, without actually modifying the value of the operands.

Source Code

```
1.    multiply:
2.        ; save registers we use
3.        push ebp
4.        mov ebp, esp
5.        push ebx
6.        push edx
7.
8.        xor ebx, ebx      ; ensure high 16 bits are zeroed out
9.        mov dx, [ebp+8]   ; second parameter
10.       mov bx, [ebp+10]  ; first parameter
11.
12.       ; eax accumulates the result
13.       mov eax, 0
14.
15.   mainloop:
16.       cmp dx, 0
17.       je done           ; no bits left in ax
18.
19.       test dx, 1
20.       jz noton          ; this bit is not on, so don't add
21.       add eax, ebx
22.       shl ebx, 1        ; ebx = ebx * 2
23.   noton:
24.       shr dx, 1         ; try the next bit
```

```
25.              jmp mainloop
26.
27.      done:
28.              ; restore saved values
29.              pop edx
30.              pop ebx
31.              pop ebp
32.
33.              ret 4                    ; pop 2 word parameters
```

Suggestions

1. What is the goal of the first iteration through `mainloop` on lines 15–25?
2. What is an input that causes `mainloop` to iterate exactly once?
3. The two numbers to be multiplied are stored in `bx` and `dx`. How come it is necessary to clear the high 16 bits of `ebx` (on line 8) but not of `edx`?
4. Does the program save/restore registers properly and access the pushed parameters at the correct offset from `ebp`?

Hints

Walk through the procedure with the following two words pushed on the stack (the current stack location is at the bottom; numbers are shown in binary for convenience):

1. Only one bit on in the second number:
   ```
   101
   1
   ```
2. Same scenario in reverse:
   ```
   1
   101
   ```
3. Two bits in each word:
   ```
   11
   11
   ```
4. The high bit is on in each number:
   ```
   1000000000000000
   1000000000000000
   ```

Explanation of the Bug

The code on line 22 to shift `ebx` to the left

```
shl ebx, 1          ; ebx = ebx * 2
```

must be executed each time through `mainloop`, not only in cases where the low bit of `dx` was on. It should be moved down one line to be after the `noton` label. Otherwise, the program works incorrectly unless the second parameter (the one stored in `dx`) is one less than a power of 2, which means its binary representation looks like 1, 11, 111, etc. For numbers like that, the missed shifts won't affect the final result.

This could be an **F.location** error, but it is more likely an **A.logic** error.

❸ Join Strings with a Delimiter

This function joins together unicode strings into one large unicode string by using a specified unicode string as a delimiter.

Unicode code strings occupy 16 bits per character.

The strings in question are stored in a special way. They are not terminated with a unicode `'\0'` character. Instead, the word (2 bytes) just before the address of the string stores the length of the string. The length is the number of characters, not the number of bytes.

This function assumes that the first argument on the stack is the address of the output buffer and the second is the address of the delimiter. After that come the strings to join; there can be a variable number of these, with a `NULL` address indicating the end of the sequence.

The program is responsible for popping the arguments off the stack, but not for preserving registers that it uses. It can assume that the output buffer is large enough to hold the result.

Remember that `rep movsw` moves `ecx` words from `[esi]` to `[edi]`. Because `movsw` increments `esi` and `edi` each time it is executed, at the end of the `rep movsw` command, `esi` and `edi` point just past the end of the source and destination strings.

Source Code

```
1.      dest        dd ?   ; store output buffer address here
2.      delimiter dd ?    ; store delimiter address here
3.
4.   join_string:
5.      pop edi          ; output buffer
6.      mov word ptr [edi-2], 0  ; length is 0 to begin
7.      mov dest, edi ; save it in a variable
8.      pop eax          ; delimiter
9.      mov delimeter, eax  ; save it in a variable
10.
11.     mov ecx, 0     ; cx holds various lengths; ensure
12.                    ; the high 16 bits are zero
13.
14.  nextstring:
15.     ; loop back here to take a string off the stack
16.     pop esi
17.     cmp esi, 0     ; NULL string, we are done
18.     je done
19.
20.     ; if this is the first string, don't add delimiter
21.     mov edx, dest
22.     cmp word ptr [edx-2], 0  ; length is 0, first string
23.     je copystring
24.
25.     ; not first string, have to copy the delimeter
26.     push esi        ; save this (next string address)
27.     mov esi, delimeter
28.     mov cx, word ptr [esi-2]  ; length of delimiter
29.     add word ptr [edx-2], cx  ; add to length of buffer
30.     rep movsw       ; copy delimeter
31.
32.  copystring:
33.     mov cx, word ptr [esi-2]  ; length of string
34.     add word ptr [edx-2], cx  ; add to length of buffer
35.     rep movsw       ; copy string
36.     jmp nextstring
37.
38.  done:
```

Suggestions

1. Describe the meaning of `edi` as it is used throughout the procedure. Is it used correctly given this meaning?
2. When the procedure exits, has it properly pulled all the arguments off the stack?
3. The length of the output buffer is not updated after the `done` label. This means that it must be kept updated during the procedure. Check that it will always match the number of characters in the buffer.
4. The procedure deals with unicode strings whose length is specified in characters, not bytes. Make sure that all string lengths reflect this rule.

Hints

Walk through the function with the following values on the stack at the beginning. (The current stack location is at the bottom. The inputs are specified as literal strings, which indicate that the address of a unicode string with that value is on the stack, with the length properly specified in the word just before the location the address points to. The output buffer is shown as an empty string, meaning the length is 0, but the location can be assumed to have enough room to store the result string.)

1. No strings to join:
   NULL
   `"+"` [the delimiter]
   `" "` [the output buffer]
2. Only one string:
   NULL
   `"test"`
   `"-"` [the delimiter]
   `" "` [the output buffer]
3. Two strings, two-character delimiter:
   NULL
   `"words"`
   `"two"`
   `"**"` [the delimiter]
   `" "` [the output buffer]

4. Three strings, empty delimiter:
```
NULL
"c"
"b"
"a"
" " [the delimiter, empty in this case]
" " [the output buffer]
```

Explanation of the Bug

Line 26 saves `esi`, which is storing the address of the next string, on the stack

```
push esi       ; save this (next string address)
```

so it can be used in lines 27–30 as the source address for the delimiter copy, as required by `movsw`. However, it never pops it back off the stack. This is an **F.missing** error. The effect is that, if the delimiter ever has to be copied, the string gets pushed on the stack at line 26, then pulled off again as the next string at line 16. This results in the program looping forever and appending the same string to the output buffer until it crashes accessing memory it is not allowed to access.

A line of code needs to be added at line 31:

```
pop esi        ; restore this (next string address)
```

The only time this bug does not happen is if the delimiter is never copied, which means that zero or one strings are passed in to be joined.

❹ Calculate Fibonacci Numbers

This function calculates the Nth Fibonacci number.

The Fibonacci numbers are a well-known mathematical sequence. The first and second numbers are both 1. From then on, the Nth number is the sum of numbers (N-1) and (N-2), so the sequence begins:

1, 1, 2, 3, 5, 8, 13, 21 . . .

Because the numbers can become large, the program calculates a 64-bit result. It assumes on entry that `ecx` contains the number in the Fibonacci sequence to calculate. It returns the result in `edx:eax`, which means `edx` stores the high 32 bits and `eax` stores the low 32 bits.

If the result would overflow 64 bits, 0 is returned.

This is a code fragment, not a full procedure. It does not worry about preserving the initial values of registers.

The program uses the `xchg` instruction, which simply swaps the two operands. The `jc` conditional jumps if the carry flag is set.

The `adc` instruction allows multi-byte/-word/-dword additions. It adds the carry flag to the result, so you could add `ebx:eax` to `edx:ecx` (storing the result in `ebx:eax`) using the following:

```
add eax, ecx    ; adc not needed on low dword operation
adc ebx, edx    ; add carry flag from previous operation
```

Source Code

```
1.    fibonacci:
2.
3.        ; ecx holds the number
4.        mov eax, 1
5.        mov edx, 0
6.        cmp ecx, 2    ; if ecx is 1 or 2
7.        jle done      ; then return 1 in edx:eax
8.
9.        sub ecx, 1
10.
11.       ; result will go in edx:eax
12.       mov ebx, 0    ; esi:ebx store previous value
13.       mov esi, 0
14.   top:
15.       add edx, eax
16.       adc esi, ebx  ; esi:ebx += edx:eax
17.       jc overflow   ; if carry flag set, we overflowed
18.       xchg eax, ebx
19.       xchg edx, esi ; swap esi:ebx and edx:eax
20.       loop top
21.
22.       jmp done
23.
24.   overflow:
25.       mov eax, 0
26.       mov edx, 0
27.
28.   done:
```

Suggestions

1. Where are the introductory, main part, and cleanup code?
2. Why is 1 subtracted from ecx on line 9?
3. Are add and adc used properly on lines 15–16?

Hints

Walk through the program with the following values in ecx to test the first few numbers in the sequence:

1. 2
2. 3
3. 4
4. 5

Explanation of the Bug

The addition of the two 64-bit numbers on lines 15–16 is incorrect:

```
add edx, eax
adc esi, ebx   ; esi:ebx += edx:eax
```

The comment on line 16 is correct in what the code should be trying to do, but the registers are mixed up. The code should read as follows:

```
add ebx, eax
adc esi, edx   ; esi:ebx += edx:eax
```

This is a **B.variable** error that actually has an interesting behavior if you walk through the code. The code still works correctly for the first and second number because those are special-cased on lines 6–7. For N larger than 2, the result depends on whether N is even or odd. If it's even, the result is 0. If it's odd, edx winds up set to N-1 and eax winds up set to 1, so the result is $[(N-1) * (2^{32})] + 1$. Maybe that's a useful sequence on its own.

The corrected program, incidentally, overflows trying to calculate the 94th Fibonacci number, which is 19,740,274,219,868,223,167. This is larger

237

than the maximum unsigned 64-bit value of 18,446,744,073,709,551,615 (both numbers have 20 digits).

❺ Check if Two Words Are Anagrams

This function checks if two words are anagrams (which means that they have the same letters, but possibly in a different order). It ignores case differences in letters.

The program counts the letters in a string by allocating a 256-byte array and storing, in index n of the array, the number of times that the letter with an ASCII value of n appears (with an adjustment for case insensitivity—all letters are upper-cased first). This means that the program can't handle more than 256 of any one letter—that is not the bug. After the letter totals for the two words are counted, they are compared to see if they match, in which case the two words are anagrams.

The main procedure is called check_anagram. It calls a procedure do_count to count the letters in a single word. The address of the two words (strings terminated with a '\0' character) are pushed on the stack as parameters to check_anagram.

The procedures are not responsible for popping their parameters off the stack. (When check_anagram calls do_count, it is the responsibility of check_anagram, as the caller, to clean up the stack.) Because do_count is only called by check_anagram and, at a point where no registers need to be saved, do_count does not preserve passed-in registers, but check_anagram does.

The program uses the following string instructions:

- **stosd**. Store eax into dword ptr [edi]
- **scasb**. Compare al to byte ptr [edi]
- **lodsb**. Load byte ptr [esi] into al
- **cmpsd**. Compare dword ptr [esi] to dword ptr [edi]

Keep in mind how the rep prefix works on each iteration. If ecx is non-zero, it performs the primitive string instruction, decrements ecx without changing flags, and then (for cmps and scas) checks the zero flag result from the primitive operation.

The following instruction

```
sete al
```

sets `al` to `1` if the zero flag is 1; otherwise, it sets `al` to `0`. (There is an entire collection of `setXX` instructions that match up with the `jXX` status-flag–based conditional jump instructions: `setne`, `setl`, and so on. They all set a byte to 1 if the condition is true, and 0 otherwise.)

Source Code

```
 1.       ; helper procedure called by check_anagram
 2.   do_count:
 3.
 4.       ; do_count expects word, then count array
 5.       ; to be pushed
 6.       mov edi, [esp + 4]    ; count array
 7.       mov ecx, 64
 8.       mov eax, 0
 9.       rep stosd            ; clear count array
10.
11.       ; find the length of word
12.       mov edi, [esp + 8]    ; word
13.       mov ecx, -1  ; start it at -1 so it won't cause
14.                    ; the repne scasb to end
15.       repne scasb  ; terminates when [edi] points to a 0
16.                    ; ecx will be -(length of word + 2)
17.       not ecx      ; ecx is now (length of word + 2)
18.       sub ecx, 2   ; ecx is now length of word
19.
20.       jecxz countdone  ; if length is zero, skip word
21.
22.       mov edi, [esp + 4]  ; count array
23.       mov esi, [esp + 8]  ; word
24.
25.   startcount:
26.       lodsb         ; put next character in al
27.       cmp al, 'a'  ; if less than 'a'...
28.       jl dontupper
29.       cmp al, 'z'  ; ...or greater than 'z'
30.       jg dontupper ; ...don't uppercase it
31.       sub al, 'a'
32.       add al, 'A'
33.
34.   dontupper:
35.       inc byte ptr [edi+eax]   ; update count array
36.       loop startcount
```

```
37.   countdone:
38.       ret
39.
40.       ; the main procedure
41.   check_anagram:
42.
43.       push ebp
44.       mov ebp, esp
45.       push ebx
46.       push ecx
47.       push esi
48.       push edi
49.       sub esp, 512  ; allocate count arrays
50.
51.       mov ebx, [ebp + 8]      ; first word
52.       push ebx
53.       lea ebx, [ebp - 528]
54.       push ebx
55.       call do_count
56.       add esp, 8              ; clean parameters off stack
57.
58.       mov ebx, [ebp + 12]    ; second word
59.       push ebx
60.       lea ebx, [ebp - 272]
61.       push ebx
62.       call do_count
63.       add esp, 8              ; clean parameters off stack
64.
65.       mov eax, 0
66.       lea esi, [ebp - 528]
67.       lea edi, [ebp - 272]
68.       mov ecx, 64
69.       rep cmpsd
70.
71.       sete al    ; eax will be 1 if it matched, else 0
72.
73.       add esp, 512  ; remove local variables
74.       pop edi
75.       pop esi
76.       pop ecx
77.       pop ebx
78.       pop ebp
79.       ret
```

Suggestions

1. It's best to focus on the do_count procedure first because it is called by check_anagram. Think of a trivial input to do_count, as well as an input that exercises all the code paths.
2. The statement on line 35 is indexing into the count array that was passed as a parameter to do_count. What ensures that this will not index past the end of the array?
3. Check that ecx is used correctly in all the rep instructions.
4. Check that the count arrays allocated as local variables to check_anagram on line 49 are correctly addressed.

Hints

Walk through the code with the following parameters to check_anagram:

1. Anagram, case differs:
   ```
   "a"
   "A"
   ```
2. Anagram, more than one character:
   ```
   "123"
   "321"
   ```
3. Not an anagram, one string is blank:
   ```
   ""
   "hello"
   ```
4. Not an anagram, differ only in count of one letter:
   ```
   "abca"
   "abc"
   ```

Explanation of the Bug

The calculation of the length of the word on lines 13–18 is incorrect:

```
mov ecx, -1   ; start it at -1 so it won't cause
              ; the repne scasb to end
repne scasb   ; terminates when [edi] points to a 0
              ; ecx will be -(length of word + 2)
not ecx       ; ecx is now (length of word + 2)
sub ecx, 2    ; ecx is now length of word
```

241

After the `repne scasb`, ecx will indeed be `-(length of word + 2)`, as the comment states. The easiest word to check this against is an empty one, where `byte ptr [edi]` is 0 the first time the `scasb` instruction on line 15 executes. In this case, based on the rules of how the `repne` prefix works, it still decrements ecx once, so after line 16 ecx ends up as –2 for a zero-length string.

The bug is on line 17. The `not` instruction inverts every bit in ecx, which is not the same as negating it. To negate a number in two's complement, you invert every bit and then add one. Since the "add one" step is missing, ecx winds up as one less than it should be.

This could be classified as an **A.off-by-one** or a **D.limit** error because the behavior is that the code skips counting the last character in the word—unless the string is zero-length, in which case, ecx winds up as `-1` and the `startcount` loop on lines 23–34 iterates (almost) forever (until it accesses bad memory).

The fix is to change line 17 to use the correct opcode to negate ecx, as follows:

```
neg ecx        ; ecx is now (length of word + 2)
```

❻ Convert a 64-Bit Number to a Decimal String

This function converts a 64-bit unsigned number to its decimal string equivalent.

Three parameters are pushed on the stack in order: the buffer that holds the resulting string, the low 32 bits of the number, and the high 32 bits of the number. The program should NULL-terminate the string it stores in the output buffer. Assume the buffer is large enough to hold the result.

The program works by producing the proper digit for each "place" (as in the ones place, tens place, hundreds place, and so on) in turn, moving from high to low place. It first calculates 10 to the appropriate power and then keeps subtracting that from the original number until it becomes less than it. The number of times the subtraction is done is the correct digit for that place.

The program "knows" that the largest 64-bit unsigned number is between 10^{19} and 10^{20}.

The main procedure is `to_decimal`, which calls the helper procedure. `mult10`. `to_decimal` is responsible for preserving register values and cleaning parameters off the stack. It uses three local variables, all of which are bytes.

The `shld` instruction shifts a certain number of bits to the left, the same as `shl`, but it fills in the bits from another location rather than putting in 0. The effect is that the sequence

```
shld esi, ebx, 2
shl ebx, 2
```

shifts `esi:ebx` left by 2 bits.

Recall that `adc` allows multi-byte additions with carry, so that

```
add ebx, eax
adc esi, edx
```

adds `edx:eax` to `esi:ebx`. The subtraction equivalent is "subtract with borrow." The `sbb` instruction adds the carry flag to the `subtrahend` (the `subtrahend` in a subtraction operation is the number to the right of the minus sign). Thus, you calculate `edx:eax -= esi:ebx` with the following:

```
sub eax, ebx
sbb edx, esi
```

If you think it through, it works. Remember that after `sub eax, ebx`, the carry flag is set if `ebx` was less than `eax`. In that case, you want to "borrow" one from `edx`, which is what happens because in that case, `sbb edx, esi` becomes `edx -= (esi+1)`.

Source Code

```
1.   mult10:
2.        ; multiply esi:ebx by 10, ecx times
3.        jecxz multret
4.
5.        push eax
6.        push edx  ; save these
7.
8.   multloop:
9.        ; x * 10 == x * 8 + x * 2
10.       shld esi, ebx, 1
11.       shl ebx, 1
12.       mov eax, ebx
13.       mov edx, esi
```

```
14.          ; edx:eax is now 2 x the number
15.          shld esi, ebx, 2
16.          shl ebx, 2
17.          ; esi:ebx is now 8 x the number
18.          add ebx, eax
19.          adc esi, edx
20.          ; esi:ebx is now 10 x the number
21.          loop multloop
22.
23.          pop edx
24.          pop eax
25.      multret:
26.          ret
27.
28.
29.      to_decimal:
30.
31.          push ebp
32.          mov ebp, esp
33.          sub esp, 4     ; [ebp-4] place we are producing
34.                         ; [ebp-3] next digit
35.                         ; [ebp-2] on if number is nonzero
36.                         ; [ebp-1] unused
37.
38.          mov edx, [ebp+8]  ; high 32 bits
39.          mov eax, [ebp+12] ; low 32 bits
40.          mov edi, [ebp+16] ; buffer
41.
42.          mov byte ptr [ebp-4], 19   ; initial place is 19
43.
44.      mainloop:
45.          ; first put 10^place in esi:ebx
46.          mov ebx, 1
47.          mov esi, 0
48.          mov ecx, 0
49.          mov cl, byte ptr [ebp-4] ; place goes in ecx
50.          call mult10
51.
52.          ; subtract esi:ebx from edx:eax until it is less
53.          ; than esi:ebx. Track number of times in [ebp-3].
54.
55.          mov byte ptr [ebp-3], 0   ; digit starts at 0
56.      subloop:
57.          cmp edx, esi
58.          jb subdone
59.          ja subandloop
60.          cmp eax, ebx
```

244

```
61.          jb subdone
62.     subandloop:
63.          sub eax, ebx
64.          sbb edx, esi
65.          inc byte ptr [ebp-3]   ; increment digit
66.          jmp subloop
67.
68.     subdone:
69.          cmp byte ptr [ebp-3], 0   ; is digit 0?
70.          jne adddigit              ; no, so add it
71.          cmp byte ptr [ebp-2], 0   ; digit is 0, so add if a
72.                                    ; non-zero part of number
73.                                    ; has already been output
74.          jne adddigit
75.          jmp nextdigit
76.     adddigit:
77.          add byte ptr [ebp-3], '0'   ; convert digit to ASCII
78.          mov bl, byte ptr [ebp-3]
79.          mov byte ptr [edi], bl      ; store digit in buffer
80.          mov byte ptr [ebp-2], 1     ; nonzero is true now
81.          inc edi
82.
83.     nextdigit:
84.          cmp byte ptr [ebp-4], 0   ; did we finish place 0?
85.          je done                   ; if so, we are done
86.          dec byte ptr [ebp-4]      ; on to next-lower place
87.          jmp mainloop
88.
89.     done:
90.          cmp [ebp-2], 0            ; is nonzero still false?
91.          jne skipzero
92.          mov byte ptr [edi], '0'   ; output a single zero
93.          inc edi
94.
95.     skipzero:
96.          mov byte ptr [edi], 0     ; '\0'-terminate buffer
97.
98.          pop ebp
99.          pop ebp
100.         ret 12                    ; pop 12 bytes off the stack
```

Suggestions

1. Look at each instance where to_decimal uses one of its three 1-byte local variables, and use that to come up with names for each of them.

2. Verify the algorithm and implementation of `mult10`.

3. The procedure treats `edx:eax` and `esi:ebx` as 64-bit quantities. If you can show that these are always used properly, you can run through the algorithm without having to use a value greater than 32 bits as an input. In particular, determine what arithmetic comparison between `edx:eax` and `esi:ebx` is being tested on lines 58–62.

4. What is the meaning of `edi`?

Hints

Walk through the program with the following inputs on the stack, with the current stack location at the bottom (assume the output buffer is correct and will hold the result):

1. Test if zero is handled correctly:
   ```
   output_buffer
   ```
   0 [low 32 bits]
   0 [high 32 bits]

2. A single-digit number:
   ```
   output_buffer
   ```
   9 [low 32 bits]
   0 [high 32 bits]

3. Three digits, all in the low 32 bits:
   ```
   output_buffer
   ```
   234 [low 32 bits]
   0 [high 32 bits]

4. One digit on in the high 32 bits:
   ```
   output_buffer
   ```
   0 [low 32 bits]
   1 [high 32 bits]

Explanation of the Bug

The "nonzero" variable stored at `[ebp-2]` is not initialized to false. It is not initialized at all, which is an **F.init** error. As a result, it randomly starts out as true or false based on what happens to be lying around on the stack. It needs to be initialized around line 43:

```
mov byte ptr [ebp-2], 0    ; nonzero starts as false
```

If the stack had a zero at that byte, the program works as expected. If not, it prints leading zeros in the output buffer.

❼ Sum a Signed Array

This function sums an array of signed dwords.

The program returns a dword as the final value, but allows the intermediate result to be larger than a dword can hold. It tracks the "result," which is the dword total of the elements in the array, as well as an overflow/underflow "counter." Each time the cumulative sum of the elements overflows (meaning it is more than 2^{31}-1, the highest value a signed dword can hold), the counter is incremented; each time the cumulative sum underflows (meaning it is less than -2^{31}, the lowest value a signed dword can hold), the counter is decremented. The net effect is that the counter functions as the high bits (above 31) of the result. If at the end of summing the array the counter is zero, then the 32-bit result is correct.

The program calls itself recursively to add up every element but the first one, then adds that result to the first element to produce the final result.

It is passed four parameters, pushed on the stack in order: the address to store the result, the address to store the overflow/underflow counter, the length of the array, and the address of the array. The length of the array is in elements, not bytes.

The procedure has to preserve registers; when calling itself recursively, the calling code is responsible for cleaning the parameters off the stack.

The program checks the carry and overflow flags (the overflow flag is checked with the `jo` instruction, the carry flag with `jc`). Because of how two's complement notation works, an arithmetic operation such as add or subtract is unaffected by whether the user is treating the variables as signed or unsigned. The carry and overflow flags can be checked depending on which interpretation is desired. The carry flag is set if the operation, when treated as unsigned, resulted in a value that was too large or too small. The overflow flag is set if the operation, when treated as signed, resulted in a value that was too large or too small (the "too small" condition is known as an "underflow," but it still affects the overflow flag).

The conditions when the carry flag is set are fairly straightforward; since all bits are treated as positive in an unsigned number, an unsigned addition can never result in a number that is too small, and an unsigned subtraction can never result in a number that is too large. An add instruction will set the carry bit if the result is greater than $2^{32}-1$, and a sub instruction will set the carry bit if the result is less than 0.

The overflow flag is less obvious; the valid range of signed numbers is -2^{31} to $2^{31}-1$. Thus, an addition of two positive numbers may result in an overflow, but the addition of two negative numbers may result in an underflow. Similarly, a signed subtract can either overflow or underflow.

Remember that in the two's complement notation, a signed number will have the high bit off if it is positive, and the high bit on if it is negative. When adding numbers, the program first checks the overflow flag to see if the result did not fit in a signed dword; it then checks the carry flag to differentiate between overflow and underflow, so it can adjust the overflow/underflow counter appropriately.

As with any recursive function, the stack will eventually overflow if the array is large enough, but that should not be considered a bug.

Source Code

```
1.    sum_array:
2.        push ebp
3.        mov ebp, esp
4.        sub esp, 8        ; local vars for result/counter
5.        push edi
6.        push esi
7.        push ecx
8.
9.        mov ecx, dword ptr [ebp+12]  ; size of array
10.       cmp ecx, 0        ; is array empty?
11.       jne notzero
12.       mov dword ptr [ebp-8], 0   ; yes, so counter...
13.       mov dword ptr [ebp-4], 0   ; ...and result are 0
14.       jmp done          ; and we're done
15.
16.   notzero:
17.       ; first make a recursive call for the rest of
18.       ; the array (not including the first element)
19.       lea esi, dword ptr [ebp-4]
```

```
20.         push esi            ; push address of result
21.         lea esi, dword ptr [ebp-8]
22.         push esi            ; and address of counter
23.         sub ecx, 1
24.         push ecx            ; and count-1
25.         mov esi, dword ptr [ebp+8]
26.         add esi, 4
27.         push esi            ; and address of array+4
28.
29.         call sum_array   ; result/counter in [ebp-8]/[ebp-4]
30.
31.         add esp, 16       ; take parameters off the stack
32.         sub esi, 4         ; point esi back to current element
33.         mov ecx, dword ptr [esi]
34.         add dword ptr [ebp-4], ecx   ; add result
35.         jo overflowed      ; did it overflow/underflow?
36.         jmp done           ; no, so we're done
37.
38.     overflowed:
39.         jc toobig          ; did it overflow too large?
40.
41.         ; no, overflowed too small
42.         dec dword ptr [ebp-8]   ; decrement counter
43.         jmp done
44.
45.     toobig:
46.         inc dword ptr [ebp-8]   ; increment counter
47.
48.     done:
49.         ; copy our updated result/counter to the locations
50.         ; passed as parameters to this call
51.         mov edi, dword ptr [ebp+16]
52.         lea esi, dword ptr [ebp-8]
53.         movsd              ; copy overflow/underflow counter
54.         mov edi, dword ptr [ebp+20]
55.         lea esi, dword ptr [ebp-4]
56.         movsd              ; copy result
57.         pop ecx
58.         pop esi
59.         pop edi
60.         add esp, 8
61.         pop ebp
62.
63.         ret
```

Suggestions

1. `sum_array` has four parameters, addressed as `[ebp+8]`, `[ebp+12]`, `[ebp+16]`, and `[ebp+20]`, as well as two local variables, `[ebp-4]` and `[ebp-8]`. Check that these are correctly indexed from `ebp`, and assign them more meaningful names that you can use when walking through the program.
2. Ensure that the recursion eventually terminates.
3. Verify that the `movsd` instructions on lines 53 and 56 actually move the correct data.
4. Check that everything pushed on the stack is eventually popped off the stack, in the proper order, before the procedure returns.

Hints

Walk through the program with the following arrays (assume the address, length, and space for the result and counter are pushed correctly to the outer call to `sum_array`):

1. Check a trivial case, a single element (the recursive call within this will test the empty case of no elements):
   5
2. Two elements, that will result in a "too large" overflow:
   $2^{31}-1$
   1
3. Two elements, that will result in a "too small" underflow:
   -2^{31}
   -1
4. Three elements, that will overflow, then swing back to the valid range (remember that $2^{30}+2^{30}$ is equal to 2^{31}):
   -1
   2^{30}
   2^{30}

Explanation of the Bug

The program uses the wrong check when determining whether the overflow flag was set because of the result being too large or too small.

Consider the case where the overflow flag is set because of the addition of two positive numbers. Positive signed numbers do not have the high bit (bit 32, if the low bit is numbered 1) set; therefore the addition of any pair of them can't set the carry flag—the most the addition of two positive signed numbers can do is carry from bit 31 into bit 32. The carry flag, on the other hand, indicates that the result overflowed from bit 32 into (nonexistent) bit 33. As a result, after a "too large" signed overflow, the carry flag will be *cleared*, not set.

Meanwhile, negative signed numbers do have bit 32 set, so the addition of any pair of them *will* set the carry flag. So if there is an overflow and the carry flag is set, it was because of the addition of two negative numbers, so it must be a "too small" underflow.

Because of this, the check for overflow versus underflow on line 39

```
jc toobig        ; did it overflow too large?
```

although it may seem intuitively correct, is actually reversed. It should be checking if the carry flag is not set:

```
jnc toobig       ; did it overflow too large?
```

This is a **D.number** error, because it is based on a misunderstanding of how two's complement numbers are stored.

The effect of the bug is that the counter goes off in the wrong direction, being negative when it should be positive, and vice versa. If the counter winds up at zero, however, the result is correct.

❽ Play the Simulation Game *Life*

This program calculates one generation in the game *Life*.

Life was invented by the mathematician John Conway. The game board is a two-dimensional grid, on which each cell is either occupied or not. The next generation is calculated according to the following rules:

- For each cell, calculate the number of occupied neighbors from the eight possible neighbors (including diagonal neighbors).
- If a cell is occupied and has two or three neighbors, it is occupied in the next generation; otherwise, it dies and is unoccupied in the next generation.
- If a cell is empty and has exactly three neighbors, a new occupant is born and the cell is occupied in the next generation.

Some fascinating patterns can come from these simple rules as the generations unfold.

The program assumes that three variables can be accessed: a (the array), xsize (the size in the x dimension), and ysize (the size in the y dimension). It also uses two variables, curx and cury, to track its position in the array. The array uses one byte per cell, laid out in memory as the first row of xsize bytes, followed by the second row of xsize bytes, up until the ysizeth row of xsize bytes. A cell that is occupied has the value 1; an unoccupied cell has the value 0.

This fragment of code calculates only a single generation. The results for the next generation must be determined in their entirety before any of the cells are updated. The birth or death of a cell mustn't affect its neighbors in the current generation. To accomplish this, the program stores the current generation in the lowest bit of each cell and the next generation in the second bit. When it is done, it shifts every byte to the right by one bit.

Source Code

```
1.        mov curx, 0
2.        mov cury, 0
3.        mov eax, a
4.
5.        ; we jump up here each time we start
6.        ; to calculate the results for a single cell.
7.        ; That cell is at (curx, cury).
8.        ; ecx holds the neighbor count for the cell.
9.  outerloop:
10.       mov ecx, 0
11.       ; Figure out where to loop from in the ydir.
12.       ; ebx holds the y loop counter.
13.       mov ebx, cury
14.       test ebx, ebx  ; is ebx equal to 0?
15.       je newrow       ; in row 1, start in row 1
16.       sub ebx, 1      ; not in row 1, start in row cury-1
17. newrow:
18.       ; Figure out where to loop from in the xdir.
19.       ; edi holds the pointer into the beginning of
20.       ; the row and edx holds the x loop counter.
21.       mov edi, ebx
22.       imul edi, xsize
23.       add edi, a      ; edi is address of row ebx
24.       mov edx, curx
```

```
25.        test edx, edx
26.        je countcell    ; in col 1, start in col 1
27.        sub edx, 1      ; not in col 1, start in col curx-1
28. countcell:
29.        mov ch, [edi+edx] ; ch is value of a[edx,ebx]
30.        and ch, 0xfd    ; turn off the next generation bit
31.        add cl, ch      ; add to running count
32.        and ch, 0x00    ; remove temp value from ch
33.
34.        ; are we done in xdir?
35.        cmp edx, curx
36.        jg rowdone      ; edx > curx, so row is done
37.        inc edx
38.        cmp edx, xsize
39.        je rowdone      ; edx == xsize, so row is done
40.        jmp countcell   ; count next cell
41. rowdone:
42.        ; are we done in ydir?
43.        cmp ebx, cury
44.        jg cellcounted  ; ebx > cury, so cell is done
45.        inc ebx
46.        cmp ebx, ysize
47.        je cellcounted  ; ebx == ysize, so cell is done
48.        jmp newrow
49. cellcounted:
50.        ; cell is done, so update and move to next one
51.        ; first get current value of cell in ch
52.        mov edi, cury
53.        imul edi, xsize
54.        add edi, curx
55.        add edi, a      ; edi is address of a[curx,cury]
56.        mov ch, [edi]   ; read current value into ch
57.
58.        cmp ch, 1       ; is it on?
59.        je cellon
60.        cmp cl, 3       ; off: turn on if 3 neighbors
61.        jne celldone
62.        jmp turnon
63.
64. cellon:                ; on: remain if 2 or 3 neighbors
65.        cmp cl, 2
66.        jl celldone
67.        cmp cl, 3
68.        jg celldone
69.
70. turnon:
71.        or ch, 0x02     ; turn on bit 2 for next generation
```

253

```
72.        mov [edi], ch
73.
74.        ; now see where to go next
75.  celldone:
76.        inc curx
77.        mov ebx, xsize
78.        cmp curx, ebx    ; if curx has reached xsize...
79.        je nextrow       ; ...go to next row
80.        jmp outerloop    ; otherwise count this cell
81.
82.  nextrow:
83.        mov curx, 0      ; back to column 0
84.        inc cury
85.        mov ebx, ysize
86.        cmp cury, ebx    ; if cury has not reached ysize...
87.        jne outerloop    ; ...count this cell
88.
89.        ; done, so just shift the table right one bit
90.        mov edi,a        ; edi is start of array
91.        mov ecx, xsize
92.        imul ecx, ysize  ; ecx is size of array
93.        dec edi          ; so loop starts and ends right
94.  shiftloop:
95.        shr [edi+ecx], 1
96.        loop shiftloop
```

Suggestions

1. Because the assembly language is not indented, loops are not obvious. Identify the beginning and end of all the loops in the code.
2. Check that the counts for the top-left element (0, 0) and the bottom-right element (xsize-1, ysize-1) are calculated correctly.
3. Verify that the next generation is properly prevented from interfering with the current generation.
4. Check that all the comparisons and resulting jumps are correct.

Hints

Because the code is complicated, there is only one hint, which is an array laid out as follows. (Cells that are on are shown as a 1; cells that are off are shown as a . for visual clarity, but really contain a 0.) This array has at least one instance of occupied cells with 2, 3, and 4 neighbors, as well as unoccupied cells with 1, 3, and 5 neighbors:

```
.1..
11.1
..11
.111
```

Explanation of the Bug

The program calculates the next-generation results incorrectly for cells that are on. Lines 64–68 appear to check it correctly:

```
cellon:                 ; on: remain if 2 or 3 neighbors
    cmp cl, 2
    jl celldone
    cmp cl, 3
    jg celldone
```

However, the cell-counting loop counts the current cell also. So, for a cell that is on, the neighbor total will be one higher than expected. Thus, the code on lines 64–68 needs to read as follows

```
cellon:                 ; on: remain if 2 or 3 neighbors
    cmp cl, 3
    jl celldone
    cmp cl, 4
    jg celldone
```

to accommodate this.

The result of this **A.logic** error is that existing cells survive if they have one or two neighbors, instead of two or three. This small change makes the simulation much bleaker—in particular, if a cell is born because it has three neighbors, it is likely that all four cells will die in the next generation because they all have three neighbors.

❾ Check if Parentheses Match in Source Code

This program checks if parentheses match up in a buffer that contains source code.

The source code is in a language similar to C. It supports the following:

- Comments that start with /* and end with */, and can span multiple lines.
- Comments that start with //, and run to the end of the line.
- Strings that are delimited with double quote (") characters.

In addition, the following rules apply:

- Inside a /* */ comment, // and " are ignored.
- Inside a // comment, /*, */, and " are ignored.
- Inside a string, comment delimiters are ignored.
- Inside a string, the two-character sequence \" indicates an escaped double quote, which means that the string contains a double quote character and does not terminate.
- A newline ends a string constant.

The program uses a state machine. The states are identified by a number:

- 0. Regular text [looking for / or "]
- 1. In state 0, hit / [looking for / or *]
- 2. In state 0, hit " [now in " string, looking for \ or " or \n]
- 3. In state 1, hit * [now in /* comment, looking for *]
- 4. In state 3, hit * [in /* comment, looking for /]
- 5. In state 1, hit / [now in // comment, looking for \n]
- 6. In state 2, hit \ [in " string, looking for "]

The program special cases the characters *, /, ", \, and newline ('\n') when they appear in the buffer. For each character, the program uses a table of which state to move to next, based on the current state:

```
 *  = "0324352"
 /  = "1523052"
 "  = "2003352"
 \  = "0063352"
\n = "0003300"
```

For example, this means that if the program encounters a * while in state 1, it should move to state 3. This corresponds to having seen a / as the previous character and now seeing a *, which puts the state machine into the "in /* comment" state.

There is also a special table for what to do if the program encounters any other character—in some cases, the state stays unchanged; in other cases, it won't:

```
other = "0023352"
```

For example, if in state 1 (just saw a /, looking for * or /) and any other character is seen, the program should revert back to state 0, normal text. But in state 2 (inside a " string), the state should remain unchanged unless one of the special characters is seen.

The program has to only track parentheses (for the purpose of determining if they are matched up) when in states 0 or 1.

On entry, the variable textdata holds a pointer to the buffer, which is terminated with a '\0' character. The variable chars points to a '\0'-terminate string that contains the special characters, in order: *, /, ", \, newline (this string would be written in C, with appropriate escape characters, as "*/\"\\\n").

In addition, the six variables startable, slashtable, doublequotetable, backslashtable, newlinetable, and othertable point to '\0'-terminate strings containing the state transition tables previously shown.

Remember precisely how repne scasb works. For each iteration, it does the following:

- Exit if ecx is 0.
- Perform the scasb (which sets the flags based on al - byte ptr [edi]).
- Decrement ecx without changing the flags.
- Exit if the zero flag is 1.

The program is a code fragment, not a procedure. It is not responsible for preserving registers. It should return the result in eax: 1 if the parentheses match, 0 if they don't.

Source Code

```
1.      mov esi, textdata    ; esi holds current pointer
2.      mov ecx, 0           ; ecx holds the paren depth
3.      mov ebx, 0           ; ebx holds the current state
4.
5.      sub esp, 24          ; allocate room for tables
6.      mov eax, startable
```

```
7.          mov [esp], eax
8.          mov eax, slashtable
9.          mov [esp+4], eax
10.         mov eax, doublequotetable
11.         mov [esp+8], eax
12.         mov eax, backslashtable
13.         mov [esp+12], eax
14.         mov eax, newlinetable
15.         mov [esp+16], eax
16.         mov eax, othertable
17.         mov [esp+20], eax
18.
19.    nextchar:
20.         cmp byte ptr [esi], 0   ; is next character '\0'?
21.         je done
22.
23.         cmp ebx, 1          ; if state is not 0 or 1
24.         jg lookforspecial  ; don't worry about ( or )
25.         cmp byte ptr [esi], '('
26.         jne checkforright
27.         inc ecx            ; increase paren depth
28.         xor ebx, ebx       ; go back to state 0
29.         jmp skiplookup     ; it's a (, so not special
30.
31.    checkforright:
32.         cmp byte ptr [esi], ')'
33.         jne lookforspecial
34.         dec ecx            ; decrease paren depth
35.         xor ebx, ebx       ; go back to state 0
36.         jmp skiplookup     ; it's a ), so not special
37.
38.    lookforspecial:
39.         push ecx           ; save this temporarily
40.         mov edi, chars     ; chars is '*','/','"','\\','\n'
41.         mov al, [esi]      ; load next character
42.         mov ecx, 6
43.         repne scasb
44.
45.         mov eax, 5
46.         sub eax, ecx       ; ecx is index in chars that
47.                            ; matched, or 5 if no match
48.         shl eax, 2         ; multiply by 4
49.         mov edi, [esp+4]   ; +4 because ecx was pushed
50.         add edi, eax       ; index into tables
51.         mov eax, [edi]     ; eax is now address of table
52.
53.         mov cl, [eax+ebx]  ; cl is table[current state]
```

258

```
54.        sub cl, '0'              ; convert digit to number
55.
56.        mov bl, cl              ; update current state
57.
58.        pop ecx                 ; retrieve the paren depth
59.
60. skiplookup:
61.        inc esi                 ; next character in buffer
62.        jmp nextchar
63.
64. done:
65.        jecxz matched           ; jump if ecx is 0
66.        mov eax, 0              ; ecx non-zero, didn't match up
67.        jmp end
68. matched:
69.        mov eax, 1              ; ecx is zero, matched up
70. end:
71.        add esp, 24             ; remove local storage
```

Suggestions

1. There are really two parts to checking this program: ensuring that the state machine transition tables are correct and ensuring that the program processes them correctly. Are the state machine transition tables correct?
2. Check that esi and ebx hold their meanings properly throughout the program.
3. Walk through the instructions on lines 42–47 carefully to verify that the comment on lines 46–47 is correct.
4. Is the return value calculated correctly?

Hints

It is easiest to test the program on small inputs that check some particular aspect of the state machine, rather than try a full program all at once. The strings are shown without escape characters or double quotes to make them clearer:

1. Make sure basic parentheses matching works:
   abc((def)ghi)
2. Check /* comments:
   (/*) " */)

3. Check `//` comments and too many left parentheses:
   ```
   (abc // def
   ```
4. Check strings and too many right parentheses:
   ```
   ( ")\")"123))
   ```

Explanation of the Bug

Line 49 is incorrect:

```
mov edi, [esp+4]    ; +4 because ecx was pushed
```

The code tries to set `edi` to be the base address of the array of state-machine transition tables that is stored in local variables on the stack. However, this statement actually puts the address of the first table in `edi`. What it should be doing is putting the address of the entire array in `edi`. Thus, it should read as follows:

```
lea edi, [esp+4]    ; +4 because ecx was pushed
```

This is a **B.expression** error. There is an extra dereference of the "pointer" on the stack. The effect is that the program, instead of looking up a table in an array of tables on line 51, looks up a table in a string, which results in a crash.

⑩ Radix Exchange Sort

This procedure performs a radix exchange sort of an array of dwords.

The radix exchange sort works by considering elements of the array one bit at a time, going from right to left (least significant to most significant). It first rearranges the array so that all elements that have a 0 in the least significant bit are before all the elements that have a 1 in the least significant bit. Then, it does the same with the second least significant bit, and so on up until the most significant bit.

The reason this works is because the algorithm takes care, when rearranging the array for bit n, to never disturb the relative position of elements that have the same value for bit n. That is, it moves elements that have bit n set to 0 up in the array so they are before elements that have bit n set to 1, but if two elements have bit n set to 0, it won't change their relative position—the one that was earlier in the array is still earlier, even though both might have moved.

It can be difficult to convince yourself that the algorithm actually works. Elements tend to move around the array somewhat randomly until magically settling into place on the last loop iteration.

However, it is not difficult to prove that it is correct. If you consider two numbers, A and B, in binary representation, they will have a certain number of most significant bits that match (this number might be 0), followed by a bit that doesn't match. The relative ordering of A and B depends only on that first bit that doesn't match. If the bit is 0 in A and 1 in B, A is less than B. If it is 1 in A and 0 in B, A is greater than B. If the "different" bit never happens, A is equal to B.

So, the algorithm proceeds from least significant bit up, moving A and B as it sees fit, until at some point it processes the most significant bit where A and B differ. At that point, it orders them properly based on that bit. From then on, because they will match in all higher bits, it won't disturb their relative order. Thus, they are properly sorted in the array. The same is true for any pair of numbers.

The program takes two parameters pushed on the stack: the length of the array and the address of the array. It has no return value. It is required to preserve the values of registers and clear the parameters off the stack.

Source Code

```
1.    radix_sort:
2.        push ebp
3.        mov ebp, esp
4.        push eax
5.        push ebx
6.        push ecx
7.        push edx
8.        push esi
9.        push edi
10.
11.        mov edx, 1      ; start with low bit
12.
13.    outerloop:
14.        mov eax, [ebp+8]  ; address of array
15.        mov ebx, [ebp+12] ; size of array
16.
17.        mov esi, eax    ; esi stores address of first element
18.        imul ebx, 4
```

```
19.         add eax, ebx    ; eax stores address of last element
20.
21.     lookforonebit:
22.         ; start at esi, find an element with the edx bit on
23.         cmp esi, eax
24.         je trynextbit   ; we are at the end of the array
25.
26.         test [esi], edx  ; does [esi] have the edx bit on?
27.         jnz foundone     ; yes
28.         add esi, 4       ; no, advance esi and loop back
29.         jmp lookforonebit
30.
31.     foundone:
32.         ; edx bit is on at [esi], now look for the next
33.         ; element where edx bit is off. Then adjust array.
34.         mov edi, esi    ; use edi as the pointer
35.     lookforzerobit:
36.         add edi, 4
37.         test [edi], edx    ; does [edi] have the edx bit on?
38.         jz foundzero    ; no
39.     checkforendthenlookforzero:
40.         cmp edi, eax    ; yes, see if we hit the last element
41.         je trynextbit   ; last element, move edx to next bit
42.         jmp lookforzerobit
43.
44.     foundzero:
45.         ; edx bit is one from [esi] to [edi-4], and zero at
46.         ; [edi]. Slide array between them down and move
47.         ; [edi] to [esi].
48.         mov ebx, [edi]  ; save to store at [esi] later
49.         push edi         ; save these three
50.         push ebx
51.         push esi
52.         mov ecx, edi
53.         sub ecx, esi    ; ecx has the count of bytes to move
54.         add edi, 3      ; edi is last target byte of move
55.         mov esi, edi
56.         sub esi, 4      ; esi is last source byte of move
57.
58.         ; esi > edi, so the move has to be done backwards
59.         std              ; set direction flag
60.         rep movsb
61.         cld              ; clear direction flag
62.
63.         pop esi          ; restore what we just pushed above
64.         pop ebx
65.         mov [esi], ebx ; put what was at [edi] at [esi]
```

```
66.          pop edi
67.
68.          ; done with the move, continue the loop. We
69.          ; move esi up one, and edi is now the last of
70.          ; the elements we moved that had the edx bit on
71.          add esi, 4
72.          jmp checkforendthenlookforzero
73.
74.     trynextbit:
75.          shl edx, 1
76.          jne outerloop
77.          ; edx shifted out to zero, we are done
78.
79.          pop edi
80.          pop esi
81.          pop edx
82.          pop ecx
83.          pop ebx
84.          pop eax
85.          pop ebp
86.
87.          ret 8
```

Suggestions

1. Because the algorithm depends on not disturbing the relative order of two elements if they have the same value for the bit being considered, verify that this is done properly.
2. Check that the main outerloop loop terminates properly.
3. Line 36 advances edi and line 37 tests a bit in it. Only later is a check made to see if the end of the array has been hit. Can this result in an access beyond the end of the array?
4. Is it okay on lines 24 and 41 to jump right to trynextbit, or is there possibly shifting of the array that has to happen before moving to the next bit?

Hints

Walk through the program with the arrays:

1. The trivial case of a single number:

```
1
```

2. A sorted array with numbers that differ in only one bit:

```
10
18
```

3. An unsorted array with numbers alternating bits on and off:

```
1
0
1
0
```

4. An unsorted array with every combination of bits 2 and 3, multiple times:

```
6
0
0
2
2
4
6
4
```

Explanation of the Bug

The code on lines 17–19 to initialize the start and end of the array

```
mov esi, eax    ; esi stores address of first element
imul ebx, 4
add eax, ebx    ; eax stores address of last element
```

produces a result in `eax` that is the first byte past the end of the array. However, the way the program is written, it expects `eax` to point to the last actual element in the array. Thus, `ebx` has to be adjusted back between lines 17–18:

```
sub ebx, 1
```

This is a **D.limit** or **A.off-by-one** error because the program winds up "sorting" one extra element in the array, whatever it happens to contain (unless it crashes trying to access the memory).

Appendix A

CLASSIFICATION OF BUGS

This appendix details the bug classifications used in this book. Appendix B, "Index of Bugs by Type," allows you to quickly find all the bugs of a particular type. (Ideally, you should only consult Appendix B after the problems are solved because knowing the type of bug in a particular example makes it easier to find.) Because of the imprecise nature of the bug classification, there is some overlap. In many situations, a particular bug can be classified in several different ways.

When talking about bugs, there are really three types—failures, faults, and errors:

- A failure is visible to the end user of a program. For example, the program is supposed to print a one and instead prints a zero.
- A fault is the underlying state of the program at runtime that leads to a failure. For example, the program might display the incorrect output because the wrong value is stored in a variable.
- An error is the actual incorrect fragment of code that the programmer wrote; this is what must be changed to fix the problem.

(This distinction between failures, faults, and errors is provided by a paper written by Andrew J. Ko and Brad A. Myers of Carnegie Mellon University.)

A failure implies at least one fault, and a fault implies at least one error, but the reverse is not true. As programmers know, errors can lurk in code that appears to run perfectly, and an inconsistent runtime state might not lead to an actual user-visible failure.

When this book (and the classification of bugs that follows) talks about "bugs," it really talks about errors. All the errors in the programs are of a type that leads to faults and failures—at least for certain inputs.

Many of the errors discussed in this appendix are demonstrated with short examples written in C, Java, or Python. With the exception of a few cases where an explanation is given, the language should not interfere with understanding the code.

Syntax Versus Semantics

Most writing on programming errors distinguishes between two basic types of errors: syntax errors and semantic errors.

Syntax errors involve the precise definition of how valid programs are formed. For example, in Python, the following code fragment

```
if i == 5
```

is syntactically incorrect because Python syntax specifies that an `if` statement must have a colon at the end of the line.

This book does not deal with syntax errors. Spotting them can involve more detailed knowledge of the language than what this book requires. More importantly, they won't sneak in unnoticed; when a compiler or interpreter encounters a syntax error, it reports an error to the user. Although one single syntax error can often cause a cascade of related errors, which makes it difficult to figure out where the actual error is (for example, if the declaration of a variable is incorrect, every reference to it might become a syntax error), it is still apparent that *something* is wrong and needs to be fixed.

Note

Arguably, another class of errors exists: Linker errors, where the compiler cannot produce a binary, can occur when an external variable or function name has a typo, or if there is a problem with how the compiler is installed, or for various other reasons that are outside the scope of this book. Because these errors are language- and system-specific, and (like syntax errors) result in an error being reported to the user, this book does not worry about linker errors.

What this book focuses on is semantic errors.

Semantic errors can be broken down into runtime errors and logic errors. Runtime errors cause the program to crash or abort in some way, while logic errors cause a program to run to completion, but produce the incorrect output or result.

This book does not distinguish between those two types of semantic errors. It is often pure luck whether a buggy program exhibits one misbehavior or the other. A runtime error leading to a crash could be considered a form of "bad output," and a program that has a logic error might run to completion on some inputs, while crashing with an error on others. For example, the following code fragment

```
int compute_average(int array[], int count) {
    int j, total = 0;
    for (j = 0; j < count; j++) {
        total += array[j]);
    }
    return total / count;
}
```

works correctly on most inputs, but crashes with a divide by zero error if `count` is 0. (It's debatable what the program should do in such a case, but crashing is not the answer.) Meanwhile, in some languages, certain bugs always cause a runtime error (using an incorrect array index is one example), but in others, they usually result in silent logic errors. So, the book won't try to distinguish between runtime and logic errors.

Classification Used in This Book

In the existing writing on programming, many articles attempt to classify bugs into types. In fact, there have been roughly as many classifications as articles. One notable feature of the bug classification literature is that *everyone* feels the need to devise his or her own system.

The categorization in this book is based on one devised by Donald Knuth, who is the author of the typesetting package known as T_eX (although as befits the field, I'll make some changes to his categories).

Knuth is an expert programmer who kept a detailed log of all the code changes he made during the development of T_eX—both bugs and enhancements. He later wrote a paper called "The Errors of T_eX" in which he grouped the changes into 15 categories, 9 for bugs and 6 for enhancements, each assigned a letter of the alphabet for reference. We'll ignore the enhancement categories and focus on the 9 bug categories, which are as follows:

- **Algorithmic Anomalies**. The code correctly follows the intent of the programmer, but the intent was wrong.
- **Blunders**. As Knuth put it, "thinking the right thing, but writing it wrong." The algorithm was correct, but the code did not implement it correctly.
- **Data Disasters**. Data was incorrectly modified in some way such that the result did not reflect the programmer's intent.
- **Forgetfulness**. A simple error of omission; leaving out some code so that the program did not do all that it was supposed to do.
- **Language Lossage**. Errors related to misunderstanding or not considering the specific features of the syntax, such as the precedence of operators.
- **Mismatches**. Calling a subroutine with incorrect parameters in a way that the compiler won't report an error.
- **Robustness**. Crashing on bad input data, reporting uninformative error messages, and the like.
- **Surprises**. Unforeseen interaction between different sections of the program.
- **Typographic Trivia**. Simple errors when typing in the program.

This book's classification merges some of these categories and ignores some others. The categories used are as follows:

- **A–Algorithm**. This category combines Knuth's Algorithmic Anomalies and Surprises. The distinction between the two is somewhat difficult anyway (this was pointed out by Marc Eisenstadt in his paper, "Tales of Debugging from the Front Lines"), and seems to be primarily related to the distance in the code between the error and the fault, or the fault and the failure. All bugs—except perhaps malicious ones introduced on purpose—are "surprises" to the code's author. So I will merge these two categories.
- **D–Data**. This category is Knuth's Data Disasters. Although you could argue that data winds up incorrect because of an **A–Algorithm** bug, the **D–Data** category refers more specifically to cases where the code reads or writes incorrect data, or accesses the wrong storage location.

- **F–Forgotten**. This category is Knuth's Forgetfulness, but generalized to include all control flow errors that occur because the statements in the program are not executed in the order that the programmer intended—the most common reason being that the statement is not present in the program, as Knuth defined it, but also including statements in the wrong location.
- **B–Blunder**. This category includes Knuth's Blunders and Typographic Trivia. The latter category exists because Knuth wrote his code on paper and then typed it, so he made occasional transcription errors in the process. Because many programmers type code directly into the computer, they would never encounter that problem. (Marc Eisenstadt also pointed out the difficulty of distinguishing between those two categories.) Some **A–Algorithm** bugs can manifest themselves as small mistakes in the code, but in most cases, it can be ascertained if the programmer intended to type it that way or not.

The book doesn't use Knuth's three other categories: Mismatches, Robustness, and Language Lossage.

- In the real world, mismatches do occur, but usually only in large programs, especially when calling functions written by someone else. To the extent that we see these in the small programs in this book, they will go under **B–Blunder**.
- T_eX is written specifically to process input and produce output, as a compiler would, so handling incorrect input and producing good error messages for the user is important. I assume this is why Knuth gave Robustness its own category. In this book they would be put under **A–Algorithm**. There is another kind of robustness, writing functions so they can handle incorrect parameters passed to them; these won't get their own category, either.
- Finally, because this book uses several languages for its examples, and I did not want to require in-depth knowledge of them, there are no bugs that would fall under Language Lossage, although as with Mismatches, in the real world, these can be common. (Knuth includes floating-point rounding errors under Language Lossage, although he says it was a "close call" over Algorithmic Anomalies. I would classify such errors under **D–Data**.)

I will not make any attempt to order the different types by frequency or difficulty. Any of them can produce bugs that are easy or difficult to find, depending on the way they manifest themselves, the techniques used to find them, and pure luck. The only thing that can be said is that the ease of *fixing* bugs after they are found can vary with the type: A **B–Blunder** can usually be patched up with a minor change, whereas the solution to an **A–Algorithm** might involve fundamental changes to the entire program.

The following sections break each of the four main categories into subcategories with discussion and examples. The subcategories are identified with the notation **C.subcategory**, where **C** is the initial of one of the main categories (**A**, **D**, **F**, or **B**) and **subcategory** is a descriptive name.

A–Algorithm

A.off-by-one

An **A.off-by-one** error occurs when the code performs a calculation or includes an expression that is one away from what it should have been, which results in the code processing the wrong number of pieces of data, or returning a value that is incorrect, or taking a branch in the code at the wrong time. "One" can refer to 1 byte, but it can also mean one element in an array, one record in a file, and so on.

A well-known **A.off-by-one** error is the fencepost error. The canonical fencepost error occurs when calculating the number of posts in a 100-foot fence with a post every 10 feet. Your first guess might be 10, but that is incorrect. (You can also reverse the question by describing a fence with a post every 10 feet and 11 posts in all, and asking how long the fence is.)

So, a fencepost error occurs when the number of elements is miscounted because of neglecting to account for the final element (or the initial element). For example, code such as the following

```
// count how many pages will be printed
pagecount = lastpagenumber - firstpagenumber;
```

contains a fencepost error.

Another **A.off-by-one** error involves using the wrong comparison operator, confounding < and <= or > and >=. The following code, which tries to check if someone is old enough to vote in the United States (you must be 18 or older to vote), is an example of this:

```
if (age > 18) {
    // OK to vote!
}
```

In languages that index arrays from 0, code can incorrectly start at the element with index 1 (the second element, that is). This error is sometimes considered an **A.off-by-one** error, but because those bugs typically involve processing the data, they are classified here as **D.index**.

A.logic

An **A.logic** error occurs if the programmer has designed a logically incorrect way to achieve the desired result.

In many cases, the error involves the incorrect calculation of a value based on some data. Often, this is caused by a bad assumption about the data in question. For example, the following code attempts to lowercase a string using knowledge of how characters are represented in ASCII. (The Python function `ord()` converts a character to its numeric ASCII value, while `chr()` does the reverse.)

```
upper = ""
for k in range(0, len(s)):
    upper += chr(ord(s[k]) - ord("A") + ord("a"))
```

The code fails because the conversion algorithm is only correct if `s[k]` is an uppercase character. It won't work properly for spaces, lowercase characters, and so on.

Loops can also be prone to **A.logic** errors, especially the code to terminate the loop. Loops usually terminate when a logical expression changes from true to false or vice versa. One error is a loop termination condition that never changes:

```
for (j = 1; j != 100; j = j + 2)
```

Because `j` has an initial value of `1` and is incremented by `2` for each iteration, it never equals exactly `100`, the logical expression `j != 100` is always true, and the loop never terminates (unless `j` is modified somewhere within the loop body, or the code exits the loop through another method).

Code can also break out of a loop at an incorrect time, or neglect to break out at the proper time:

```
while (1) {
    if (end_of_line) {
        cleanup();
```

```
        // probably missing a break statement here
    }
    // more processing
}
```

The previous examples could be fixed with minor changes. In other cases, the logic is simply flawed in a more general way, and needs to be redone. This code attempts to walk through an array and find the difference between the two values that are furthest apart (`Math.abs()` is a Java library function that calculates absolute value):

```
biggest = 0;
for (k = 0; k < a.length-1; k++) {
    distance = abs(a[k] - a[k+1]);
    if (distance > biggest) {
        biggest = distance;
    }
}
```

The code does what the programmer intended, but the algorithm is incorrect. It assumes the two values that are farthest apart will be in adjacent elements of the array, which isn't necessarily true. This code can't be saved with a small adjustment; it needs to be fundamentally reworked.

A.validation

Many blocks of code that need to be debugged are functions that take parameters passed from other code. Often, the function documentation restricts the range of values allowed for certain parameters. For example, a function that takes an argument `percent` might specify that the value should be between 0 and 100.

The compiler usually does not check such restrictions (depending on how they are specified), and the question becomes whether checking the validity of arguments should be part of the function's algorithm—in other words, whether parameters should be checked for validity within the function or if it is the caller's responsibility to ensure that parameters are valid before calling the function. If the function is supposed to check this, not having this code is a bug in the algorithm. (As previously mentioned, Knuth has a separate category, Robustness, which arguably includes such parameter checking, although he does not present it as such.)

A standard example is a function that is passed a pointer to a string. A function that was supposed to do nothing on an empty string might have code to check the validity of the string that was passed in:

```
void my_function(char * my_string) {
    if (my_string == NULL) {
        return;
    }
    if (strlen(my_string) == 0) {
        return;
    }
}
```

Nobody would argue about the second check, about the length of the string. Clearly, the function should check that. The first check, about the pointer being NULL, is there on the theory that the function is more robust if it makes that check, but of course, there are plenty of "not NULL but still invalid" pointer values that would make the function crash. (NULL just happens to be a common invalid value.) Calling the function as follows

```
my_function((void *)0x12345)
```

probably still causes a crash.

The extra check doesn't take much time to execute. On the other hand, it does add code that needs to be processed by the brain of the person reading it. The good news is it can usually be dismissed quickly, unless the code has the classic C/C++ error in it, of using = instead of == for a comparison:

```
if (my_string = NULL) {
    return;
}
```

The question of "who should check for an invalid pointer" is one this book doesn't discuss. In the interest of simplifying the code and saving space in the source code listing, in general, the examples don't have validation code such as what's shown here, and this book doesn't have any **A.validation** bugs in its examples.

A.performance

Performance problems occur when a program performs its task properly, but uses far more resources than it needs. Often, the resource is time, but it could also be memory, disk space, network packets, or any other limited resource.

Because different programmers can solve the same problem with different algorithms and one of them is likely faster than the other, the question of when inferior performance becomes a bug is highly subjective. If the code is 10% larger than it could be, that is often not an issue, unless memory use is critically important. On the other hand, a program that is 100 times slower than necessary is generally considered to have a performance problem, no matter what the situation.

Knuth, when categorizing the performance fixes he made to T_eX, listed them as enhancements, not bugs. As he noted, "I felt guilty when fixing the bugs, but I felt virtuous when making the enhancements."

Performance problems are included in this list for completeness. None of the bugs in the book are **A.performance** bugs.

D–Data

D.index

A **D.index** error occurs when an invalid index is used when walking through an array or other data structure.

Many languages use zero-based arrays; that is, the valid indices for an array of size n go from 0 to n-1. This leads to a common indexing error when looping through such an array, starting at 1 instead of 0. (In the Python example here, note that range(1,n) includes numbers from 1 to n-1.)

```
for i in range(1, n):
    # code that processes array[i]
```

Beginning the indexing at 1 instead of 0 causes the code to miss the first element of the array. (In Python, you can write range(n) as a shortcut for range(0,n), which makes this error less likely to occur.)

Similarly, you can make the same mistake on the other end, going past the end of the array:

```
for (i = 0; i <= n; i++)
    // code that processes array[i]
```

As mentioned earlier, such errors can be categorized as **A.off-by-one** errors, but here they will be listed as **D.index** instead. An index error does not have to be off by one. It can be off by much more, especially when the index is part of a calculation:

```
int process_array(int my_array[]) {
    int index_to_check;
    for (int k = 0; k < my_array.length; k++) {
        if (k < my_array.length / 2)
            index_to_check = k;
        else
            index_to_check = my_array.length + k;
        check(k[index_to_check]);
    }
}
```

This code miscalculates `index_to_check` in the `else` clause of the `if`, which leads to an index error.

D.limit

A **D.limit** error involves failing to process data correctly at the limits: the first or last element of the data set (or possibly, the first few or last few elements).

An index error often leads to a limit error. It may cause the code to not process the first or last element at all (if the indexing is too restrictive, as in the preceding example where the `range()` starts at `1`). Or, it may cause the code to crash accessing past the end of the data (if the indexing is too expansive, as in the previous example where the loop termination check is `i <= n` instead of `i < n`).

Other **D.limit** errors occur when the code makes assumptions that are true except on the first or last element. For example, code that is parsing lines in a file into sections delimited by lines containing `"###"` might have a section like this:

```
String line;
while (true) {
```

```
line = getnewline();
if (line.equals("###")) {
    break;
// other code
}
}
```

If the file ends without a "###" line the code might loop forever.

I also include as a **D.limit** error cases where the code works incorrectly on certain inputs near the beginning or end of the range of valid inputs. That is, unlike the previous examples, which tend to slightly misprocess all inputs, these are cases where the code works fine on most inputs, but completely fails on a small subset near the limit. For example, this code attempts to print a baseball player's batting average to three decimal places. (The Python function `str()` converts a number to its string representation; `string.zfill()` pads a string with zeros up to the number specified as the second argument.)

```
def print_average(hits, at_bats):
    average_string = str((1000 * hits) / at_bats)
    print "." + string.zfill(average_string, 3)
```

The code has a **D.limit** error. It works except when `hits` is equal to `at_bats`. In that case, it prints out ".1000" instead of "1.000".

D.number

The **D.number** class of data errors relates to how numbers are stored on a computer. Knuth mentions floating-point rounding errors and calls them Language Lossage. However, **D.number** errors are usually not specific to a particular language, but rather to how a particular processor stores numbers (and because different machines use the same processor, the same type of error can occur in many languages on many machines).

I won't use any floating-point numbers in the examples, but certain types of errors occur because of how integers are stored in memory.

The most basic of these is an overflow, which is when a program attempts to store a number in an area of memory that is not large enough.

One form of an overflow error is an assignment between variables of different sizes:

```
long a_long;
short b_short;
b_short = a_long;
```

Assuming that a `long` holds 32 bits of data and a `short` holds 16 bits of data, this assignment results in `a_long` being truncated down to 16 bits, which causes loss of data if `a_long` holds more than 16 bits of information (and might cause a signed/unsigned error if `a_long` has exactly 16 bits—see the discussion below). Most compilers give a warning about this or require that the programmer make the conversion explicit, for example, through a cast in C:

```
b_short = (short)a_long;
```

The cast does not change the problem of overflowing `b_short`. It merely quiets the compiler and hopefully forces the programmer to realize that something risky is occurring.

Another form of overflow can happen with types of the same size. In an expression such as the following

```
int c, d, e;
c = d + e;
```

if `d` and `e` added together are larger than the maximum number that can be stored in `c`, this causes an overflow, or possibly a signed/unsigned error. Compilers won't warn about this type of error. The programmer must be careful about storing values close to the size limit of a certain data type.

A signed/unsigned error happens because most computers store negative numbers in what is known as two's complement. To negate a number, invert all the bits (`0` becomes `1`, `1` becomes `0`) and then add `1`. For example, using 8-bit values, the number 11 is stored in binary as

```
00001011
```

and −11 is stored as

```
11110101
```

The problem is that the positive number 245 is also stored as `11110101`.

A signed 8-bit variable can hold values from −128 to 127; an unsigned 8-bit variable can hold values from 0 to 255. For both signed and unsigned variables, the numbers from 0 to 127 are stored the same way—using values from `00000000` through `01111111`. The signed versus unsigned difference is whether the values from `10000000` to `1111111` are interpreted as the range from 128 to 255 or the range from −128 to −1.

277

Thus, languages often require that a variable be declared as either signed or unsigned (with signed usually the default). It doesn't affect how the data is stored. It's just a convention for how to interpret them when displaying them (and affects some operations such as extending them to fit in a variable with a larger number of bits; for example, converting a `short` to a `long`). Writing the following

```
char j = -11;
unsigned char k = 245;
```

results in `11110101` being stored in both `j` and `k`.

As you can see, in signed notation, a negative number has the high bit (the leftmost bit in the binary representation) set to 1. A signed/unsigned error can happen when two signed numbers are added and the result has the incorrect value in the high bit. For example, adding 127 + 3 with unsigned 8-bit values results in the value 130, but with signed values, it results in the value –126. Negative numbers can improperly wind up positive: An 8-bit addition of the values –100 and –100 results in the value 56.

Programmers sometimes have to be aware of another detail of number storage that concerns how the bytes in a number are arranged in memory. A machine that stores the least significant byte first is known as *little-endian*. Machines that store the most significant byte first are known as *big-endian*. That is, the 32-bit number whose hexadecimal representation is `0x12345678` would be stored on a little-endian machine as four consecutive bytes

```
0x78 0x56 0x34 0x12
```

while on a big-endian machine, it would be stored as follows:

```
0x12 0x34 0x56 0x78
```

Normally, these differences don't matter, but they become important in C code such as the following:

```
long l;
short s = *((short *)&l);
```

If you don't write code like that, you probably don't have to worry about little-endian versus big-endian.

Finally, errors can occur because of truncation or rounding—even with integers. During integer division, the remainder is not preserved, so a routine that attempts to compute an average by recalculating the "current total" for each iteration

```
integer count = 0;
integer avg = 0;
for (j = 0; j < array.length; j++) {
    tot = avg * count;
    count = count + 1;
    avg = (tot + array[j]) / count
}
```

would likely generate an incorrect result because of the intermediate conversion of the division result back to the integer avg.

D.memory

The **D.memory** error involves mismanaging memory. One way to cause this error is to attempt to access memory that is not accessible to the program, by improperly manipulating an array index or pointer:

```
int a[5];
int j = a[200];
```

Another way to cause this error is to allocate memory after it is freed. (The C functions malloc() and free() allocate and free memory; memcpy() copies bytes of data.)

```
char * k = malloc(200);
char * kcopy = k;
memcpy(k, buffer, 200);
// k is processed...
free(k);
// at some point later...
do_something(kcopy);
```

Both these examples are contrived and obviously incorrect at a quick glance. Real invalid memory bugs are better disguised and more difficult to find.

Instead of freeing memory too soon, programs can forget to free it, which causes a memory leak. (This is impossible in some languages where the user does not have the ability to explicitly allocate and deallocate memory).

A section of code might leak all the memory it allocates

```
for (k = 0; k < buffer_count; k++) {
    void * temp_buffer = malloc(80);
    // some processing using temp_buffer
}
```

or it might leak only memory in certain situations:

```
for (k = 0; k < buffer_count; k++) {
    void * temp_buffer = malloc(80);
    // some processing using temp_buffer
    if (unexpected_endoffile())
        break;    // oops, don't free(temp_buffer)
    free(temp_buffer);
}
```

Code with memory leaks often works for a long time and then fails unexpectedly when new memory cannot be allocated. This is an unpredictable situation based on the hardware being used, what other applications are running, and other hard-to-predict factors.

A final way to mismanage memory is to use the same variable for two different reasons in different sections of code, but later discover that the logical scope of the two areas overlaps. One example of this is using the same loop counter in a nested loop:

```
for (i = 0; i < count; i++) {
    length = getnextbuffer(buf);
    for (i = 0; i < length; i++) {
        process(buf[i]);
    }
}
```

This error can occur when code is cut-and-pasted into the middle of a larger section of code that uses the same variable. It can also happen when programmers reuse the same variable name for different functions on the theory that it saves memory. In fact, modern compilers can often figure out if two variables have scopes that do not intersect and reuse the same storage for them. Therefore, it is best to use separate variable names for separate purposes.

Although **D.memory** errors can cause some of the hardest-to-find bugs in the real world, it is hard to create a short example with a non-obvious case. Therefore, none of the programs in this book have a **D.memory** error.

F–Forgotten

F.init

Many errors are caused by the programmer wanting the computer to "Do what I mean, not what I say." The most basic case of this is an instruction that is accidentally left out of the program. One of the most common types of instructions to leave out are ones that initialize variables. This is an **F.init** error.

Many variables are not initialized when they are defined, and many languages do not assign a default value in this case, which results in the variable containing whatever value happens to be in the memory location the variable is stored at. An uninitialized variable becomes a bug when it is actually used in code that expects it to be initialized. Usually, this error happens because certain paths through the code avoid the initialization, although in some cases, the variable is never initialized. The more unusual the uninitialized path is, the less likely such a bug will be found early. In code such as the following

```
int a;
if (somethingunusual()) {
    // code that does not modify a
} else {
    a = 12;
}
// code that expects a to be initialized
```

the error might go undetected for a while, depending on how often `somethingunusual()` is true.

A common case is the loop counter not being properly initialized:

```
int k;
while (k < max_tables) {
    // some code: k was never initialized
}
```

Some languages make this impossible, depending on the type of loop command used, and the level of checking that the compiler or interpreter is asked to do.

It's also possible the initialization code is correct for the loop counter, but is missing for a different variable that is compared in some way

281

against each of the values that are being looped through. Code such as the following

```
for (i = 0; i < 20; i++) {
    if (array[i] > biggest)
        biggest = array[i];
```

must ensure that `biggest` is initialized properly before the loop begins. For example, there might be some known value that would be smaller than any value in the array.

F.missing

Other statements besides initialization can be left out; the case of missing initialization is just so common that it deserves its own subcategory. **F.missing** is the general case.

Programmers can neglect to type in a statement, or accidentally delete it while moving code around, cleaning up comments, and so on. Finding these types of bugs can be tricky unless a comment makes it obvious:

```
//
// First read a, then tokenize it, then store it.
//
read(a);
// perhaps a call to tokenize(a) is missing here?
store(a);
```

Problems with loop counters can occur when the loop counter is improperly modified. For example, a loop might look like the following:

```
while buffer_index < 100:
    # some code
    if doublebyte:
        buffer_index += 2
    else if singlebyte:
        buffer_index += 1
```

If `doublebyte` and `singlebyte` are both false, `buffer_index` won't be incremented and the code might get stuck in an infinite loop.

Keep in mind that loops can have more than one variable that is logically acting as a "loop counter," even if it doesn't appear in the statement that defines the loop. For example

```
pointer = first;
```

```
for (count = 0; count < maxcount; count++) {
    // code
    if (jumptonext)
        continue;
    // more code
    pointer = pointer->next;
}
```

`count` and `pointer` are both logically functioning as loop variables. Because `count` is modified in the `for()` statement itself, it will always be updated for each iteration of the loop. But `pointer` is modified by code within the loop body, and it is possible that the code might iterate the loop without advancing it (such as in the previous example if the `continue` statement is executed).

F.location

The **F.location** refers to code that is in the wrong sequence within the program. One example is initializing a variable inside a loop rather than outside it:

```
while somecondition():
    count = 0
    # code that updates count
```

Another example of **F.location** is when the sequence of instructions does not match the intended order of operations. Often, two instructions are swapped. This code tries to zero out an array element after it has included it in the total, but has the statements in the incorrect order:

```
array[f] = 0;
total += array[f];
```

An arithmetic operation can also have swapped statements, such as these two attempting to compute the hypotenuse of a triangle:

```
result = Math.sqrt(c);
c = Math.pow(a,2) + Math.pow(b,2);
```

Instructions can be placed in the wrong block of code, particularly if blocks are nested several layers deep:

```
if (found_blank) {
    if (string_done) {
```

```
            clean_up();
            if (buffer != NULL) {
                free(buffer);
            }
        }
        return;
    }
```

In this case, it's likely that the `return` statement should be one layer deeper in the nesting (that is, the function returns only if `string_done` is true, not just because `found_blank` is true). Of course, the code could be correct as written. The point is that it is easy to miss such an error when looking at the code because the only difference is the order of the tokens in the code.

I'll also use **F.location** for cases where the code in question should not be present at all:

```
// sort the list
list_head = sort(list_head);
list_head = null;    // what is this doing here?
display(list_head);
```

The extraneous statement might have been a remnant of a previous algorithm, a cut-and-paste error, or simply a programmer's mistake.

B-Blunder

B.variable

An easy and common mistake is using the wrong variable name. For example, the author meant to write

```
i = 5;
```

but instead wrote

```
j = 5;
```

In many languages, this generates an error unless j is defined and is the same type as i, but the existence of two variables of the same type and similar names can be the *cause* of the **B.variable** error (because the programmer is thinking about both variables), so this is more common than you might expect. Often, when first typing in code, there will be typos. For example, your finger might slip off the I key and hit the adjacent key to wind up with:

```
io = 5;
```

Whether this is caught quickly might depend on how the language specifies that undeclared variables should be treated.

One source of **B.variable** errors is cutting-and-pasting similar code. For example, in code that looks like the following

```
// adjust the endpoint of the line
x1 = transform (x1, x2, current_transform);
y1 = transform (y1, x2, current_transform);
```

the second line was likely copied from the first and each occurrence of x was changed to y by hand, with one of them being missed, which generates legal but likely incorrect code.

Anywhere a variable is used, it's possible to use the wrong one—on the left or right side of an assignment, as an argument to a function, as a return value from a function, and so on. One situation that arises is switching two variables in the parameters to a function, which passes unnoticed by the compiler as long as they are the same type. That is, calling:

```
draw_dot(y, x)
```

instead of:

```
draw_dot(x, y)
```

Knuth calls this class of errors Mismatches, but I won't define a separate category for them. If your code has two functions with similar names (or even dissimilar names), it might also use the wrong function name instead of the wrong variable name.

B.expression

The **B.expression** is a more general form of the previous category, **B.variable**. A variable on its own is an "expression," but the case of just using the wrong variable name is so common that it was separated. **B.expression** covers other cases in which expressions are incorrect not because of the algorithm being wrong, but because of a momentary cramp in the programmer's brain.

The most basic of these errors is when the code uses the wrong operator

```
a = a + 2;
```

instead of:

```
a = a * 2;
```

Given that expressions can be arbitrarily complex, there is an arbitrary opportunity to make mistakes. One place that bad expressions may appear is in an `if` statement:

```
if ((count < min) && (count > max))
```

This example is almost certainly not what the author intended (assuming `min` is less than `max`, the expression will never be true). At times, it is not clear if the mistake is a typo or simply a bad algorithm. In these cases, a nearby comment might help differentiate:

```
// Make sure a is less than 100
if (a > 100)
```

That code is likely a typo, but:

```
// If these are equal, k is divisible by five
if (((k-1) / 5) == (k/5))
```

is more likely to be an **A.logic** error because the comment matches the code (but both are incorrect). In general, if the mistake is simple, only occurs in one place, and is inconsistent with the rest of the program, it probably belongs in **B.expression**.

The logical "and" and "or" operators are common areas where the wrong operator is used in an expression, usually by using `and` instead of `or` or vice versa. For example, the example above might have been intended to be as follows:

```
if ((count < min) || (count > max))
    // code to handle an invalid count
```

Conversely, the `&&` might have been correct and the `>` and `<` might have been reversed (another error that occurs often)— the intent was to write the following:

```
if ((count > min) && (count < max))
    // code to handle a valid count
```

In the first case, the `if()` was checking for a count that was out of range. In the second case, it was checking for a count that was within the proper range. (Although it is more likely in that case that the proper comparison operators would have been `>=` and `<=` instead of `>` and `<`.)

In the end, it does not matter why the code is wrong; it has to be fixed. Still, a typo is arguably more likely to be a single localized mistake (unless it was duplicated elsewhere through cut-and-paste) while a logical error might indicate more fundamental problems.

B.language

Some languages have syntax features that can lead to improper expressions. This is what Knuth calls Language Lossage. For example, expressions that depend on the precedence of operators can be interpreted in a non-intuitive way. In C, the following statement that uses `&`, the boolean "and" function

```
if ( i & 1 == 0 )
```

is parsed by the compiler as:

```
if ( i & (1 == 0) )
```

This is unlikely to be the author's intention.
Another example is the following C fragment:

```
if (i == 5); {
    i = 0;
}
```

This fragment is syntactically correct, but the semicolon (`;`) after the `if()` is interpreted as the entire `if()` body, which means that the `i = 0;` statement always executes. Other cases of this in C include neglecting to include a `break` after a case in a `switch` statement, and using `=` instead of `==` in a comparison. If that didn't make sense to you, don't worry—none of the bugs in this book depend on such quirks of the language.

Summary

A–Algorithm. The algorithm that the programmer designed is incorrect.

A.off-by-one. The program makes a calculation that is off by one.

A.logic. The algorithm has a logical flaw.

A.validation. Variables are not properly checked to ensure they are valid. [*]

A.performance. The algorithm has severe performance problems. [*]

D–Data. Data is not properly processed.

D.index. An array is indexed into incorrectly.

D.limit. Processing is done incorrectly at the beginning or end of the data.

D.number. A bug related to how numbers are stored in memory.

D.memory. The program mismanages memory. [*]

F–Forgotten. Statements are not executed in the intended order.

F.init. A variable is not properly initialized.

F.missing. A necessary statement is missing.

F.location. A statement is in the wrong place.

B–Blunder. A simple mistake in the code.

B.variable. The wrong variable name is used.

B.expression. The calculation of an expression has a mistake.

B.language. A bug specific to the syntax of the language. [*]

[*]: This book doesn't have any bugs of this type.

Appendix B

INDEX OF BUGS BY TYPE

As previously mentioned, bugs can appear multiple times in this list because the classification is somewhat fluid. Each bug is listed by title, with the language and number of the page on which it appears.

A.off-by-one. The program makes a calculation that is off by one.

Language	Title	Page Number
C	Memory Free	60
C	Kanji Backspace	71
Python	Alphabetize Words	90
Python	Print the Month and Day	95
Java	Convert a Number to Text	133
Perl	Sort a File by Line Length	179
x86 Assembly	Check if Two Words Are Anagrams	238
x86 Assembly	Radix Exchange Sort	260

A.logic. The algorithm has a logical flaw.

Language	Title	Page Number
C	Selection Sort	41
C	Memory Copy	50
C	Memory Allocator	56
Python	Parse Numbers Written in English	110
Python	Assign Gift Givers	113
Java	Quicksort	149
Perl	Print the Prime Factors of a Number	182
Perl	Tab Expansion	184
Perl	Find Repeating Parts of a Fraction	190
Perl	Play the Game *Mastermind*	207
x86 Assembly	Multiply Two Numbers Using Shifts	230
x86 Assembly	Play the Simulation Game *Life*	251

D.index. An array is indexed into incorrectly.

Language	Title	Page Number
C	Memory Free	60
Python	Find a Substring	87
Java	Convert a Number to Text	133

D.limit. Processing is done incorrectly at the beginning or end of the data.

Language	Title	Page Number
C	Recursive Word Reversal	64
Python	Is a Number Prime?	85
Java	Reverse a Linked List	143
Perl	Simple Database	187
x86 Assembly	Check if Two Words Are Anagrams	238
x86 Assembly	Radix Exchange Sort	260

D.number. A bug related to how numbers are stored in memory.

Language	Title	Page Number
x86 Assembly	Make Change for a Dollar	227
x86 Assembly	Sum a Signed Array	247

F.init. A variable is not properly initialized.

Language	Title	Page Number
C	Parse a String into Substrings	53
Java	Is a Year a Leap Year?	129
Java	Play the Game *Pong*, Part II	157
Perl	Sort All the Files in a Directory Tree	196
x86 Assembly	Convert a 64-Bit Number to a Decimal String	242

F.missing. A necessary statement is missing.

Language	Title	Page Number
C	Linked List Removal	47
x86 Assembly	Join Strings with a Delimiter	232

F.location. A statement is in the wrong place.

Language	Title	Page Number
C	Calculate All Possible Routes	68
Python	Go Fish, Part II: Ask if Another Hand Has a Card	102
Java	Draw a Triangle on the Screen, Part II	140
Java	Check if a List Has a Loop	146
Perl	Calculate Student Test Averages	200
x86 Assembly	Multiply Two Numbers Using Shifts	230

B.variable. The wrong variable name is used.

Language	Title	Page Number
C	Selection Sort	41
C	Linked List Insertion	44
Python	Go Fish, Part III: Play a Full Game	105
Java	Draw a Triangle on the Screen, Part I	136
Java	Compute Bowling Scores	161
Perl	Merge Sort of Multiple Files	203
x86 Assembly	Calculate Fibonacci Numbers	235

B.expression. The calculation of an expression has a mistake.

Appendix C

REFERENCES

Classification of Bugs

Here's some background information for the classification of bugs used in this book (Donald Knuth's paper being the most direct ancestor). A lot of the studies of bug types are based on observing inexperienced programmers, which tends to skew the results in a certain direction. Nonetheless, they make for interesting reading, particularly the series of *Empirical Studies of Programmers* workshop proceedings.

Eisenstadt, Marc. *Tales of Debugging from the Front Lines.* Paper submitted to Empirical Studies of Programmers V, 1993.

Fergusson, Kymberly. *Research Readings: Archived Category—Programming Errors.* http://www.csse.monash.edu.au/~kef/research/readings/archives/cat_programming_errors.shtml.

Knuth, Donald. "The Errors of T$_e$X." p. 243 of *Literate Programming.* Center for the Study of Language and Information, 1992.

Ko, Andrew J. and Brad A. Myers. *Development and Evaluation of a Model of Programming Errors.* Human-Computer Interaction Institute, School of Computer Science, Carnegie Mellon University, 2003.

Pennington, Nancy. "Comprehensions Strategies in Programming." p. 100 of *Empirical Studies of Programmers: Second Workshop*. Ablex Publishing Corporation, 1987.

Spohrer, James C., and Elliot Soloway. "Analyzing the High Frequency Bugs in Novice Programs." p. 230 of *Empirical Studies of Programmers*. Ablex Publishing Corporation, 1986.

Spohrer, James C., Elliot Soloway, and Edgar Pope. "A Goal/Plan Analysis of Buggy Pascal Programs." p. 355 of *Studying the Novice Programmer*. Lawrence Erlbaum Associates, Inc., 1989.

General Sources for Bug Types

This section covers more generic information than the previous section, dealing with syntax versus semantic errors and the like. There are a lot of pages like this on the web.

Acorn Corporation. "What to Do if Baffled." Chapter 12 of *Atom Theory and Practice*. http://www.howell1964.freeserve.co.uk/Acorn/Atom/atap/atap_12.htm.

Dassen, J.H.M. and I.G. Sprinkhuizen-Kuyper. "Types of Bugs." Chapter 3 of *Debugging C and C++ Code in a UNIX Environment*. http://oopweb.com/CPP/Documents/DebugCPP/Volume/debug.html.

Green, Roedy. *How to Write Unmaintainable Code*. http://mindprod.com/unmain.html.

Pitts, Robert I. *Compiler, Linker and Run-Time Errors*. BU CAS CS Notes, Boston University Computer Science Department. http://www.cs.bu.edu/teaching/cpp/debugging/errors/.

Raymond, Eric, et al. *The Jargon Dictionary*. Version 4.2.2. http://info.astrian.net/jargon/. (Original version available at http://www.jargon.org/.)

Robust Programming + Testing, Profiling & Instrumentation. CS 217 Course Notes, Princeton University. http://www.cs.princeton.edu/courses/archive/spring03/cs217/lectures/Robust.pdf.

Shaw, Greg. *Types of Programming Errors*. COP 2210 Notes, Florida International University. http://www.fiu.edu/~shawg/2210/errors.doc.

C

There are many books on C. The two listed here are the original classic (also known as "K&R") and a book that was hailed as its possible replacement as the "one C book you must have." The author learned C from earlier editions of both of these.

Harbison, Samuel and Guy Steele. *C: A Reference Manual*, Fifth Edition. Pearson Education, 2002.

Kernighan, Brian and Dennis Ritchie. *The C Programming Language*, Second Edition. Prentice Hall, 1988.

Python

Python also is discussed in many books, or you can learn it from the web. Mark Pilgrim's site has a good quick introduction; then you have the tutorial and reference straight from the creator.

Pilgrim, Mark. *Dive Into Python*. http://diveintopython.org/toc/index.html.

van Rossum, Guido and Fred L. Drake, Jr. *Python Tutorial*. http://www.python.org/doc/current/tut/tut.html.

Python Library Reference. http://www.python.org/doc/current/lib/.

Java

The official documentation from Sun, both online and in printed form, is as good a place to start as any. The API reference details all the classes available, which is critical information for getting the most out of the language.

Campione, Mary. "Trail: Learning the Java Language." *The Java Tutorial*, Third Edition. Addison-Wesley 2000. http://java.sun.com/docs/books/tutorial/java/index.html.

Java 2 Platform, Standard Edition Documentation.
http://java.sun.com/j2se/1.4.2/docs/index.html.

Java 2 Platform, Standard Edition, API Specification.
http://java.sun.com/j2se/1.4.2/docs/api/index.html.

Perl

This is a standard introductory Perl book; there are lots of others to choose from, but it's the one the author used.

Schwartz, Randal and Tom Phoenix. *Learning Perl*, Third Edition. O'Reilly & Associates, 2002.

x86 Assembly Language

Assembly language books are becoming more rare. The first two listed (which focus on the x86 specifically) are out of print, but the information in the first one is available online from various web sites.

Intel Corporation. *Intel 80386 Reference Programmer's Manual.* Intel, 1986.

Nelson, Russ. *The 80386 Book.* Microsoft Press, 1988.

Carthy, Joe. *An Introduction to Assembly Language Programming and Computer Architecture.* Thomson Learning, 1996.

Index